Finding Your Voice

A Woman's Guide to Using Self-Talk for Fulfilling Relationships, Work, and Life

By the W2W Psychologists Group

Dorothy Cantor, Psy.D.

Carol Goodheart, Ed.D.

Sandra Haber, Ph.D.

Ellen McGrath, Ph.D.

Alice Rubenstein, Ed.D.

Lenore Walker, Ed.D.

Karen Zager, Ph.D.

with

Andrea Thompson

WILEY

John Wiley & Sons, Inc.

Published by John Wiley & Sons, Inc., Hoboken, New Jersey
Published simultaneously in Canada

Photo of Dorothy Cantor by Alan Fox; photo of Carol Goodheart by Pryde Brown; photo of Sandra Haber by Mary Elmer DeWitt; photos of Ellen McGrath and Lenore Walker courtesy of the author; photo of Alice Rubenstein by Leichter Studios; photo of Karen Zager by the Associated Press

For general information about our other products and services, please contact our Customer Care Department within the United States at (800) 762-2974, outside the United States at (317) 572-3993 or fax (317) 572-4002.

Wiley also publishes its books in a variety of electronic formats. Some content that appears in print may not be available in electronic books. For more information about Wiley products, visit our web site at www.wiley.com.

Library of Congress Cataloging-in-Publication Data:

Finding your voice : a woman's guide to using self talk for fulfilling relationships, work, and life / by the W2W Psychologists Group ; Dorothy Cantor . . . [et al].
    p. cm.
Includes bibliographical references and index.
   ISBN 0-471-43075-7 (Cloth)
  1. Women—Psychology.   2. Interpersonal relations.   I. Cantor, Dorothy W.
II. W2W Psychologists Group.
   HQ1206.F4657 2004
   158'.082—dc22

                                                          2003025751

Printed in the United States of America
10 9 8 7 6 5 4 3 2 1

To our amazing women clients,
who have given us so much
and helped all of us to understand
the complexity of women's lives.

Contents

Preface

Finding Your Voice began a few years ago, when we seven psychologists walked out on a dull presentation at a winter conference, deciding that sitting in the sun beside the pool and talking was a far better use of our time. We discovered in the course of that talk that we were a group of presidents, each of us having been elected head of a national professional association. We talked about our goals, the significance of our work, the value of our friendships, and what paths might be desirable in the future. Our conversation that afternoon was personal, intense, and meaningful to each of us. We became aware of a process of self-talk—a clarifying of each of our internal conversations—followed by respectful sharing and listening to one another. We wondered how to use this experience, and what kind of project might emerge from it.

Sharing our backgrounds, here's what we found. Our areas of specialization include children; family therapy; health and fitness; relationship issues; domestic violence; depression; women and power; eating disorders; adolescent development; breast cancer; health psychology; sexual assault, harassment, and exploitation; and the psychology of women. Among us, we have authored or coauthored over two dozen books and counseled more than fifty thousand clients. We work or have worked in universities, medical schools, hospitals, public schools, courtrooms, community advocacy groups, and our own independent practices.

Regarding our personal lives, we've been married, some of us have divorced, and some of us have remarried. We've raised eighteen children and have seventeen grandchildren. We've coped with our own serious illnesses and with the illness or death of a family member. We've been poor and we've had money. We have traveled around the world, learning about women's lives in other cultures.

In short, as professionals *and* as women we have confronted and continue to confront the challenges and choices of women's lives in this century. And so *Finding Your Voice* began to take root.

One more thing: While developing the ideas for this book—gathering in our homes for weekend meetings or after conferences, in New Jersey, Washington, New York, California, and Mexico; putting all of our talk on tape; and transcribing the tapes—we wanted to have fun. We wished to enjoy one another's company, even as we learned more about ourselves as individuals. It is our hope that you too, alone and with others, will find the pleasure and excitement in the journey of self-discovery that follows.

Acknowledgments

First and foremost, we want to thank our families and dear ones for their ongoing love and support, including our parents, our partners, our children, and our grandchildren. Without them there would be no book.

We gratefully acknowledge the American Psychological Association, whose governance structure provided each of us with a place to be leaders, and which gave us the opportunity to meet one another and learn how to work and play together, despite our very different backgrounds.

Special thanks to our agent, Harvey Klinger, who took a casual airplane conversation and parlayed it into the sale of this book; to Tom Miller, executive editor at John Wiley & Sons, Inc., who saw the power to help women in the proposal we sent to him; and, of course, our enormous respect and gratitude to the extraordinarily talented and patient Andrea Thompson, for taking multiple voices and making them sing in unison.

—The W2W (Women-to-Women) Psychologists Group

1

Introducing Self-Talk

This is your life. Is it what you want it to be?

Maybe your answer to that question would fall somewhere along a continuum from "Sort of" to "This isn't what I had in mind at all." If you're like most of the women we talk to, probably the last thing you'd say is, "Things are working out exactly as I want."

The fact is, we're faced with a thoroughly modern-day conundrum that is both exciting and maddening. Arguably, there's never been a better time to be a woman. In this day and age, in this culture, a woman has unprecedented opportunities to chart a course according to her own lights. But along with the abundant possibilities comes the need to make abundant choices, many of them tough ones.

More than ever before, defining what it means to be fulfilled as a woman, living the life you want to be living, is a personal challenge, one that you must meet on your own terms. We've written this book to help you meet that challenge. Rather than listening to myths, men, mother, the media, and other influences that are all too ready to tell you what you should want, we will encourage you to trust yourself, ask some good questions, and begin to reason and act your way toward the answers that are true for you.

"We cannot solve our problems with the same thinking used when we created them," wrote Albert Einstein, who also said that if he were given one hour in which to deal with a difficult situation (we are, of course, paraphrasing here), he would spend the first fifty-five minutes asking himself the questions that defined the issue; once that was accomplished, he'd solve the problem in the remaining five minutes. To you, we say: Once you get the questions right, the answers—or better answers—become clear.

We call that process self-talk.

Initially, we considered using the title "1,000 Hours of Therapy for the Price of a Book." That notion was prompted by these facts: As seven psychologists who have spent countless hours listening to our patients' worries and frustrations, we bring to the dialogue that follows a deep and varied understanding of women's lives. We hope you will feel as if you're sitting in the comfortable chair across from our collective selves, and as if we're talking. We will pose some questions and suggest some avenues of thought that may not have occurred to you. We will work with you at sorting out messages that are perhaps clouding the picture of your life, and at considering the options you have.

Self-talk is no mystery. It's actually something you do all the time, for it is the internal conversation that points you in one direction or another, toward this choice or that one. It is a force you can take charge of and harness—but only when you know who's doing the talking. Are you actually following others' voices, thinking they are your own? How do you know? And what do you do about it?

The self-talk you will go through in the following chapters is the process by which you learn to better understand what you really want, how you really feel, and what may be the consequences of particular actions. Before we tell you how it works, let's briefly consider the major factors that conspire to create feelings of discontent in so many women today.

Under the Face of Things

There's a kind of popular image of twenty-first-century woman we have all somehow absorbed—from magazines, TV shows, and news items, perhaps from the coworker in the corner office down the hall. The image tells us that today's woman is strong, sexual, confident in her femaleness. She's accomplished and assertive, aggressive when necessary. Whatever road she's on—married or unmarried, career woman, professional, homemaker, mother—it's one of her own design. She is also a bit smug about all this; she handles her days with a casually competent, I'm-on-top-of-my-game attitude. In the words of a professor of media studies, today's woman is often pictured as "tough and smart-alecky as well as really self-aware."

And why shouldn't she be? After all, women have become liberated. We have benefited from a few decades of consciousness raising and role change. We have more money, more information, more power, and, most significant, wider options in all areas of life. The sky's the limit. Or, as a popular actress told us recently in a magazine interview, "We can have absolutely anything we want now." *All is achievable.*

At the same time *all is permissible.* The roles that defined the generations of women who came before us are no longer carved in stone. Unmarried? Embrace your singleness! Working mother? Good for you! Happy homemaker? That's great! Lesbian? Why not? Or, as a popular media personality told us, "Women have the power to be themselves."

There is truth and much that is good in this. The measureable gains made by women in the workplace, for example, and the lessening of old taboos, constraints, rules, and notions relating to a woman's place and presentation in the world—are real and to be applauded. We have, indeed, arrived at something that looks like freedom. And yet, for our clients—and, we're guessing, for you—the *experience* of freedom is not great. Things have indeed changed, but not that much (and in some areas, not much at all). What *has* changed are the expectations we bring to what it means to be a success as a woman living in this world.

The fact is, being free to do or be as you choose does not inevitably make life easier or more pleasant. On the contrary, the apparent freedom that is suggested by an abundance of choices can feel more frustrating than exciting, and more frightening than empowering. And so, many of us ordinary women end up disappointed in our own degree of confidence and our own range of accomplishments. We're caught in a new kind of oppression.

The New Oppression

If all is *achievable,* if no one and nothing is any longer holding a woman back, then it is entirely up to her to feel satisfied. When she feels less than satisfied, she assumes it must be her fault and quietly berates herself for her mistakes. She looks beyond herself to the handful of women who seem to have pulled it all together and gotten it right. Then she wonders what's wrong with her.

Today's woman is encouraged to believe:

- Managing money is a good thing.
- Being a career woman is a good thing.
- Repairing your own leaky faucet is a good thing.

To herself, she may be saying: "Thinking about investments makes me break out in a cold sweat." "I really would like to just stay home and cook." "I expect *him* to take care of the faucet, and it infuriates me when he can't or won't."

If all is *permissible,* if a woman has the power to shape her life and control her destiny, then happiness should be the outcome. When she's not happy, she wonders what's wrong with her.

Today's woman is encouraged to believe:

- It's okay to be single.
- It's okay to be overweight—in fact, come right out and call it fat!
- It's okay to stay home with the kids.
- It's okay to have a different color skin and different hair from the people around you.
- It's okay to wear clothes that reflect your ethnic background, even though it makes you stand out or invites comments.

To herself, she may be saying: "But I'm terribly lonely." "But I hate my fat body, and I can't stand looking at myself." "But I feel as if I'm lacking in ambition and I get defensive around people who are 'out there' in the world." "But I fear that people won't understand my culture, and think I'm so different they won't want to be with me."

As psychologists, we ask: If the freedom to do and/or be has created an increased level of psychological health (call it self-assurance, confidence, or contentment), why do so many competent women suspect they're not doing very well at all? The fact is, while it may *look* like a woman's world has undergone a sea change, many of the stumbling blocks are still as true as ever, if perhaps somewhat camouflaged and disguised.

Apparent progress notwithstanding, external obstacles or societal attitudes still limit our possibilities or make us unsettled about our choices. Internal barriers still hinder us.

Complicating the picture, interpersonal developments in our puzzling new world—including the fragility of the couple, the blurring of sexual attitudes, the changing nature of the parent-child relationship—leave us without a sure relational compass.

We've been riding the wave of feminism for thirty-five years—and we're still confused. The old oppression, as defined by Betty Friedan and railed against by a cadre of determined women who marched on matters ranging from forced sterilization to job equity, was clear and tangible. There was much on which to hang our hats and enable us to conclude: "I can't get to where I want to be, because society won't let me because I'm not a man." Today, we live with the new oppression and its consequences: "I can succeed, I can even have it all (everybody tells me). But in my heart of hearts I don't feel like I'm succeeding at much of anything and I certainly don't have it all, so what's wrong with me?"

The Women You Will Meet in *Finding Your Voice*

In the pages that follow, we look under the image to the real experiences of real women. You will see that matters are far more complex than the image suggests—and that, whatever your suspicions of inadequacy may be, you have much company.

You *know*—indeed, you can hardly have escaped absorbing—all the ubiquitous advice on how to have a better relationship and satisfying sex, trim down and firm up, balance work and family, and so on. What *we* hear every day in our practice is the disconnect—

how and why women feel they are failing or paying lip service or putting up a good front—and the forces, internal and external, that make it so difficult to change, adjust, or simply accept themselves as perfectly good enough. The women we talk to feel stuck, even though they wish to be unstuck and to move forward. That's especially true for women of color, who have been marginalized all their lives.

Each chapter lays out the expectation, the high-bar, popularly promoted image or images of the modern woman—how the expectation is expressed, how it seeps into our collective cultural consciousness and into our individual, often dissatisfied sense of self. Each then presents several profiles, real stories based on real women we counsel, that reveal what's actually going on in many people's lives. The profiles illustrate the most common issues that women present in our practice. And it is a vast and varied landscape.

Do not be overly concerned about the variety of those histories and perspectives. Do not focus just on the woman whose age is similar to your own, because the themes are universal. They may be more subtle or present themselves in different ways at different points in the life cycle, but they're there. And we believe you will find in these women's stories an echo, maybe even a carbon copy of your own reality.

What's bothering you?

Many of our clients come to us with this presentation: "Things are just not where I want them to be, and I thought that talking them over with you might be useful." If that's where you're starting from, fine. Perhaps you too are aware only of a feeling of malaise, or a generalized anxiety or discontent. You are far from alone.

On the other hand, maybe you have focused with laser intensity on a specific problem, such as a man in your life, the lack of a man in your life, a horrible job, or a troubled child as the source of your pain. A number of our clients enter our offices quite certain they know what's bothering them. "I just broke up with my boyfriend, and I'm really upset," says a woman who's hoping for suggestions on how to get past her immediate unhappiness. Yet quite often, the problem—the issue she believes she has a clear fix on—is only the most obvious blip on the screen. The problem brings her in the door, and then over a bit of time she may come to recognize its offshoots and ramifications. And so the deeper issues for the woman who broke up with the boyfriend may include: How does she choose men? How quickly does she allow herself to become attached? Is she living with a fantasy?

If you are dead sure what's bothering you or, on the other hand, you don't know where to start, don't worry. This book will help you clarify your personal story, and you may end up in a place very far from where you started. One intention of self-talk, ideally, is to encourage you to be open enough to realize that not every happening in one's life is the outcome of a clear cause and effect. Where one is "at" at any point in time—the events, behaviors, and choices that shape the day—is the result of the coming together of many factors and forces.

At the same time, we are not suggesting that every woman has problems in every category we discuss. We are not saying that as a woman, per se, your life is troublesome in these particular ways. (That would be promoting still another voice, the voice of the therapist.) You may find that after doing some self-talk questions in one area, you're perfectly fine; this isn't an issue that requires rethinking or working through on your part.

How Self-Talk Works

We describe a three-step process, what we call:

- Voice mapping
- Reframing
- Movement strategies

Although we talk about "steps," these are in no way discrete phases, carved in stone, with one opening up before you only after the previous one has been completed. You will go back and forth, in and out.

Voice Mapping

When describing *Finding Your Voice* to friends and colleagues, we've been saying, "It's a book to help women find their own voices instead of listening to lots of others." And people instantly get it; they understand what we mean. What are those other voices and where are they coming from? Listen to the following randomly gathered comments from some famous and not-so famous women.

In her address to a college graduating class, the author and columnist Anna Quindlen said, "When I quit the *New York Times* to be a full-time mother, the voices of the world said I was nuts. When I quit it again to be a full-time novelist, they said I was nuts again."

In a newspaper interview, the actress Jane Fonda, newly divorced from her third husband, said, "Before each of my marriages, I had this feeling in my stomach that something wasn't right, and I ignored it. I always thought, I'll fix it. It's what happens when you lose touch with your own voice."

Flipping through a magazine, our friend Chloe came across a photo of a well-known political activist, a woman much in the news for many years. Chloe said, "My first thought was, God, she's really looking old! And sometime later, my second, third, and fourth thoughts were something like this: Actually, what she looks like is a woman of her age. What she looks like is a woman who hasn't had plastic surgery and isn't getting Botoxed every three months. And that translated into a look that said *old* in my head."

Our Episcopalian friend Ellie said she thought she'd attend church one Sunday morning, and then decided to skip the service after seeing that the sermon would be delivered by one of the associate ministers, a woman. "I'm embarrassed to admit this," said Ellie, "and I have no idea where it comes from, but I don't like to listen to a female minister, especially one who speaks English with an accent. Although I've heard some women give terrific sermons and some men give deadly dull sermons, it's just some little voice that tells me women aren't supposed to be ministers. Go figure."

There they are, some of them. The voices of the world—of myths, men, media, friends, and enemies, all the great "they" out there—are constantly buzzing in our brains, advising us of how our lives "should" be proceeding. Ms. Quindlen, Ms. Fonda, Chloe, and Ellie recognized them clearly, with feelings that might be described as insightful but rueful self-annoyance. The voices, however, are not always so easy to spot. Indeed, many of our feelings, reactions, and decisions are more externally controlled than we would ever dream.

As you read through the chapters to come and perhaps zero in on some problem areas in your own life and what our case histories have to suggest, you'll see that some voice mapping is obvious. Who-is-doing-the-talking will jump right out and hit you between the eyes. Other "shoulds" are more difficult to discern, because the messages are at once pervasive but diffuse and subtle. (Who told us a middle-aged man looks like a middle-aged man and a middle-aged woman looks old? Who told us ministers aren't supposed to be women?)

First, you will do your due diligence on whatever issue it is you're working on or bothered about. Ask: What's directing me here? What are the messages that have me doing what I'm doing about all this (dating, money, jobs, parenting)?

There may be more than one; indeed, you may become aware of a muted cacophony of voices, some of them conflicting, that have been propelling you along (an old family role as "the smart one," with a sister who was "the pretty one"? A husband too much or too little like your father? Magazine images of gorgeous women that leave you discouraged and dispirited?). Make some notes, if that seems useful; write down the voices and messages, so they're not just passing through your brain, and so you can return to look them over and give them some thought. Keep in mind that your voice mapping may reveal messages to you that are different from those influencing the women we use as examples. It's important to hear your own realities and recognize their sources.

The fact is, once you start thinking about it and asking the right questions, you may discover an astonishing number of "shoulds" in your life—how you should act in a relationship, what job you should have, whether you should have a job at all, how you should handle your money, how you should look. The trick is figuring out where the "shoulds" are coming from. Who or what is conveying them to you? The answer will be different for different women. This is what voice mapping is all about.

Are those voices all wrong, misguided, irrelevant, or unimportant? Do you turn them off once and for all? Certainly not. Obviously, what your love partner, your parent, your boss, or your child wants or needs from you or of you must be something of a critical factor in the decisions you make. But in order to feel genuinely in control of those life issues over which it is appropriate for you to be in control, in order to reason and then act your way into paths that are right for you, you must figure out who is saying what. That, simply, is what we mean by voice mapping—recognizing your current self-talk and where it's coming from, separating out the "they" from the "me." What do *I* think and want?

Once you have voice-mapped, identified where you learned what you learned regarding a particular issue, cleared away some of the cobwebs, and come to where you think *your* still, small voice is speaking up, you're ready for the next step.

Reframing

Reframing is a period of transition, exploration—basically, what we call in therapy the "working through." You will take a step to the side and tune out some of the voices that have always been there, the better to hear your own. Watch yourself, as best as you can. Toy with some fresh ideas. Envision new ways to deal with the same old stuff in your life. Come at a nagging issue from a slightly different perspective. The following is a metaphor that may be helpful.

Think of this as the fitting room phase. Your old clothes aren't working for you anymore. Maybe your weight has changed and they're too big or small, or too ethnic or stylized for the occasion, or they're outdated, or they're just not right for you at this time. And so after a little window shopping, looking around to see what else is out there, you choose a variety of different but appealing pieces. You bring them into the fitting room and try them on. You decide to stick with some and eliminate others.

In therapy, this is the point at which we suggest that our client look at alternative ways of thinking and acting, based on what we have learned about the messages that have been influencing her. We will ask, in effect: Have you ever considered the situation from this angle, or that one? What would happen if you take that step? What would happen if you do nothing at all? Who stands to lose and who stands to gain? How bad is this situation really? Why do you have to solve it? Who could help you with it?

These are some of the questions you will pose for yourself. Think of it as a self-debate, being your own devil's advocate. The fact is, some of what you can achieve in the context of therapy you can learn to do by yourself—with careful listening, honest questioning, and the willingness to consider framing the past and the present in another way.

You will consider, Now that I think I know where that message came from, I wonder: Does it serve me, does it reflect who I really am? Have I ever challenged it?

Perhaps you will find it helpful to turn the approach around, as we frequently do when talking with our clients. It is so often easier to view options and choices from another's perspective, especially for someone who habitually tends to come down hard on herself, or who might be said to have an unusually harsh conscience. (And in our experience, that's the average woman. She'll let other people get away with much more than she allows herself to get away with, partly because of the expectation that a woman should be all things for all people, all the time—one of the voices we've taken in.) So we might ask our client, "If your daughter or your best friend were having that problem, what would you tell her?" And she'll reply, "Oh, I'd probably say, don't worry honey, it'll work out fine for you. Just . . ." to which we might respond, "Okay. You have that voice in you. You just don't have it for yourself. Try to find it."

Reframing, trying out a different mindset or another angle, is an active process. Some of the process will be quiet reflection, internal musings that no one else sees or needs to know about. On the other hand, it may include reaching out to others in a new way—maybe calling the sister you haven't talked to in a year and suggesting lunch; maybe saying no when you've always said yes; maybe not taking the bait when a friend tries to bully you into doing something you don't want to do. The reframing period may involve spending less time at one pursuit and more time at another.

Movement Strategies

Begin thinking in a different way; stop operating by rote, doing the things you've always done because that's what you think you "should" be doing. Which doesn't mean *not* responding to the others in your life. Tuning in to the voice that is "the real me" is anything but subscribing to the popular image that defined the so-called "me generation." Rather, you learn how to deal simultaneously and satisfactorily with the self *and* with others.

There's risk involved. With the old way, you can be pretty sure how something's going to play out; even if the old way is not necessarily getting you anywhere, there's ease in the familiar. Try something new and different, on the other hand, and you may experience equal measures of exhilaration and anxiety. New behaviors are often awkward and uncomfortable in the beginning. Deciding to take another approach to some aspect of life doesn't mean all the pieces will fall into place. With practice, however, new strategies flow more easily.

And then, of course, if your dilemmas are intrinsically involved with other people, your movement strategies will be complicated by interlocking relationships. Psychologists use the analogy of the dance to refer to the interplay between two (or among more than two) individuals: When one partner changes the steps, so must the other—and not necessarily to his or her pleasure.

There's something else to consider as well: The society we live in still holds women in a bind. For example, we've learned over the past several decades that women can be taught to be more assertive, trained in the skills needed to be effective in Fortune 500 companies. And, listening to our clients' experiences, we then learned that so often a woman is slapped down for behaving in just those ways. The assertive woman is still viewed as pushy; the glass ceiling still exists. The point is, when you begin to adopt new behaviors you may not necessarily or immediately hit a system of rewards from the world. The receptivity may not be there. In some of the scenarios that follow, we hope to explore movement strategies that help you reach for new achievements *and* avoid being harmed for moving forward. We do know this: You will feel more powerful and empowered because you have some control over your responses. You will feel good about your ability to make whatever choice you make, as difficult as that choice may be.

In working out the processes of voice mapping, reframing, and new movement strategies, allow for revision and adjustment. If it doesn't work or you're not satisfied, it's time to ask:

- How else might I come at this?
- Do I need to modify what I'm after here?
- What do I really want to change?

Don't think that you must be 100 percent committed to a particular decision you reached, or that if you revert back to some old feelings your decision was therefore misguided, the whole business was an exercise in futility, and you're a washout as a human being.

Revision—revisiting choices—may go on for a lifetime. The writer and poet Maya Angelou, in "Wouldn't Take Nothing for My Journey Now," talks about a woman's inner journey, and what the woman who navigates it successfully needs to do: "She must have convinced herself, or be in the unending process of convincing herself, that she, her values, and her choices are important." Moving on, through the right-for-you strategies, may be an unending process.

Women to Women: Our Goal
and Our Wish for *Finding Your Voice*

In thinking through, talking over, and writing this book, we've kept in mind three overriding goals.

First, if you know that your life is not where you want it to be, we'll help you think and act your way to a better place, or into a good or better outcome of a bad situation. In the process, you strengthen your preventive muscles, so that you'll feel confident, competent, and capable despite the curves that life will continue to throw at you. This is what we do with our clients, who invariably are individuals with genuine strengths and who simply need a bit of help in sorting out complicated lives. Our work with women in our offices is the process we give you in these pages.

Second, if you discover after some voice mapping and reframing that you really don't need or wish to do anything very differently at all, great! The process of change is a choice, and it may be one you elect, with absolute confidence and conviction, not to make. To decide to do what you've always been doing is as powerful a choice as changing. But now you own your decisions and actions. We can't think of anything more satisfying than encouraging a woman, after her careful self-examination, to feel more accepting of and more comfort in who she is, *just as she is.*

Finally, in some of the chapters that follow, we talk about taboos and silences, how so many women don't open up to other women in their lives—out of shyness, perhaps, or self-consciousness, competitiveness, pride, shame, or embarrassment, as much as because of too many distractions and too little time. We want to urge you to start talking, which is the subject of our final chapter. Get together with a friend or a small group and do some self-talk in the company of women, and you almost surely will find others are going through or have experienced some of the same doubts, worries, and frustrations, as well as successes. As our own group of seven, we know that joining forces and sharing our thoughts and experiences has informed us as individuals, and validated and encouraged us as well. We wish the same for you.

In the address to the graduating college seniors, Anna Quindlen went on to say that, despite the voices telling her otherwise, she was not nuts at all, but a success on her own terms. To her audience of twenty- and twenty-one-year-olds, she gave this advice, which rings true for any woman, of any age and at any stage of her life's journey: Do not be caught up in lockstep, going along with the crowd, because lockstep "tells us there is one right way to do things, to look, to behave, to feel, when the only right way is to feel your heart hammering inside you and to listen to what its timpani is saying."

2

The Friendship Expectation:
"I've Always Got My Girlfriends"

The expectations surrounding women's friendships have to do with an assumption of universal sisterhood, which tells us that men come and go, romantic affairs are iffy, blood relations carry a lot of emotional baggage, but a woman's friends are always there for her.

For one thing, women are the great communicators. Starting back in third or fourth grade, we were the gender that loved to talk. Studies in child and adolescent development confirm what most of us remember from our own lives: girls seek connection through intimate disclosure—telling each other their secrets, sharing their problems, offering shoulders to cry on. Young girls are more likely than boys to form intense, same-sex "best friends" relationships. While girls have "face-to-face" friendships, boys have "side-by-side" ones, connecting through activities like sports and video games.

And then, women think alike. Stub an emotional toe and your best friend will understand how you feel. Go through a difficult time, and she will know just when you want her to call and check in on you, and just what you need to hear from her.

This warm, appealing picture of women with women is reinforced throughout the popular culture. For every *Heathers*, the blackly comic account of high school female bitchery, we can see or read many versions of the opposite—the understanding, beauty, and strength of women together. Actress Sarah Jessica Parker describes *Sex and the City*, the popular cable TV comedy-drama, as "a love story for women looking for relationships with men that are as fulfilling as their friendships with women." A reviewer of the bestselling *Divine Secrets of the Ya-Ya Sisterhood* calls it a book about three generations "trying to survive marriage, motherhood, and pain, relying always on their love for each other."

Reality, once again, is somewhat more complex.

First, however: Do women value their friends? Of course. A close female friend is so often the person we find it easiest to be with and talk to, the one we turn to for support or comfort. For many unmarried or unattached women, a sense of personal well-being actually centers on the quality and the number of their friendships. Do we need those friendships in our lives? Probably even more than we realize.

When you're under intense pressure, call a girlfriend to talk or meet for lunch and you're doing your mind and your body much good. Research has provided us with this intriguing suggestion: The familiar "fight or flight" reaction to a stressful situation may hold true for men, but not necessarily for women. According to a study conducted by UCLA scientists, release of the hormone oxytocin at a tense moment encourages a woman not to do battle or run the other way, but rather to care for children and gather together with other women. They call it a "tend and befriend" response, which further helps her calm herself and lessens the stress she is naturally experiencing.

Less stress translates to a longer life. It is possible that the fact that we outlive men stems in part from our instinct and ability to form wider and deeper friendships. The long-term Nurses' Health Study at Harvard Medical School concluded that the more friends a woman has, the fewer physical impairments she experiences as she ages, and the better able she is to cope with losing her husband. In fact, not having a close friend or two may be as detrimental to your health over the long run as smoking or being seriously overweight.

Also, by nurturing female friendships, a woman may ensure that her safety net stays woven. In our work with battered women, we hear again and again that one of the batterer's first efforts is to isolate the woman from her friends. But having other women to turn to enormously helps the woman in an abusive relationship, contributing to her resilience and providing a reality baseline from which to determine whether her views of the relationship are distorted.

So, solid social ties are critical. But friendships are not always so easy to foster and maintain, sometimes for reasons that may be uniquely female. In this chapter, we look at several difficulties many contemporary women experience:

- Old friends drifting away; difficulty finding new ones
- Friendships that turn sour
- Handling conflict

Caroline's Story

"The people I thought were my friends seem to have just disappeared."

Caroline, forty-eight, had gone through what she called "the worst thing I could have imagined. I was devastated." Her husband of twenty years had left her, abruptly, almost two years earlier for another woman. "I did know for some time that the marriage wasn't what I'd call in great shape," she said. "Henry traveled a lot. When he got back from a business trip, things between us were always strained for a while. I'd sort of turn myself inside out to be accommodating and amusing, to keep the house humming along." Still, there was no talk of going for marital counseling, no specific indications from her husband that he might be wanting out. "There were a few little things. Once I tried to get him to make vacation plans for the next summer, and I could never pin him down. I did notice this. Anything having to do with the future, he just seemed to want to avoid getting into it." She brushed it all off.

The breakup occurred in what Caroline thought was a particularly brutal way. "Our son was gone for the weekend. This was a Friday. I got home from work at my regular time, around six, and I was surprised to see Henry sitting there in the living room. Usually he didn't get in until much later." With no preamble, he announced that he was leaving, "that he thought this was really the best for both of us, he had a lawyer and he recommended I get one too. And that was it. As far as he was concerned, it was a done deal. I had no say."

The following months were painful, confusing, and sometimes chaotic. There were bitter discussions about finances, whether the house should be sold, and which parent their fifteen-year-old son should spend most of his time with. It was, Caroline said, "really a good year or year and a half before I began to feel that things were settling down and I was going to get back to a normal life eventually." She had been hashing all this out in therapy over that time; especially of late, however, what she wanted to talk about was not what she perceived as her husband's betrayal and not her child's adjustment ("he's really doing okay, by all indications"), but her social life or lack of it—in particular, friends who had fallen by the wayside: "I've really been hurt by women I thought I was close to."

She described some of her grievances. "Right after Henry left, and of course most of the people we knew heard about it almost instantly, a couple of women we socialized with called me and were really great. They were comforting, they let me vent, and they sort of said to tell them if there was anything I needed. That was in the first month or two. Then I never heard from them again. Once I actually did want some help—I didn't have a car for the week and needed a drive somewhere, and I called this one woman who'd made the offer. She had a lot of excuses about why she couldn't do it."

Another woman kept in touch sporadically. "But if I called her to get together, she was never available, which I understand. She was caught up in family stuff. Then she phoned me a couple of times and said her husband was out of town and her kids were away for the weekend, and did I want to meet for a glass of wine. It seems she thought of me only when she had nothing more important to do."

Old friends were dropping out of her life, and new ones weren't materializing. "I'm not looking for another man at this point," Caroline said. "I just need a wider circle of people. That's turning out to be hard to find."

Her discomfort, sense of abandonment, and loneliness actually had roots in both her past and her present. Caroline wanted to understand: Why do I feel deserted by people I thought were my friends? And how can I form new meaningful connections?

Voice Mapping

"I've always got my girlfriends."

Caroline believed what has almost become an adage. She was sure that her female friendships superceded other relationships. So it was something of a shock to her that other realities in the lives of women she knew were taking precedence over their relationships with her.

"Friends should stick by you, thick or thin and through the ages."

And if they don't stick by you, according to the way Caroline was seeing things, they probably didn't care for you a whole lot in the first place. She'd been deeply wounded by what she called the "brush-offs" from people, and then she was bitter. It felt like a further betrayal on top of what had happened with her husband.

Reframing

Where did my old friends go, and why?

Or here's another way to put it: What has changed most dramatically—me, them, or the situation?

In many cases, it's going to be the situation. Caroline's experiences pointed to one major reason friends drop away or simply become less available: a major life transition alters the unspoken basis of the old connection. A woman who enjoys her group of three best pals, all together since their college days, gets married, and her friends remain single. A married woman who enjoys her group of three also-married women has a baby, and her friends remain childless. A woman comes out as a lesbian, and her friends become reluctant to be alone with her, thinking her sexual orientation may have changed her personality. A woman, like Caroline, goes through the trauma of divorce or widowhood, and her friends are still attached to living, breathing husbands. And between that woman and her friends, maybe nothing can be quite the same as it was before.

Perhaps especially when a romantic relationship—a boyfriend, a fiancé, a husband, or a partner—enters one woman's world, the feeling of solidarity and comfort within her cadre of good girlfriends often lessens. Jealousy, fear of abandonment, or the competitiveness that girls are *still* socialized into colors the atmosphere. Sometimes the friendship between two women will span a male-female or romantic relationship, but not always. Here's where the expectation that "lovers come and go, but girlfriends are forever" gets undermined. The fact is, just as is true in most species, in the human drama mating usually out-trumps friendship. When push comes to shove, the primary relationship will win out—the high school girl drops her friends when the cute boy calls for a date on Friday night; the lesbian forgets her girlfriend/pal when a potential partner comes along.

This is hard to accept. We anticipate better; a friend is supposed to be happy about your happiness. Sometimes she isn't, not entirely. And the woman who expects her old friendships to stay unchanged after one of those major life transitions can end up hurt, angry, or disappointed.

Even not-so-major transitions often result in a loss of people who once felt like friends. For many women, the majority of friendships are situation-specific, or related to shared experiences. When they're no longer shared as time goes on, the women drift apart or maybe discover there's not enough else between them to sustain the connection. One client said that of all the mothers she'd known and made friends with during their children's school years, only one "stuck." Despite all the talks over coffee, the playdate and birthday party arrangements, and working together on school committees, she found that "there's just one woman from that time I still talk to and who I consider a friend. Now that our kids are young adults, we're not talking about the kids so much anymore, and the relationship has evolved into a real woman-to-woman friendship."

So, considering the situation, am I being unreasonable or unrealistic?
A woman who's feeling brushed off needs to evaluate her own thoughts and emotions:

- Do I have unrealistic expectations about how others should act toward me? Am I not taking into account the bigger picture?
- Are my voices of hurt and disappointment overly sensitive?

Caroline decided maybe she *was* being too sensitive or not reading situations accurately. For example, she described socializing with her old crowd a few times since her divorce ("dinner parties with small groups of people") and said she felt "like a third wheel or an add-on, like maybe they were sorry about me being on my own." She thought she was "not truly wanted there."

Maybe she wasn't truly welcome or the atmosphere was a bit tense. The divorced, unattached woman who still circulates in the company of couples might be viewed warily by one or two wives who feel a bit unsure of their husbands, or themselves. Caroline needed to give some thought to how she could dispel such suspicions, maybe by befriending the women and consciously not being too chummy with the husbands. One client in that situation said she "put it right out there on the table. After my separation, I made a point of telling my women friends, 'Trust me, I'm not after your guy, you don't have anything to worry about.'"

On the other hand, maybe those dinner invitations were extended out of real affection and enjoyment of her company, and Caroline needed to get past her self-consciousness and third-wheel perceptions.

What exactly does having or being a friend mean to me?
As she tried to look at her old social contacts realistically and figure out how to make new ones, Caroline asked herself, "What do I mean by a friend?" It was something she hadn't thought through before, and it was a good question. In other words, am I looking for:

- Expressions of caring?
- Inclusion in a wide circle of peers?
- Understanding?
- Just one or two people I can talk to about personal issues, without feeling anxious, guilty, or embarrassed?
- One or two people who want me in their lives as much as I want them?
- A few smart and funny women to get together with regularly, although I'm not necessarily going to tell them all my woes because that's not something I need?

Questioning your personal definition of friendship can be a revealing exercise. For one thing, if for one reason or another you gravitate to people who approach friendship in a way that's very different from yours, you're likely to continue to feel disappointed or misunderstood. It's also true that friendship needs may shift over time. One client, a busy professional woman, decided she would concentrate on several close friends and consciously not encourage involvements with other people. She found various polite ways to let these second- and third-tier acquaintances know that she wasn't able to be so available to them.

Movement Strategies

I need to redefine my social parameters.

In talking about her changed social circumstances and the difficulty she was having connecting with new people, Caroline echoed the experiences and feelings of many women. A surprising number of our clients say they really don't have good friends. That may partly reflect our mobile society, in which environments and the people in them change rapidly. But the older you get, the harder it gets. In college, making friends is a pretty natural process—they're the people sharing a dorm room or a sorority house, a biology class or a lacrosse team with you. Later on, the accessibility of potential friends usually diminishes. You may need to be more pointedly intentional.

To be more intentional, start by taking a reading of where and how you've amassed the friends you do have or the women you see on a regular basis. If everybody you know comes out of a tight, clearly defined social circle, you might need to stretch your ability to accommodate women in different circumstances as friends.

Maybe you struck up some good talk with the others in Lamaze class, and now you've all progressed to Mommy and Me groups and preschool. Hence, child-related activities define the population of women you know.

Maybe you can't remember a time in years when your social life did not revolve around your partner's business associates or your own coworkers.

Maybe, as was the case for Caroline, your friends are almost exclusively "couple friends," the wives of the men you and your partner socialize with. When her own couplehood ended Caroline found herself in that changed landscape, and she questioned whether she and those women were ever really close in the first place or whether they fit what she was looking for at that point in her life. "There's been a lot of 'starting over' for me in the last couple of years," she discovered, "and part of that is wanting to know new people—ideally, I hope, those will be some individuals who didn't go to all the same dinner parties for the last twenty years, don't know all the same people I know, who point me in some new directions."

Maybe it's time to let go of friendships that have withered on the vine.

One client, a woman who thought of friendship in terms of mutual kindness and caring, realized that she remained within a circle of women largely because they'd all known each other for thirty years. And those women weren't especially kind and caring people. Within the group, she saw nastiness, negative gossiping, and exclusionary behavior. Many women find themselves maintaining connections that have stopped being pleasurable because it feels disloyal to say "no thanks" to the monthly bridge games. Old friends, according to the adage, are the gold; new friends are the silver. But not always.

Sometimes it makes sense to let go, and letting go can be an added impetus to start looking elsewhere. Caroline, for example, decided she'd stop feeling rejected by her former friends; she'd try to maintain connections with one or two women from the "old life" whom she genuinely enjoyed and include them in her "new life," and not worry about the rest.

I should try to reach out more—my health depends on it.

This movement strategy applies to anyone, across the board: When a woman is caught up in busy, overscheduled days, one of the first items to drop off her "to-do" list is keeping in touch with a girlfriend (which may be one of the reasons so many of our clients claim they have no close friends). It's not that she doesn't want to. But overseeing her children's homework, getting to the job on time, throwing in another load of laundry, maybe running errands for aging parents, all take priority. Working women tell us they make certain to carve out time for their families; their friendships, however, feel elective, something that can go on the back burner. Since, as we mentioned earlier, friends are apparently a critical component of good mental and even physical health, it makes sense to *increase* their value and their place on the to-do list.

But the woman who's feeling somewhat friendless or who needs to re-create a social life can be daunted by another issue. When friendships don't come easily, when it takes being pointedly intentional, she can feel there's something wrong with her: Should it be this difficult? Maybe people don't like me.

There's a process for making friends; trust and intimacy develop over time, but the process starts with reaching out, perhaps in ways that initially feel awkward. For example, Caroline described herself as "on the quiet side, somebody who waits to be invited. I'm trying to overcome that a little. I go to church pretty regularly, but I usually skip the coffee hour afterward. Lately, I've been staying for that, and I introduce myself to people I haven't met before. Just making myself get through that momentary discomfort of being with unfamiliar people or joining a group that's already engaged in conversation."

Here's an even more pointedly intentional way to promote new friendships: Spend a half hour thinking of individuals you've met once or twice and would like to know better. Draw up a list. Set yourself the goal of making one phone call a day or one a week with the specific aim of widening your circle of associates. Join a new activity. Take pottery classes or try out a biking club, and see if anyone else attending might be someone you could cultivate as a new friend. Get involved with a project with other women, such as the walks organized around finding a cure for breast cancer. Fighting a common enemy creates a bond from which friendships may grow.

Especially as we get older, we cannot simply count on life circumstances to help us build friendships. Sometimes it's necessary to be more of a go-getter, to overcome the feeling that we don't want anyone to know we're looking for friends, and just to do it. Any such strategies mean you are being proactive, making a choice that puts you more in control of your life.

Eva's Story

"I do everything for my friends, and then they constantly let me down."

People took advantage of her, said Eva, thirty. "I give a lot to my friends, but I don't always get back." Eva had a philosophy about friendship that she described this way: "I accept people as they are. I don't try to reform them or change them. You see where they're coming from, what they need, and you're there for them." But her friends weren't there for her, it seemed, or not in the way she expected them to be.

As an example of the kind of behavior that bothered her, Eva described her relationship with Kelly, a woman who'd taken a job at Eva's company a year earlier. Kelly had relocated from another city and stayed with an aunt while she hunted for an apartment. Eva helped her. "I spent practically every evening and most of the weekends for over a month running around with Kelly, checking out places. When she found one she could afford, I went back up to Boston with her, and she and her brother and I hauled all her stuff down to the new place." Eva contributed some additional items she thought her friend needed or would like, including a Moroccan rug that she wasn't using herself. She included Kelly in many of her own social plans, meeting for drinks after work and taking her along to Halloween and New Year's Eve parties.

Eva was a woman who felt the urge to talk at all hours, and she often called Kelly in the early morning, "just to tell her about something weird that happened when I was out that evening." As the months went on and Kelly met more people on her own, she started to turn down some of Eva's invitations and wasn't so willing to gab late at night. One recent incident had brought the growing strain between them to a head.

"Kelly asked me at work one day if I wanted to come over and pick up the rug I'd loaned her, that she didn't need it anymore," Eva said. "It turned out she was planning to take a bigger apartment, with a roommate." She thought it was rude that Kelly hadn't said anything to her about the move and, especially, that she expected Eva to retrieve the rug herself. "I called her that evening, and I told her I thought it was really up to her to get the rug back to me. She apologized and said, sure, okay, she would. Then I asked her, if she was moving into a bigger place, didn't she still want the rug?" That precipitated a conversation that gave Eva a look at how Kelly perceived their friendship.

Eva explained, "She told me she'd never really wanted this rug or the other things I brought over, but I had pressured her into taking them. I didn't think that was true. Then she said she liked me, she appreciated how helpful I'd been to her, she didn't want to hurt my feelings, but I was too 'domineering' or 'unpredictable' for her to be really comfortable with. She needed to back off a little. Those were the words." Eva was fuming; she felt used. As far as she was concerned, that was it for Kelly.

As Eva described other friendships that had gone sour, a pattern emerged. She was "there" for her friends, she believed that she did all the right things, yet sooner or later people didn't want to be around her so much anymore. Over the years she'd had a string of quickly formed, intense friendships that fizzled or burned out.

Interestingly, Eva was invariably late for her therapy sessions, sometimes as much as half an hour. When we raised the issue (pointing out that although she insisted she wanted to be there, she was often, in fact, *not* there), her response was, "Oh, that's me, I'm always late for everything." We pressed a bit further, asking what she thought the impact of that behavior might be. "Well," she said, "I guess your time is valuable too. I guess in a sense I'm taking away from your time or from what you do." Her moment of insight helped her begin reframing the whole issue of her troublesome friendships: What did giving and taking mean? What boundaries might need to be recognized and respected? What constitutes boundaries in the first place?

Voice Mapping

"If somebody's your friend, you accept everything about her and she accepts everything about you."

This belief system of Eva's left little room for sensitivity to the nuances of relationships and appropriate responses to them. It wasn't that Eva didn't sometimes recognize that she stretched the limits. She was always late ("I know it drives people crazy"); she liked to call friends in the middle of the night; she could be "a little bossy with my friends." But "that's just me, that's how I am," Eva said. How she was, however, seemed to push people away or wear them out.

"A good friend anticipates and meets all her friend's needs."

Eva believed that women just understand each other—because they're women. In her relationship with Kelly, she sometimes jumped in where Kelly hadn't expressed a wish or need for her to do so. She was certain she had pleased her friend, while Kelly actually felt intruded upon.

Reframing

In a friend, am I looking for too much, too fast?

Sometimes when we meet a new person and, with delight, recognize similarities (she laughs at the things I laugh at, she can't stand the same people I can't stand), we're ready to expect all from her and from the budding relationship. Describing "our depth-charged levels of capacity for intimacy," and how in that regard we women differ from men, psychologist Phyllis Chesler, the author of *Woman's Inhumanity to Woman,* said in an interview: "Men are happy in a middle-distance ground toward all others. They don't take anything too personally, and they don't have to get right into your face, into your business, into your life. Women need to do that. Women, the minute they meet another woman, it's: she's going to be my fairy godmother, my best friend, the mother I never had. And when that's not the case we say, 'well, she's the evil stepmother.'"

That's a description that characterized Eva's running-hot, then running-cold connections with her friends. While some friendships run their course and others perhaps were never destined to be especially stable or lasting in the first place, it's also true that sometimes an intensity of feeling simply isn't reciprocated. Eva tended to think of anyone she liked as a "best friend," but they didn't all feel the same way about her. Or they weren't really permitted sufficient time to develop trust and intimacy, before feeling invaded by Eva's "in your face" behavior.

What's the dominant flavor of my friendships?

Any woman who suspects that she offers or asks for friendship in a way that keeps her from getting genuinely close to others, or who is repeatedly disappointed because hoped-for connections never take root, can help herself by thinking about her typical interpersonal behavior. Consider the following:

- Am I the endless giver, doing too much for the friends I choose? And do I feel I get the short end of the stick?
- Am I giving out to others a quality of time or attention I myself might be desperate to get back?
- Do I make assumptions about what my friends want, without allowing them room to inform me about their needs?
- Do I spend a lot of time listening to others' sob stories and problems?
- Do I subtly invite the sob stories and problems by suggesting my friend always *must* have something going wrong in her life (perhaps by starting every conversation, "Is everything okay? You look so depressed lately.")? If so, maybe you perpetually tend to present yourself as a counselor and a helper, the person who's there to fix things. Obviously, expressions of concern are appropriate at times. But if you are only a foul-weather friend and relish the role, the woman you consider yourself close to may drift away to cheerier companions when her foul weather has lifted.
- Am I an obsessive ruminator, constantly wanting to chew over the details of this or that event with my friends? Do I turn a friend into a therapist? That can be a kind of neediness that others tolerate for a short while, but eventually wish to escape.
- Am I persistently wounded? One friend lets me down so I turn to another; once again I'm hurt, and so I move on to the next individual, carrying along the same old expectations.

Movement Strategies

I need to stop feeling like a victim and become a friendship problem solver.

If you blame others, you place yourself in the role of victim—maybe you feel constantly used by people, as Eva felt about her relationships. Victims don't have much power to change things. It helps to sort out all that perceived bad behavior you're on the receiving end of. Think about particular times you've felt angry, abandoned, used, misunderstood, or like a doormat. What was going on? What role did you have in creating the disappointing behaviors?

Eva had no difficulty describing incidents that got her fired up: One friend broke two movie dates in a row (she did have reasonable excuses, however); another elected to spend a last-minute summer weekend at the shore with her boyfriend, instead of meeting Eva for Sunday brunch; a couple of friends besides Kelly let her know they weren't thrilled about the 2 A.M. phone calls. Just mentally running down this list of her friends' "sins" enabled her to see them as personally aggravating, and not demonstrations of the degree of attention and availability she wanted (or needed)—but actions that were not intended to inflict pain.

The point is to stop perceiving yourself as victim. Analyze your emotional and behavioral patterns, measure your expectations as objectively as possible, and decide how much a particular friendship really does mean to you. Criticism is often painful, but many times it is constructive. When it is destructive, the remarks or actions may be so genuinely hurtful that it's difficult to continue the friendship. Others might need to be met by a more accommodating point of view, because the rewards of the relationship outweigh the annoyance factor. Then it is within your power to make good changes. Stop hoping the other person will "improve," and figure out what in particular you can do differently.

I must establish better boundaries.

Doing things differently might mean trying to be less of a ruminator or a fixer, the endless giver or the endless taker. For Eva, and for many women, the issue was largely one of boundaries—what's going too far, getting too close, moving too fast? When does what is meant to be friendly behavior feel to the recipient like "in my face," "in my life"?

Proxemics, the study of how people use and arrange space in their daily comings and goings, gives us a definition of four "personal distance zones." In *intimate* relationships, a comfortable distance between two people is 18 inches or less. An individual wants only lovers and the best of friends to enter that space. The *personal* zone, from 1½ to 4 feet apart, is the degree of separation friends try to maintain, or people caught up in close conversation. Further away still is the *social* zone, 4 to 10 feet apart, typically sought by acquaintances in a relaxed environment. Finally, the impersonal *public* zone is 10 feet or more. Cultural differences come into play, too. While in the United States two people feel just right carrying on a conversation with somewhere from 4 to 7 feet separating them, many Europeans take up a position half that distance, which tends to make Americans start backing up.

Friends have their psychological personal distance zones. What distance feels most comfortable to a friend can be perceived with sensitivity to her temperament, needs, and maybe life stage. And sometimes—this was true for Eva, although it took her a while to figure out—friends give specific feedback by their actions or even their words. The pals who stopped answering the phone at two in the morning, the woman who called her "domineering," all were sending out clues that Eva might be taking over an intimate psychological space, when she'd be better liked and appreciated if she moved back into a personal or social zone.

Maria's Story

"I don't know if she and I can be close again."

Maria, forty-one, and Juliette met in graduate school. They shared an apartment for a year and a half, and commiserated over course loads, professors, and boyfriends. Maria left after obtaining her master's degree, and took a job in publishing in New York. Juliette finished a doctorate and began teaching in a midwestern university. By their late thirties, Maria was married, had two children, and worked as a writer for a medical newsletter. Juliette, who had not married, was a professor of English.

From the start, said Maria, the friendship was "lopsided in terms of who did most of the talking and who did most of the listening. I was the listener, mainly about her wild and crazy love life." Juliette occasionally bemoaned her unattached state. One July 4 she sent Maria a postcard that said: "Here it is a holiday and here I am at my desk when I should have a normal family like you do and everyone else does. Right now, I'd settle for one guy and some sparklers! Where are they?" But Maria always suspected that her friend actually relished her single life, which had included a series of exciting affairs. During summers and sabbaticals, Juliette took off for distant places. Passionately interested in a dozen different things, she'd been on archaeological digs in Central America, researched medieval poets on one break in Oxford, and studied the cello. There was usually a new man and a vivid, short-lived romance in the various pictures.

Maria said she herself had never had many friends. "I've never particularly liked most women, for some reason," she said. "Julie was different. She was completely unlike me, and I think that was part of the attraction. She was always a Roman candle, shooting off in all directions, full of life and adventure, and I was kind of the plodder. I was thrilled that we hit it off right from the start, back in school. She was like a gift to me."

Over the years of their friendship, they met whenever Juliette came to New York for professional meetings, and they talked on the phone. Maria was happy with her husband, her children, and her life in general, but she loved hearing about her friend's adventures and romantic involvements. "Julie can be the drama queen, but that's part of her charm." And she was always good with Maria's kids: she sent them offbeat and perfect gifts from her travels, and she took Maria's daughter out for grown-up afternoons when she was in the city.

Then Maria experienced "a string of body blows, one after the other," stretching over a year and a half. Her mother died suddenly; her father suffered a clinical depression and was briefly hospitalized; Maria had a breast cancer scare; and her preteen son started getting into trouble after school. "I felt we were all barely keeping our heads above water for a while there," she said. "Of course, I told Julie what was going on. I wouldn't say she was unsympathetic, exactly. It was more that she had nothing much to say, or her affect was all wrong. She shouldn't have been so cheery!" The last time Maria and Juliette saw each other was over lunch, right in the middle of a time Maria and her husband were deciding whether to send their son to a boarding school. "I started to talk to Julie about this, and she said something like, 'Oh brother, kids, huh?' Then she launched into a description of this next trip she was planning."

Maria felt tears spring to her eyes. Barely able to speak any longer, she cut the lunch short. Soon after that, Juliette left for two months in Europe, and there'd been no communication between the two friends since. Maria believed their old closeness had been damaged beyond repair. "I'd actually like to tell her off, let her know she's been about as sensitive as a rhino during this period in my life. But maybe I should just let it drop."

Here's an interesting reality concerning women and how they handle anger, conflict, or misunderstandings. Some women will fight with their husbands; with their female friends, however, they have a tremendously difficult time of it, and so they tend to distance, not dealing with differences overtly and directly. But conflict resolution is a key skill in maintaining and even strengthening relationships. Maria needed to think through what choices she did have about the friendship that had meant so much to her for so long.

Voice Mapping

"She's my best friend. She should know and share my emotions."

Even if she'd always done most of the listening and Juliette most of the talking, Maria believed that as best friends, they should be on the same emotional wavelength. Many women feel this way; because we do share so much, it's easy to project ourselves onto a friend, assuming she'll feel the same or simply "know."

Maria noted, "Once I read somewhere about the solar system as a metaphor for levels or qualities of friendship. You're the sun. Nearest to you is Mercury, the friend who's always there, even if she's halfway across the country or the world—the friend you don't have to explain things to, who feels your pain like her own. Other people are more distant, like Venus and Jupiter. Then the Pluto friends, who move in elliptical orbits. Sometimes they're right nearby, emotionally speaking. Then, they shift into some outer orbit, and maybe some of them are never seen again. I'd have to say, I think I've always been a Mercury friend to Juliette, and that's what I thought she was for me. But maybe she's really a Pluto friend."

Reframing

Am I looking for something my friend isn't able to give?

Maria pondered this question: Was I expecting my friend to extend herself in ways she didn't need to previously in our relationship? She decided that was so, and that maybe Juliette simply didn't have the capacity to respond fully or sensitively to stress, fear, or worry. That was a disappointment to her, and hurtful, but one aspect of the total picture of their friendship. "It's part of her personality or persona to be lighthearted, the one who's always got funny stories to tell. To my daughter, she's kind of an Auntie Mame. And I love all that about her."

That was a useful perspective to reach. If you have passed through or are experiencing a period of crisis, you may very well find that the friend you thought you could count on, the one who'd come through, wasn't there; she didn't call, she was not sympathetic, she wanted to talk about anything but what was happening. This is another hard truth: A woman may be a loyal, trusted, and delightful friend, and yet not deal with times of crisis in a nurturing way. Or her own life or emotional state is such that she just doesn't have it in her at the moment to offer what you hope for. She may need to move into one of those more distant orbits. Thus the questions are: Can I accept this person's honest limitation, and find the resources I need elsewhere? Can I accept that the friendship might go on hold for a while, but I'll come back to it later, now knowing its parameters—what I can expect from her and what I can't?

Do I value this friendship enough to express my feelings?

Any woman dealing with her anger over a close friend's behavior has three choices:

- End the friendship—usually by withdrawing, not calling, not writing, and being coolly less responsive or less available.
- Remain in the friendship, keeping up the old routines of connection, but saying nothing and feeling forever hurt or resentful.
- Deal with the conflict in some way that will help the relationship survive and perhaps even move to a more intimate, trusting level.

The choice really does depend on the value of the friendship. If it's highly valued, then almost surely it makes sense to convey your true feelings. That's not necessarily an easy thing to do;

confrontation—even when it's well thought out and kindly delivered—can make you anxious, and there may be concerns about losing the friendship. But saying nothing usually produces greater stress in the long run. And buried anger often ruins the friendship anyway.

If you allow behaviors you don't like to persist while you remain mute about it, you're likely to be a whole lot angrier when you do finally mention what you've been feeling. Conflict resolution is a critical social skill; it's a friend's responsibility to learn how to tell another person how she feels. The woman who instinctively avoids any and all confrontations may need to practice that skill.

Movement Strategies

I need to write it out.

Try a dry run. Pro and con lists—what you want to say, what you think better of saying—are helpful in evaluating the efficacy of an action strategy.

This is where Maria started: She'd write her friend a letter, although not send it. "I just want to put my thoughts down on paper, and then when Julie is in town next maybe I'll find it easier to talk a little about my feelings."

Not a bad strategy. Women often report that writing it all out—in a letter or a journal—helps to clarify emotions and allows them to feel they're taking action. Of course, what's said depends on the individuals involved and the nature of the conflict or misunderstanding, but here is what the gist of the letter will probably be:

- I want to talk about something important between us, and it's difficult to do that.
- I value our friendship so much, but I have been upset about this matter and I don't want to let it go.
- This is my concern, this is the issue that's been bothering me.

I can follow some good rules that will help everyone come out feeling okay.

In person, you'll have the best chance of getting your feelings across, resolving any misunderstanding, and improving the friendship if you keep certain ideas in mind:

- Plan a good time to talk. Don't launch an impetuous or sneak attack in the middle of something else going on.
- Describe what you've been feeling. Don't assume your friend will automatically know or should be able to guess.
- Be specific, and stick to "I" statements as much as possible. They convey the information you want to convey without sounding as if you're blaming your friend for everything. "I felt hurt because I was going through a hard time and I desperately needed some comforting and support" is probably a lot better than "You really hurt my feelings because you didn't seem to care about what was happening with me."
- Don't ask "why" she behaved the way she did or said the things she said. Listen to her, accept any apologies or explanations, and reassure her of what's most important to you and probably to her as well: you value her and your friendship enormously.

A close, nurturing, trusting friendship with another woman is one of the joys of life. Good girlfriends really can take a place in your days and your heart that no one else occupies in quite the same way. And one of our stated goals in writing this book has been to encourage you to talk to your friends—more often and more openly. Maybe more than anyone, friends may offer the buffering, support, and encouraging push that will help you navigate the choices you're considering as you reach toward your own voice.

3

The Dating Expectation: "I Can Find the Perfect Partner (but If I Don't, I'll Be Just Fine without One)"

Expectations about our love lives fall along two lines. First, a life's companion is out there for each of us, and with this individual a woman can fashion the ideal relationship. Today we're looking not only for the *total* partner—domestic, financial, and sexual—but for the *perfect* partner, which has to do with an anticipated meeting of souls. In a poll of about a thousand twentysomething men and women, almost all stated they hoped to marry eventually. And just about every one (94 percent) fervently believed, "When you marry, you want your spouse to be your soul mate, first and foremost."

On the other hand, if her soul mate doesn't materialize, a heterosexual woman should be perfectly happy without a man. Gone is the curse attached to making one's way through life alone. And gone is the belief that being alone means one will never have children: significant numbers of unmarried women over age thirty say they'd feel fine about giving birth to a child and raising him or her on their own.

Certainly, it's excellent news that being unattached no longer brands a woman as a social misfit. But does every woman really want a partner?

A few individuals, women and men both, do not seek out or wish to be in romantic relationships. For some, the choice may stem from an intensely independent nature or deep commitment to an all-absorbing life occupation. For most, and especially women, actively shunning love relationships typically reflects a fear of vulnerability. The woman who has sustained trauma, such as physical or psychological abuse, for example, experiences the potential for hurt and loss as too great to take the chance of intimacy. Absent a traumatic experience, however, most women want connection. They want to be in relationships.

The idea that a woman doesn't need one may be something of a myth. It runs counter to who we are and to all that we know, not only about female psychology but about male psychology as well. A woman's sense of self comes primarily in relation to others; a man's sense of self, traditionally, derives primarily from his achievements. Lately, of course, many men are becoming more attuned to their needs for connection. (Interestingly, an unstable job market is the factor that has brought home to many their core sensitivities; a number of our male clients first sensed the primacy of love, family, and emotional expression when they were laid off or fearful of being laid off from work.) At the same time, as achievement-oriented women assume equal positions in the workplace they're likely to define themselves increasingly by what they do.

Still, all the psychological literature talks about women in connection, the self in relation to others. It starts early. A little girl will announce that her grandmother is "my father's mother." A little boy isn't thinking in those terms.

So, assuming that a woman naturally will seek connection, what about the soul mate expectation ("my perfect partner is out there")? From our clients, women in their thirties through women in their seventies, we hear many discouraging stories about dating, relationships, and the possibilities of forming commitments that are lasting and satisfying. Here, we consider three of those stories:

- What's wrong with men?
- Who am I without a man?
- What's wrong with me that I can't get a man?

Liz's Story

"Where are all the good men?"

In many respects, Liz, twenty-nine, was doing extremely well. An MBA with an excellent job as a financial analyst, she'd recently bought her own condo. She indulged in a spectacular wardrobe. And although she believed she hadn't met anyone "really decent yet," Liz had been involved with a number of men over the years. In fact, she'd never had a shortage of dates, which wasn't surprising—a lovely-looking, articulate, vivacious, and fit young woman, she attracted much positive attention. What brought her into therapy was her situation with Jake.

Liz had been seeing Jake on and off for a year, and recently he had announced that he thought they should end it. Liz quickly came up with reasons why she and Jake weren't a good match anyway: he was too flighty, not sufficiently serious about his career; he lapsed into "frat boy mode" when he and his friends got together; he was three years younger than she and had a lot of growing up to do.

She had explained all this to her best friend, Janice, one evening over a bottle of wine, and griped about the absence of nice, reliable, available men in the world. After listening to this litany of complaints, Janice made an observation that brought Liz up short. "You were very into Jake at the beginning," Janice said, "just like you were into Charles and Ethan before him. And you found something wrong with each of them. So all these guys just don't measure up? You say you want to be in a committed relationship, you want to get married. Have you thought that maybe you really don't want any of that at all? You just *think* you do or you think you *should*?"

Liz didn't see things that way. And for some time after we began to talk, she resisted the idea. The real issue, she was convinced, had to do with the lack of decent men. Some of her romances lasted longer than others. "It's true, sooner or later," she said, "I start to lose interest. But I really believe I'm just not connecting with real men who have the capacity to move into a real relationship."

There seemed to be fewer opportunities to connect with those real men, however, now that Liz was nearing thirty, and this worried her: "The candidate pool is shrinking. Most men my age are already in committed relationships, or married, or else they're losers." Many women do feel a suddenly intense internal pressure as they approach a milestone birthday while they remain unattached. Typically, those feelings fade once the big milestone has come and gone. Many also report the upset feelings that come from external pressures—a relative at a family wedding asks the single woman if she's met someone yet, if she'll be "next," or a parent makes remarks about hoped-for grandchildren.

Liz was starting to wonder: Did she need to rethink her requirements? Was she looking in all the wrong places, accepting dates with men whom she could actually determine from the start were not going to be right for her? Was she too picky or actually not picky enough?

Voice Mapping

"I shouldn't have to compromise my standards."

Because there's bound to be someone better just around the next corner. Liz was one of a generation of women who have much to offer—they're highly educated, accomplished, self-supporting strivers, and they anticipate much in return. Some come bearing an overloaded agenda: of course he must have a professional degree, a big income, and a caring nature, *and* he must have a full head of hair, a good sense of humor, and terrific friends, *and* he'd better love skiing and hiking.

One client, with a rueful laugh, said she and most of her friends were searching for "an extremely rare commodity. This is the compassionate, emotional, and connected man, who's also got a spine, isn't too feminine, looks as beautiful as the gay guys in the magazine ads, does his laundry, knows what you want and brings it to you, has a mind, isn't a mush, will protect you, and doesn't snore." In a recasting of the old Prince Charming myth, the woman has raised the ante on the men—expecting more, unwilling to settle for anything less.

Liz was aware enough to realize that some compromising was inevitably an element in any lasting partnership. She just continued to be unwilling or unable to make compromises that she could stick with.

"Men just don't want to commit."

And if she *did* meet a man she thought had potential, chances were he would resist the possibility of a "real" relationship. "I truly believe that men these days don't want to get serious," she said. "They cling to their autonomy."

Liz began her reframing with the following question.

Reframing

What exactly do I mean by a really decent guy?

Liz described her objections to the men in her recent past, repeating the observations she had made to her friend Janice. Jake, the latest ex, had "an adolescent taste in movies and music. He also liked to play video games, the kind of thing guys should get over in college." Another man she'd dated briefly was "extremely fussy about his clothes and the way he dressed. He always looked like he was on his way to a memorial service." Liz, to her credit, started to smile. "Actually, what I didn't like about another man I saw for a few dates was that he wasn't fussy *enough* about his clothes. I used to badger him to wear a jacket and tie more often."

We suggested that she put aside for the moment specific men and describe the qualities and characteristics she believed should comprise the "decent guy," her ideal of someone with whom an accomplished woman would be happy to pursue a relationship. Does the resume make the man? Are good looks important? Liz was willing to imagine the picture, what made a man desirable to date and a potential partner for a more lasting connection. He should have a good education, a good job, and a good income. He should be assertive without being aggressive. Sensitive. Fun to be with, sympathetic to her needs and goals. Tall, definitely. He'd make a good father someday. It was a long checklist.

We suggested she rank her "decent guy" characteristics in terms of the four or five she'd consider most critical, the ones she knew in her heart she most valued. This was a difficult challenge for Liz, but she concluded that what was most important to her was "a man who's engrossed in some pursuit, who's good at what he does. I need to admire him. Someone who will challenge me intellectually, keep me on my toes. Someone with curiosity and a sense of adventure." Several of the ideal characteristics actually didn't end up high on the list, somewhat to her surprise. Making a lot of money wasn't especially important; being a good father sounded like an appealing quality, and yet having children wasn't something Liz was sure she wanted.

One or two men she'd dated seemed to have potential, she said. But she experienced that waning interest, which started with focusing on matters like the way he dressed or the music he liked. Indeed, she could see that as the man became more interested in the relationship, the more vividly his "faults" loomed in her mind.

If I'm setting up an impossible standard for my soul mate, is there something I'm afraid of or avoiding?

This line of reframing brought Liz to considering her beliefs about men's unwillingness to commit. Was that true of all men? Or was *she* the reluctant one? If so, what motivated her reluctance?

Typically, we think of men as the resistant gender, with some justification according to various surveys. If not opposed to marriage, men are not rushing to get to that stage of their lives. The median age at which American men marry for the first time is now twenty-seven, older than at any previous period in our cultural history. According to a study conducted by the National Marriage Project at Rutgers University in New Jersey, men's reasons for delaying are several, including the ease of obtaining sex as an unmarried man; few social pressures to settle down; no burning desire for children, at least not for a long time; the ability to gain the benefits of having a wife by living with a woman, not necessarily marrying her; and the fear of divorce and the financial risks that would involve. Men also tell us about the time constraints and pressures of demanding jobs. (Said one, "My life is going to work, going directly from work to the gym, sometimes stopping to meet a friend for a beer, falling into bed, and getting up to go to work.")

For the resistant woman, the issues may be somewhat different. She, too, may wonder if there's a troublesome road ahead if and when she does make a choice: to be a mother or not, to pursue her career with the former intensity or not, the possibility of divorce—all the variables women once didn't worry about. But in addition, the woman, like Liz, who shies away from relationships—perhaps by measuring every date against her endless checklist—may have concerns around her need for control and independence.

She may need to consider these questions:

- How can I maintain the right to make decisions in aspects of my life?
- Is remaining independent the only way of keeping my power as an individual?
- How can I strike a balance between independence and merging, keeping some control and ceding some control, compromising on some issues and not on others?
- Will he expect me to give up my friends?
- Will his family take precedence over mine? His job over mine?
- Do we only see people as a couple?

Movement Strategies

It might be time to change my dating patterns.

As she continued to reframe her thinking around the issues of standards, control, and independence, Liz did reach one early conclusion: she'd been dating indiscriminately, perhaps even subconsciously choosing to see men who were unlikely potential partners so that she'd never be pushed to the point of making a choice. What turned out to anchor some new dating behaviors she wanted to establish was the reassessment she'd done of her "ideal guy" needs list. She sharpened her self-understanding by thinking it all through in a focused way. One big realization was that although she'd previously believed that she'd have kids eventually, she saw that it wouldn't be so necessary at all for her to have a child. And it was tremendously freeing when she took the mother piece out of the picture. Liz started to think it would be fine to meet a divorced man with a child or two.

For another woman, changing her dating behaviors might evolve out of beating back those internal and external pressures to meet someone. It takes work to develop an inner voice that says, "I'm not going to date a man (or woman) who's not good for me, even though I'm pushing thirty (or thirty-five or forty) or my biological clock is ticking."

I need to consider whether living together would be a good idea.

Once Liz got her priorities clear, things became simpler. She started dating less, because she no longer allowed herself to be pursued by men she knew in the long run weren't going to meet those priorities. Several months into our sessions, Liz had begun seeing Alex, an architect several years older than she, who happened to be a divorced father of a ten-year-old son. "We got serious very fast," she said. Alex had recently suggested they live together in his loft, which combined a spacious living space and a small work studio. She was excited; it felt right. But she was still hedging her bets. "I'm not selling my apartment, I can afford to hold on to it. If things don't work out with Alex, it won't be complicated to end it." Marriage was the big step, Liz believed, and maybe there was no strong reason to possibly spoil a lovely relationship by making it legal.

It may be the big step. Certainly it's true that when marriage is added to the equation, life is not precisely the same afterward. For one thing, the world does view the married couple differently than two people who are sharing a home. And while the illusion of greater freedom without marriage may be true for some, the notion that simply living together makes it easier to stop living together, to separate, isn't quite true. Emotionally, individuals usually have just as difficult a time detaching from long-term relationships as they do from marriage—because any move into a committed relationship, usually a conscious choice, inevitably creates a shift in the nature of the connection.

For Liz, it would probably continue to be necessary to reexamine and wrestle with issues of individual power, control, and independence. She might need to answer her own questions and address her internal voice before she was able to negotiate those necessary compromises with the man who might, after all, be her soul mate.

Alice's Story

"I just feel empty without a man in my life."

Alice, sixty-five, widowed for six years, had for five of those years been dating a highly narcissistic man; her wishes were met only if and when they happened to coincide with his. Fully aware of his demanding personality, this competent, recently retired woman put up with it all. Mentally, she worked hard to focus on what was good about her boyfriend. "Steve really can be sweet at times—for example, he'll walk my dog early in the morning when I want to stay in bed longer." She worked hard, too, to explain away what was not so good. "He doesn't like to spend time with my children and their kids. He'll leave when they're coming over, or maybe just stay in another room, which is a bit rude. But I understand. They're not his family, and I'm perfectly all right visiting with them on my own."

Their relationship had been chugging along virtually unchanged for most of the time Steve and Alice had been together. They sometimes took extended weekends out of town attending estate sales and flea markets, hunting up items of Americana for Steve's collections. She enjoyed those jaunts for the most part, although the main appeal was having him all to herself for a while, and he was always in a cheerful mood when they went antiquing. The trips were usually spontaneous; Alice never knew until the evening before that they'd be taking off the following morning. Often Steve essentially dropped out of sight for three or four days—he had his apartment, Alice lived in her house—and she wasn't sure when they'd be getting together next. He didn't like to be pinned down, she said.

In many respects, Alice had followed a pattern typical for her generation, the one following the immigrant generation; she was proud, as her parents had been, to be the first in her family to attend college. She became a teacher, an honorable job and a good profession, part of the gender expectations of her age. Marrying shortly after college, believing herself the most fortunate woman in the world to have found Martin, a good man, Alice had two daughters. For the last year of her marriage, she had been caretaker to her husband, who suffered from a degenerative disease. He died, her two daughters had married and started their own families, and Alice stayed in the house she'd lived in for thirty years. And felt lost. There was no man; she wasn't quite whole without a male in the house and in her life. Being Martin's wife had given her not only legitimacy, but a sense of self, and she hadn't realized that until after he was gone.

When Steve entered the picture, Alice was thrilled. Here was an attractive, healthy, and robust man, in that way so unlike her husband in his last year. She threw herself into the pursuit—losing weight, coloring her hair, and generally making herself more attractive than she already was, so Steve would pick her over the other woman he was seeing at the time. He did, but their subsequent relationship wasn't what Alice had envisioned. Steve needed to have his way. When he didn't, he'd initiate a temporary breakup, actually slamming the door on his way out of Alice's house.

She started therapy at the recommendation of her daughters, who were urging her to get out more, meet new people. "Actually, they've been very pointed about it. They're telling me Steve is no bargain." But without him, or at least someone, Alice felt "at loose ends," and she disliked that feeling. "My so-called love life," as she put it, seemed to leave her diminished.

Twenty years ago the title of a best-selling book posed this question: "Why do I think I am nothing without a man?" That was a question Alice needed to answer for herself.

Voice Mapping

"A woman needs a man to have a life."

Younger women hear this voice too; they just hide it better. For Alice, who had gone almost directly from her college years and her parents' house to her home and husband, there had hardly been a time when she was on her own as an unattached woman. Despite her accomplishments—a satisfying teaching career and raising two good children—she felt, in her word, "empty" in her newly unmarried life.

"An older woman needs to take whatever she can get."

Half the time, Alice thought she was lucky to have any kind of love life at all, and if she let go of Steve, there'd surely never be anyone else coming along. "Of course I think this is my last chance," Alice said. "How many women in their sixties do you know who can get a man?" That belief led her to make large accommodations to her boyfriend, adapting herself to his moods and wishes in order to keep the relationship happy for him.

But the last-chance scenario was clouding her vision. Alice admitted she didn't know if she genuinely cared for Steve. Nor could she be rigorously honest with herself about whether or not *he* actually wanted an emotional connection.

Reframing

What do I want from this relationship?

To gain better control of her emotions and her days, and maybe to make some new choices, Alice would help herself by reframing the voice that told her she *needed* a man. There is a world of difference, after all, between these two statements: "I have to be in a relationship with a man or else I'm not a whole person," and "I've enjoyed being in relationships with men, and I prefer to have a man in my life than to be alone."

To begin moving out of desperation mode, Alice was willing to try naming what she wanted from her relationship, ignoring for the moment the likelihood of actually receiving it from the elusive and self-centered Steve. "What do I want?" sounds like a simple question, but for Alice it wasn't simple at all. She recognized that she'd like it if Steve could be a little friendlier toward her daughters; she'd appreciate it if he gave her more advance notice about their weekend getaways; when they went out to a movie, it would be nice if sometimes it was a movie she wanted to see rather than always one he picked.

Gradually, she began thinking about issues that touched on her sense of self, her memory of the past, and her visions of the future. Alice wanted a deeper commitment from her boyfriend. "I'm actually not entirely sure that I'm the only woman he's seeing. But I'm afraid to push him and say I think we should have an exclusive understanding." She spoke of the affectionate communication she and Martin, her late husband, had enjoyed, and she wanted to find that again. "Pillow talk. Just that nice time of getting ready for bed, telling each other about our days, talking about people we ran into." It was a sense of emotional intimacy, she said, "feeling relaxed and safe with somebody you know so well."

Do I have other people in my life who give me emotional sustenance? And if I don't, can I find some now?

Interestingly, although Alice felt not entirely whole without a man, one of the facts that came out as we talked was the presence of wonderful female friends in her life—great connections, women she'd known for years. She and her women friends did have fun together. With one friend, Alice attended the spring flower shows each year; she and another woman treated themselves every New Year's to a Broadway show and dinner out. But Alice didn't talk about Steve very much to her friends. When she thought about it, she realized she had never been particularly confiding with her friends. When Martin was alive, her needs for emotional intimacy were largely satisfied. It seemed that as before, she was relying on a single source for that kind of connection, but this time her needs were unmet.

A trade-off assessment: What am I giving up to maintain this relationship? And how much does that mean to me?

One client, a woman in a situation almost identical to Alice's, said she knew exactly what she had. "I go to a lot of evening affairs, fund-raisers and so on. I have a somewhat important social position and I'm involved in several causes that are important to me. The man I've been seeing for the last three years owns his own tux, looks great, can carry on an intelligent conversation, and be charming to women. I need a date and he's a wonderful one. Also, I like to have sex every now and then, and he's pretty good in bed." She described the other side of the coin: "He's kind of a horse's ass. He needs to be told regularly how smart, handsome, and terrific he is. He requires a fair amount of catering to, like making sure I stock the particular wine he likes. I can deal with all that. It's an acceptable tradeoff."

Unlike Alice, this woman didn't feel empty with no man in her life; she just preferred having one there, for several reasons. But the woman who holds onto a less than satisfying relationship out of a degree of desperation would be wise to consider this equation: What is the tradeoff? What price am I paying, or, what am I giving up for the sake of having a man? Is the value of what I'm gaining greater than the value of what I'm ignoring?

Alice began to acknowledge that she often simmered with resentment over the accommodations she made to suit her friend. She also expended much mental effort trying to figure out what Steve wanted and when, and that often left her jittery and uncertain. What bothered her most, however, was her fear of pushing him, and how that was making her a passive participant in her own emotional life, and eroding her good feelings about herself. She decided that her wish for an exclusive relationship was reasonable. "Maybe it's time for me to speak up, and let the chips fall where they may."

Like many women who reached older middle age before the year 2000, Alice experienced the effects of limiting socialization from the society in which she grew up. The message was that girls should never be assertive; men always take the lead. Even the woman who achieves recognizable success in the worlds of business, politics, or the professions can still assume the all-accommo-dating role within her primary relationship, with a man. To her, asking for a greater voice can be tremendously difficult. Some married women of that generation who would like more say in the relationship never think of requesting it, even when the men they're married to might be receptive.

A risk assessment: If I press for my needs, what might happen?

Every action, of course, has a consequence. Alice had framed the action of speaking up, airing some of her thoughts and feelings with her boyfriend. She then had to consider just where those chips might fall, and if that was an outcome she was willing to risk.

Steve was getting all his needs met; he was well taken care of; he was not pressured. If Alice elected to change the balance of power, to ask for greater accommodations to *her* needs and wishes, one obvious risk was that she'd soon see the end of Steve in her life. She decided that if that indeed turned out to be the consequence, it didn't say much for their relationship in the first place.

Movement Strategies

I'd like to share more with my friends.

Any woman who's in the process of seeing if she can improve an unsatisfying relationship with the man she's dating, or perhaps working her way up to ending it, will help herself by shoring up her emotional ties with other welcome people in her life. The almost inevitable effect of overvaluing a relationship with a man is *devaluing* friendships. A period of reframing can be an excellent time to turn to those wells of support, and perhaps even ask for caring feedback.

Alice decided to spend more time with her women friends, and also to share with them some of her concerns and disappointments about Steve. Several of them had met Steve; they'd seen him and Alice as a pair at one or two social functions. When Alice began to open up with a couple of close friends, they helped her obtain a clearer perspective on her situation. "When I told one friend some of what's been going on, and my feelings about how Steve kind of comes and goes at his pleasure, she said it seemed I got despondent when he went off for a while but I wasn't tremendously happy when he was there. That was certainly true."

Another friend gave her an earful. "Delores and I had a talkative lunch, and at one point she said, 'Alice, you know what they say about guys like Steve, they're looking for a nurse or a purse. A caretaker to get them through their old age or a lady with some money.' We had a laugh about that, but later I started thinking she had a point. I'd have to say with Steve, the nurse thing might be part of the picture. Not that he needs one now, but he's eight years my senior."

Talking about her concerns in this way had an added benefit: Alice began to feel closer to a couple of her friends. Sharing vulnerabilities in the way she was now allowing herself builds intimacy in a friendship; the connections deepen.

I will take steps to expand my social circle, or my range of interests.
Here is a specific assignment we often suggest to the woman who senses she's spinning her wheels in an unsatisfying romance. Find two new activities you think you might enjoy, and decide you will pursue them. Ask yourself, Is there something I've always wanted to try out? A class in public speaking at the adult learning center? A photography course? Acting lessons?

Choose an activity that's not likely to involve an all-women venue. But don't choose an activity with the thought of meeting available men; the thing must hold the possibility of being a pleasure in itself.

One client took a class in clowning. "You know what?" she remarked. "It didn't matter who I met, because I met myself." Another, thinking out loud, stated, "I've always wondered if I'd be any good at painting. Watercolors and pastels, just pretty flowers and landscapes." She took an introductory painting class—trying not to focus on whether she'd be "any good," but allowing herself to relax and enjoy, and maybe to meet some new people.

I'm going to investigate new dating possibilities.

Alice was caught up in her last-chance scenario, believing that at her age she'd never have another opportunity to bring a romantic partner into her life. Clearly this wasn't entirely certain, and even more clearly, such negative thinking prevented her from adopting possibly useful movement strategies.

Statistics may be in the older woman's favor. The thirties and forties are not promising for finding potential romantic partners, but the odds improve after that. For one thing, older women are having great success with dating services on the Internet. Men after age fifty aren't typically going to bars and rock concerts to meet women, and computer dating can be a comfortable approach for both sides. A relationship, if there is to be one, unfolds in stages. You don't have to show what you look like, but you can reveal yourself slowly, control the situation, and decide if you do or do not want to approach.

It's time to address the fact that I may be in a developmental arrest.

At the time we stopped meeting, Alice was making progress, as she put it, "at weaning myself off Steve, or actually off this feeling that I desperately need him in my life." She hadn't yet pushed him for the firmer commitment she thought she wanted; in fact, she was starting to wonder if her daughters were right that he was "no bargain," and if she wished to give herself the chance to meet another man—she still hoped to find love again, but not quite so urgently as before.

If Alice did venture out, she might find herself undertaking another kind of reframing, of her notions of herself in a relationship and whether she might need to move beyond an emotionally arrested state of development.

Wherever a woman *stopped* as a dating person—perhaps at age twenty-five or age thirty, when she settled on her partner, became engaged or married, and left the dating scene—that's how she will tend to see the world of singles. Emotionally, although it's three decades later and she's that much older, she's back where she was. Former feelings can reemerge full blast. In addition, a woman's worldview may be seriously out of date. For example, thrown again into the mode of unattached female, she may feel deeply uncomfortable about being the one to extend a "harmless" invitation to a man; she may find herself waiting for the phone to ring. She may need to think about how she's perceived by other people, and give herself the kind of pep talk she might have once given her teenaged daughter: project confidence, even if you don't feel that confident; smile and look welcoming, even if you feel nervous and awkward.

Start from where you used to be and catch up. It's never too late.

Stacey's Story

*"What's wrong with me? Every other woman
is finding a man, but I'm not."*

Stacey, in her late thirties, was another high-achieving woman. She had recently made partner in her law firm, and now that she was able to ease up on the intense efforts needed to reach that position, she was taking stock of the nonprofessional aspects of her life. She was lonely.

Stacey had married her college boyfriend immediately after they both graduated; the marriage ended in divorce two years later. For a couple of years after that, she said, "I had a few stupid affairs with guys who were completely unsuited to me, and me to them." The decision to go to law school was "my salvation." Since then, she had had no serious romances, and hadn't been on a date in a long time when we began to talk. Now she believed that all likely relationship candidates were gone, and said, with a note of regret in her voice, "If I ever do get married, I'll probably be the fifty-year-old second wife of some seventy-old divorced man with grandchildren."

Much of her story was one we've heard from a number of women her age, the generation who pushed for careers, trusting that love, marriage, and children would follow. Later they looked for husbands and wondered if they would ever have families. The notorious male "fear of commitment" may, in fact, have some root in demographics and socialization: the older he gets, the larger the population of available women, while the reverse tends to be true for her. But the woman who's fifteen or more years out of college and absorbed in her work, like Stacey, may need to consider whether her dating difficulties have more to do with her own relationship skills, and perhaps how she learned them in the first place.

Some social commentators suggest that young people today may be missing a reliable training ground for meeting people, developing interpersonal connections over time, learning how to get along with others and compromise. The new configurations of our offices and our lives mean that computers and telecommuting eliminate the need to communicate one-on-one, relationships are spelled out in cyberspace, and a younger worker is likely to remain in the same job for only slightly more than a year.

Over the course of our meetings, two patterns that shaped much of Stacey's life began to emerge. She effectively positioned herself so that she remained invisible to men who might be appealing dates. And she had an intense, sometimes troubled relationship with her mother, who conveyed messages about men that might have played a part in the development of what Stacey called "my generally pathetic life when it comes to romance."

In her short-lived marriage, in the affairs she'd had years earlier, Stacey had never experienced real companionship or love. "My husband and I connected over sex in college. Getting married seemed to be the natural linear progression. Then we turned out to be two needy children, basically." Understandably, she was wary about making another wrong choice. She felt men weren't entirely to be trusted—or she didn't trust her own judgment about them. She wanted to understand these emotions, and had been thinking a lot about her father lately.

He had been "invisible." Stacey had never felt his presence deeply in her life. He was quiet; although he had little to say when he was home, which wasn't often, he gave off a vaguely disapproving air. When Stacey was young, she thought her mother "hung the moon" and her father was "ineffectual." As she grew older, however, she began to see her parents in a different light. "My mom always was and still is extremely forceful and argumentative. My dad rarely tried to stand up to her, and if he did, she just beat him down. That's still true. But I began to think the predominant truth of his life was that he was simply, miserably unhappy."

One of the issues she wondered about was whether a woman looked for a man just like her father or for a man exactly unlike her father? How much does her relationship with him figure in her own love connections?

Voice Mapping

"Don't expect much from a man."

Some women who carry around a negative message about men can trace that conviction back to a primary source—the image of the two genders they received within their family of origin.

Stacey had absorbed powerful and contradictory voices from her mother, who appeared to be a somewhat self-righteous and possibly frustrated woman. They might be summed up like this: "Getting married, having children, and staying married is what a woman does—as I, your mother, have done and as our religion tells us we should do. And yet you, Stacey, are so smart and accomplished, with your good grades and your law degree, that you don't need anything from a man. Which is all for the best, because men are basically incompetent, mainly interested in sex, and have nothing to say. Anyway, your sister got married and has children, so she's filled that role in the family and you don't have to."

"Relationships turn out badly."

The woman who looks to her parents' union and sees years of unhappiness and disconnection brings a poor model and huge reservations to her own prospects for meeting an appropriate partner. The only marriage she got a firsthand look at didn't seem so great. But a woman may be risk averse for other reasons. She might have come out of a first marriage because of divorce, like Stacey. She *knows* about marriage, the good, bad, or indifferent of it. It's easy to conclude that it's in the nature of relationships to go sour. They don't work.

Reframing

Maybe men are not actually rejecting me, but not getting much of a chance with me.

In talking about her barely existent social life, it seemed that aside from taking a part-share in a beach house over the summers ("something I've done for the last ten years, with the same group of people") Stacey didn't make many efforts in that direction. She came up with some possibilities on how she might get herself out in the world a little more, but it struck her as "high-schoolish and artificial and also a little demeaning" to pursue activities solely for the purpose of meeting men. We suggested that instead of focusing on meeting men, she consider some other questions:

- What am I projecting for people to respond to?
- Am I friendly, willing to allow myself an opportunity to get to know someone and allow him to know me—without worrying about where it will lead?
- Do I too quickly conclude that an individual I meet will be a bad choice?
- What sort of courting behavior—say at a social gathering or in the office—would be comfortable to me, not so "artificial" that it doesn't feel real, but still welcoming?

What would happen if I take more chances?

Many women who today are in their thirties and forties grew up in families that included both strong, working-women mothers who modeled achievement, and supportive fathers who admired their daughters, thought they were intelligent and lovable, and encouraged them to have confidence in their own abilities. In adulthood, those women often tend to do well with men, being attracted to individuals who will respond to them in the same way their fathers did. They're relaxed in dating or predating situations—a bit risk-taking but not reckless, playful but not trying too hard, with realistic but hopeful perspectives on the men they're meeting.

For the woman like Stacey, there's a bumpier path. She might need to talk herself into taking more chances, some of those small risks—like initiating a conversation, and tell herself there's little to lose and maybe much to gain.

Movement Strategies

Could I be spending my spare time in a better way?

Stacey claimed that she didn't have spare time, and as she described her typical day, month, and year, it became clear that virtually all she did was work at her job. Only two other women had made partner in her firm, so Stacey felt her workaholic ways had been justified. They paid off; they kept her safe in the area of her life she knew she was good at.

Outside of the job, in the available time she did have, Stacey was busy enough. She didn't like being at home alone in her apartment, and so for years she'd seen to it that she went to the gym regularly, where she worked out intensely on her own. Before she felt secure in her career position, she had given herself the assignment of studying accounting, real estate law, and tax codes in case she ever did need to explore a related career.

Stacey had to decide how many nights a week she was going to make sure she was occupied. Keeping on that route, she wasn't likely to have any time to pursue new horizons, perhaps accept some invitations. In addition, all her busyness revolved around activities that were achievement oriented, another way of reaffirming her sense of accomplishment and maybe continuing to ignore her lack of a social life.

Could I interact with my work colleagues in a better way?

People at work didn't know very much about her at all, Stacey thought, although she'd worked at the firm and with many of the same people for almost seven years. She had one woman pal at work, and one man had always been friendly toward her. But she was able to recognize a tendency in herself that had the effect of keeping others at a distance: she was all business, discouraging any conversations about personal matters—even what new movies were good, or where somebody was taking a vacation. She had a narrow area of specialization that required few people skills, and that suited her. Now she began asking herself: Have I adopted some behaviors that are actually designed to keep men at arm's length? Am I not allowing myself the chance to become friendly with people who might introduce me to some available men, invite me to their homes, help me broaden my circle?

Stacey decided to try to connect more personally with the people she was around all day, and find ways to reveal herself more. She made a point of talking to the coworker who'd always been friendly, and although it was a bit awkward, it worked out well, because he was a warm and pleasant individual and because she felt good about taking a small risk.

I must forge a changed connection with the primary male in my life.
For Stacey, as for many women, knowledge of her father came through her mother. Growing up, she rarely had direct conversations with this rather remote, hard-working man. Even now, her mother would remain on the phone if Stacey asked to say hi to her dad when she called home.

She took an action that amounted to a huge step. She invited her father to meet her for lunch one day, something they'd never done before. It was an eye-opening and relationship-shifting hour and a half. "We were a little shy with each other at first. But we ended up having some wonderful talk. My dad told me about the possibility he had when he got out of engineering school to take a year-long job in South America. He'd never mentioned that before. But he was seeing my mother by that time, and he didn't do it. It was clear that he's always regretted it, and I think maybe he's always wondered if his life might have taken another turn. If he might have been happier." When they left the restaurant, Stacey's father said he'd like to treat her to lunch the following month.

Gradually, she created a little more separation from her mother, and at the same time, a deeper understanding of her. Stacey mentioned her earliest dating experiences, as a teenager, and the fact that she'd always told her mother about the boy she currently liked. Her mother never approved of any of them. "I'd bring a boy over to the house," Stacey said, "and my mom wouldn't say anything much. Just look kind of suspicious. Then later she'd make some disparaging remark to me—he didn't seem very bright. Or that one had a weak chin!" She believed those votes of no confidence had had a destructive effect, but now Stacey recognized that her mother had her own disappointments, and that maybe she too sometimes wished her life had turned out differently.

Here's the great beauty of identifying old parental patterns and how they might be influencing your current reality: those voices can be silenced. Better than that, it becomes possible to come into your own voice without assigning blame to those individuals who may have conveyed unfortunate messages, and who are still people you love.

In an increasingly multicultural world, in the broadest sense of the word, women have many possible dating choices. Some women date across ethnic minority lines. Some date people from different religious or cultural backgrounds. Some date younger men. Same sex and cross-group and -age dating patterns are gaining in social visibility and acceptance, but they still raise eyebrows. These choices have repercussions for women in their families, social circles, and work settings. The search for a soul mate can easily become entangled with the internal and external "push me–pull you" messages that encourage a woman simultaneously both to reach out and grow in new ways, and to draw back and stay within the "comfort zone" of family, colleagues, and friends.

Lesbians are faced with a relatively small community of out lesbians, so their pool of potential partners is smaller than for heterosexual women. In addition, because most potential candidates were someone else's partner previously, the woman who dates within the same town or circle faces the difficulty of being "mature" about accepting a lover's former husband or partner. Family dinners and other events at which potential partners can get to know each other and each other's world are so often more problematic for lesbians than for heterosexual women. Gossip adds another dimension.

A woman who dates a younger man, an immigrant, or a person of a different color may find herself also a target for disapproval and gossip. This can push a dating couple into a secret arrangement or an "us against the world" stance, either of which may throw a monkey wrench into a dating relationship. But dating someone different can work well and develop into a secure and lasting relationship, if the woman and her partner each has a clear and solid inner sense of self and if together they maintain strong shared life values.

In this chapter, we barely skimmed the surface of the complex matter of love relationships. The experiences we've discussed are typical but by no means inclusive of the many and diverse choices possible. Keep in mind that the emotional issues they touch on might apply to your story, even if the dating pattern itself does not fit you exactly.

4

The Sex Expectation: "I'm Healthily, Happily, Wildly Sexual"

Female sexiness, even lasciviousness, is put before us as the modern norm. Magazine articles are startling not only in the degree of graphic description ("twenty ways to make a man moan"), but in the larger message, one that often urges a woman to pursue what was typically considered a man's path—experiment, have lots of sexual fun with lots of people before you settle down with one partner.

We're presented with advice on the best vibrators to buy. When an extremely popular brand (described by one woman as a device with the power to "shake the enamel off your teeth") was temporarily unavailable from its manufacturer, countless women experienced "major panic," according to a newspaper report on the catastrophe.

At a meeting of hundreds of scientists and sex therapists, conference goers heard reports on how the search for the female Viagra was progressing, surveyed new products intended to enhance sexual response, and (as reported in an article in the *New Yorker*) listened to "a French team who had introduced a copulating couple into an M.R.I. machine in an attempt to take precise anatomical measurements of the beast with two backs."

Our popular culture tells us that orgasm—or at least, an evergreen sex life—should be every woman's goal, age no impediment. After reporting that, at the age of seventy-eight, she had sex the previous night with her husband, who was eighty-three, a magazine editor wrote, "Sex keeps you connected to the human race, prevents you from being a prim, stuffy, correct, respected, respectable, *finished* old person! It makes you a functioning female instead of a sexless old crone."

That's the expectation. It is simple (and damaging): sex is normal, enjoyable, and easy; if you're not having it, not enjoying it, or finding it complicated, you're abnormal—not a functioning female and maybe not even quite a member of the human race. What's missing is acknowledgment of a huge history and reality that go directly to the experience of what it is to be female. More than any other stories we hear in our practices, money and sex remain the private ones, the issues about which women feel most furtive. They reveal their deepest truths with reluctance or difficulty, because those thoughts and feelings and behaviors often are experienced by the women themselves as shameful. If guilt is what one feels about something one *does* (or *doesn't* do), shame is what one feels about something one *is* or *is not*, and that can be much harder to deal with. (Later, we have more to say about this matter of shame and its power in our lives.)

In this chapter, we look beyond the sexual expectations of the popular culture to some realities with which so many women are familiar:

- Not enjoying sex
- Enjoying it but not getting much of it

We suggest self-talk that might clarify what you feel about the whole matter and what you want to do about it. Yes, women these days do talk to one another about "the beast with two backs," certainly to a greater degree than our mothers and grandmothers probably did. Especially young people, in their teens and pre-serious-relationship twenties, don't seem to find it a struggle or embarrassment to trade news about their sexual experiences and questions. But for many women—we'd say the majority—the level of disclosure remains superficial. They'll joke about how a little sex goes a long way; they'll suggest they're not taking the matter all too seriously. ("That movie *Annie Hall* got it right," said one client, with a forced laugh, "where Woody Allen says something like, 'She never wants to have sex, we do it only twice a week,' and Diane Keaton says, 'All he wants is sex, sex, sex, we do it twice a week!'")

In the twenty-first century, it's easy to ignore or understate a reality that still influences our psychological makeup, a reality that still comes across directly or indirectly: over generations, women have been taught to feel shameful about sex or their sexual needs and responses. We learned we weren't supposed to enjoy intercourse or at least, to enjoy it too much. We were made to understand that sex is what men want, not what women want.

Contrast that deep internal reservation with the popular "everybody's doing it" message, one that is underscored by the seductive outward appearance and openly sexual body flaunting of so many current media stars. The disconnent can produce strain and confusion for the woman who wants to (or thinks she should) address the sexual aspect of her life, and maybe change it for the better.

Jan's Story

"Sex . . . I don't really like it; I put up with it."

After the first couple of years of marriage and the birth of her children, Jan, forty-two, "went totally bed dead. The truth is, I never really enjoyed the actual sex with my husband, although I didn't mind the holding and cuddling." Her husband, Bill, every now and then suggested that maybe they could be more active in the bedroom, but he didn't insist. And that was fine for Jan, in one way; in the bigger sense, however, she believed that something was wrong with her ("sex just feels messy, and I know that's not normal") and that something was definitely going to go wrong with the marriage in the near future.

Jan and Bill had married nineteen years earlier and had two children within the first three years. Now the older child had left for college, and the younger would be following him out of the house shortly. Then it would be just the two of them at home for long stretches of time, and that prospect was suddenly alarming—and saddening her as she thought about how the marriage had gone so stale. They were a good pair in some ways—raising a couple of terrific sons, having some common interests. But mostly what they shared was all about the kids. Jan realized she didn't like to go out for dinner just with her husband, because there wasn't a lot to talk about.

Something else was on her mind: "We're both forty-two. I'm starting to look middle-aged, and Bill still looks ten years younger." She'd been feeling pangs of insecurity and an odd jealousy about the fact that he was around women all day in his office. She wasn't sure anybody would find her attractive again, even though, para-doxically, she didn't especially *want* to attract anybody.

As therapists, we have all seen this woman. Her situation is almost generic. We repeatedly hear from women who simply don't have sex anymore, and maybe haven't for a long time. (Such is the case not only in heterosexual relationships. Perhaps we wrongly identify lesbians by their sexuality. In fact, many lesbian relation-ships are largely asexual too.) It's men, however, not women, who usually come to therapy specifically because they're dissatisfied with their sex lives. The man will state on day one, "Here's my prob-lem. We don't have sex anymore." The woman in therapy may even-tually get around to revealing that the sex isn't so great, or she hasn't in fact had intercourse in twelve years. But at first, we're likely to hear, "My problem is, I'm depressed, I'm anxious."

That was pretty much how Jan began to describe her emotions and the quality of her current life. Before long, she was talking about her lack of sexual interest, and her feelings of embarrassment and worry over whether she was "normal."

Voice Mapping

"Real women have great sex."

For starters, it helps to recognize that the popular images con-stantly in our faces—real women, great sex—insidiously pressure us. Said Jan, "You just can't get away from it. Movies, TV, I'm con-stantly seeing these stories of a woman and a man just seeming to be so intimate and physical with each other. It makes me sad to watch certain ads even! Like one about an older couple, I think they're supposed to be retired, and they're in a canoe boating along a lake, just glowing in each other's presence."

"Sex is dirty."

Think back to what you may have learned about sex as a child or teen: What were you told about sex? Where did you pick up that information? What were the earliest lessons about your body—how to care for it, what it could do? Was menstruation something secret and vaguely shameful?

Growing up with negative messages about sexual activity or your own physicality (even if the messages were subtle—such as nobody told you anything) can amount to a history that leads to adult disinterest in or fear of sex.

Jan, an only child, had few thoughts or memories about any of this, but hers was a troubled childhood in some ways. Her father died suddenly when she was eleven; her mother, always an anxious woman, had various health problems after that. Jan, by her own admission, grew up "a worrywart, always expecting some disaster, usually a physical one. Some terminal illness." She never remembered a time when she felt "really happy in my body."

"Good sex isn't what you should look for in a husband."

The woman who's concerned that she's gone "bed dead" in her marriage or relationship needs to think about the beginnings of it, and what importance, if any, sex played in her choice of a partner. There are various possibilities.

With Jan, it was a story of choosing a man she didn't "want" in a sexual sense, but a man she "needed" for other reasons. When Bill appeared in her life, Jan felt a wave of relief. Here was someone with all the right credentials, "and a guy I sensed would be loyal and true, and also make a terrific father, which he has been." He would also be her consoler and soother, maybe in some way the father who would take care of her, although these were never conscious and articulated thoughts. She wasn't highly attracted to him in the first place; the sex (he was her first and only lover) was never very pleasurable, but the marriage wasn't for that reason. And he didn't disappoint her, comforting her and talking her through her anxieties.

For some women, the opposite scenario holds true. This might be the woman who marries a man because of intense physical attraction, then fairly quickly feels empty and disappointed, maybe even miserable; once sexual passion fades, she discovers there's not much else there. Many women in this category have some childhood history of sexual abuse, perhaps with a sibling or other relative. That history may not necessarily interfere with active and satisfying sexual behavior throughout adolescence, college, and dating. Then it comes streaming out once they enter a committed relationship or marry, and again feel trapped as they did earlier.

The point is that placing sex somewhere in your original list of needs, wishes, or pleasures concerning the relationship ("It was never great but it wasn't why we got together," "It started off great and now it's not") can help lead you to some current decisions, including whether or how to bring up the issue with your partner.

Turned Off to Sex?

Sex problems, or female sexual dysfunction, are identified in four categories:

- Little or no desire for sex, or lack of libido, which may have physical or psychological roots, and may stem from stress, anger, or depression
- Difficulty becoming aroused, as when a woman feels no stirring of excitement or fails to lubricate
- Lack of orgasm
- Pain during sex, which is particularly common in women past menopause

Occasional bouts of any one of these difficulties may be experienced by perfectly *healthy, normal women.* Ask yourself two questions:

1. Is the trouble you're having persistent?
2. Are you deeply distressed by it?

If you answer yes, to either or both, the self-talk questions and action strategies we outline here will help.

Reframing

Many women share my low interest in sex.

Here is a fact that might be the first step toward change or acceptance: not all real women have great sex. Jan has a lot of company. Forty million married American women, according to some estimates, say they don't really want sex; one in four are nonorgasmic. According to a study reported in the *Journal of the American Medical Association*, close to one-half of American women consider themselves sexually dysfunctional.

So there's a starting point for any woman who's trying to reframe the picture of her nonactive sex life. Jan was able to acknowledge that she felt "like a freak because of this kind of sexual atrophy." Normalizing her feelings and recognizing that she was not alone in having them, was a critical piece of self-talk, one that helped her begin to sort out more clearly, for one thing, whether they were actually disruptive to her relationship, or might be in the future.

Do I not like sex in general, and did I ever? Or do I not like sex with this partner?

The question gets at the "me" or the "we" in the situation: Is it me? Am I truly sexually blank, never interested in sex, never aroused? And is this an issue I may want to work on privately, by discovering and developing my own sexuality? Or am I feeling inhibited because of changes in my body—such as weight gain, a surgical scar, a loss of breast firmness after having a baby? Can I talk to my partner about my self-consciousness? Or is it something in the "we" equation? Possibly an emotion I'm feeling toward my partner that's getting in the way of my sexual enjoyment?

When a woman isn't dealing with a difficult issue, or maybe a raft of issues, she has with her partner, the sex may shut down as part of anger, and this is hard to see. What's lurking behind or just underneath "I don't like sex, I put up with it" may be the fact that a woman is really enraged with her partner, perhaps because she's overwhelmed and stressed by family responsibilities or for any number of reasons. Here's where men and women differ: Men tend to want to have sex to stop the anger in the air. Women stop the sex because they're angry, which in fact is the most common theory for female sexual lack of interest.

Another possibility is that a woman in a heterosexual relationship who doesn't like sex with her partner may really wish to be in a same-sex relationship. Despite any shame or denial, if present, her orientation is elsewhere.

Consider that my sexual self is there, if buried.

In other words, maybe it's not that you're uninterested in sex, as much as that you're out of touch with your body. Every woman does not have the same sex drive. If you think or know your drive is lower than your best friend's or your sister's, do not conclude there must be something wrong with you.

However, while women do differ widely in the amount of sex they desire, that does not mean you don't ever wish or have never wished for it. Actually, the most unlikely cause for your low libido is that you truly don't like sex. (And isn't that nice to know!) Sexual abuse (which is not always the same as incest or actual intercourse) in childhood, negative voices from the family, a disastrous introduction to sexual activity earlier in life—these and other experiences may have left you not really knowing if you like sex or not. Now is the time to find out, starting with this reframing notion: My sexual self is alive, if not necessarily so well at the moment.

Improving our sex life is important to me.

Jan recognized that to some extent she had looked to her husband over the years to comfort her; she had married him for his parentlike qualities, and perhaps had difficulty seeing the one man as both nurturing and sexual. But she felt herself in a time of transition, at least partly because of her changing family circumstances.

"It's important to me to improve our sex life" is the conclusion she came to. Not every woman will reach the same conclusion. An active sex life with her partner may be an important value to one, and not necessarily to another.

Movement Strategies

I need to work on the "me" part of the equation and explore my own sexuality.

"Sex has never been a real part of my life," Jan said. She had never masturbated, and felt self-conscious about touching her body in ways intended to arouse. She decided to make what was for her a bold move. "There are regular times I'm in the house on my own for long stretches, when the boys are gone and my husband visits his parents on Sundays. In private, maybe I can try getting more comfortable with my body."

Examine your own awareness:

- Do you masturbate to orgasm? (Some women basically need to be taught, or to teach themselves.)
- Watch porn movies?
- Experiment with sex toys?
- Buy and enjoy sexy underwear?
- Fantasize? About what?

Does any of this sound tempting, and worth giving a try? Are you willing to make exploring your own sexuality a priority, to carve out some time to see whether and how much you might actually enjoy sexual arousal? (Even the woman with three young children running around can indulge in sexual fantasy.)

It's time to ask for more of the hugging.

Jan "didn't mind the holding and cuddling," and she needed to appreciate the importance of that in the overall picture of the sexual side of her marriage. Putting greater value on such contact, she decided to request it—and just that—when her husband suggested they get "more active in the bedroom," giving her something she enjoyed and relieving some of the pressure of needing to perform.

It's what many women want. A common complaint we hear: "He never wants to just cuddle and snuggle." But snuggling can be an invaluable step in leading to more active sexuality. Studies show that monkeys engage in "lick and hug" behaviors before the two partners can feel safe; the lick and hug calms them down. For the woman who meets the beginning of a possible sexual encounter with reluctance, prolonged cuddling can provide necessary soothing and express affection. And affection makes a woman feel connected.

She might ask for some more hugs during the day too, just to reinforce the safety and comfort of presexual physical contact. In fact, daytime hugs that are clearly not a prelude to intercourse can be wonderful for the woman who wants more physical closeness but not necessarily more sex, at least for now. Women tell us that hugs at night, in bed, lead the man to sex.

If Childhood Sexual Abuse Is Part of Your Past

Childhood sexual abuse, especially incest, produces enormous complications. An individual who may have loved you and/or treated you well was also an individual who harmed, exploited, and betrayed you. It is the betrayal, in fact, that is so difficult to treat. With girls, incest often does not involve physical abuse, in the sense of force. A girl may be mentally coerced into the activity, which may range from fondling to intercourse.

Here's what you should know while you are going through the healing process:

Ambivalent feelings are normal reactions to this abnormal situation. Although in retrospect you rightly blame your coercer—and maybe also your mother for failing to protect you, whether or not you ever explicitly told her—you may also obsess about your role in what happened: Perhaps you believe you were seductive and inviting in some way. Perhaps you even experienced a degree of pleasure at times (horrifying to acknowledge). Perhaps you think you should have been stronger. All such feelings lead to lingering self-guilt: "Why didn't I stand up to him?" "I shouldn't have liked it, there's something wrong with me that I felt that." "Why did I want the gifts he gave me so much? Now they seem so trite."

Self-defeating or negative behaviors are common reactions. A victim of early sexual abuse may later take steps to make herself less attractive, such as by gaining weight. She may "turn off," not allowing herself to become aroused, because she fears she cannot control arousal.

The abuse was not your fault. Even if you believe you were seductive—in fact, even if you were—sexual abuse is never the child's fault.

Catharsis, such as "confessing" to a friend in adulthood, has limited benefits. In fact, it may reopen an old wound and only leave you feeling more upset. It's common to seek out a sympathetic friend or reveal the episode to a minister or other trusted acquaintance. But venting is not a solution to this problem.

Support and advice from an expert or experts in the field will help. Certain issues cannot adequately be tackled through self-help alone, and this is one of them. But a woman may be so paralyzed by shame that she's reluctant to seek support, or she may consult with a therapist who's not especially helpful and give it up. Sexual abuse is an event you can't get over by yourself. You do need a trained guide. When seeking a therapist, the American Psychological Association Working Group on Investigation of Memories of Childhood Abuse advises that you be wary of two kinds of therapists: those who offer instant childhood abuse diagnoses (no single set of symptoms automatically means that a person was a victim of childhood abuse) and those who dismiss claims or reports of sexual abuse without exploration (most people who were sexually abused as children remember all or part of what happened to them). Find a licensed practitioner with training and experience in abuse issues. This individual may suggest:

- Specific strategies, such as visualization techniques, that are proven effective with many women
- How to talk to and involve your partner in working through the emotional residue of abuse, in ways that will strengthen you as a couple

> • How to address with relatives what is probably a long-buried issue, without demanding changed allegiances or in other ways destroying the family and causing more grief

Linda's Story

"I want sex, my partner doesn't."

Linda, thirty-five, and her fiancé, Frank, had been together for six years, engaged for two. They shared an apartment, and weren't in a huge rush to marry. Although she described "a wonderful partnership," sex had been unsatisfying, especially lately. She was keeping count: "Sometimes a week or more goes by with no sex, unless I cajole him into it."

What brought Linda to therapy was an action that deeply troubled her: She was considering starting an affair with a coworker at the auction house where she worked. "We're together a lot during the day," she said, "and we often go out with a bunch of other people from the company to have a few drinks after one of our sales. He and I work late a lot of evenings, and one of these evenings we suddenly got caught up in a wild makeout session." He had let her know he wanted to take it a step further; he'd asked her to come up to his place, but only if she wanted to. "He's a decent guy," Linda said, "he's not putting a lot of pressure on me. And fortunately, we're okay with it all during the day at work."

She felt guilty, "pretty shabby, actually. Frank and I are committed to each other. It's always been understood we'll have an exclusive relationship. I'm sure he's never cheated on me, or wouldn't even think about it." But the coworker was on her mind. It wasn't love, "just lust," and yet she was wondering, did she really want to start an affair?

Before she tried to answer that question, Linda wanted to figure out what was behind her behavior—specifically, what it said about the state of her relationship with Frank. "I've tried talking to him a little bit about my sexual needs," she said, "but nothing much has changed." Lately, in fact, she thought he'd been actively avoiding her, leaving their apartment earlier in the morning and working late most evenings. She also was questioning the wisdom of their "exclusive relationship" and their planned future. "Sex is a big deal to me, I guess," she admitted. "And I think it would just be terribly sad if this wasn't going to be a vital and vibrant part of our life together."

Voice Mapping

"There's a normal amount of sex."

Many women do hold preconceived ideas about what constitutes normal frequency. To counter the voice that says we're all "doing it" all the time, here are some useful findings from an extensive 1994 survey of over three thousand individuals ages eighteen to fifty-nine: On average, Americans have sex about once a week; one-third of adult Americans, however, have sex a few times a year or not at all. Many people also think men (unlike women) possess ravenous sexual appetites. In fact, some don't. Low libido is clearly identifiable not only in women but also in men, who reflect a wide range in normative sexual desire.

Consider what is or might be a "normal" amount for you and your partner, remembering not only the continuum of sexual appetites but what's going on in your lives in general. Before kids or after kids, financial stress, one partner with a job or both with a job—all these variables obviously have a lot to do with sex or no sex. For some couples, having good sex once every two or three weeks or every month may be normative. For some, sex every other day is normative.

Despite the proliferation of data on frequency of sex, however, the *main* consideration—the issue that causes the greatest problem—is whether a mismatch exists in the sexual needs of the partners. Is the amount of sex that's occurring acceptable to you both? If so, just about anything goes and just about anything should be considered normal. Is the amount of sex unacceptable to one of you? If so, which was the case with Linda and Frank, some strategies we describe in the following paragraphs are a possibility.

"The man should be the one to make the first move."

As she described how sex happened (or didn't) at home, Linda thought that her fiancé, understandably, was often simply too tired to be interested in sex. He would usually respond if she approached

him. Yet taking the lead seemed to be an impediment to her enjoyment; she felt less desirable when she was the one to get things
going. Or maybe Frank seemed less attractive, since, Linda
explained, "I don't know if sex is a big deal to him at all, which
makes me wonder if there's something wrong with him."

Those are two cultural messages about the absolute sexual roles
of men and women. First, men are supposed to be the initiators. Second, men who aren't the initiators aren't so manly. The woman
who's unhappy about lack of sex from her partner might need to
think her way through these messages and put them to rest.

Another voice, one we hear often from married women, says it's
a little wrong to make an issue of all this. "With our jobs, everything
going on at home, the kids and whatnot, wishing my husband
wanted to make love to me more often doesn't seem like something
I should bother him about." In other words, we've been persuaded
that a woman really shouldn't uphold sex as a priority. Or that she
can rate her sexual desires up there with her other wants and needs
until she's in a committed relationship or marriage. After that,
everything else takes precedence. Forty years ago women weren't
supposed to have sex until marriage—and then not like it. Today,
it's okay to have it and like it, but then you're to give it up, if necessary, because other things count more.

"Intimacy is the same as physical contact."
Many women fail to distinguish between sexual contact, including orgasm, and affectionate contact. Linda was calling what she
wanted more of "sex," because sex is the only name we have for
physical intimacy in our culture. But was it something else she
was longing for and missing? If she decided she'd enjoy more fre-
quent and more sustained physical contact—the hugging and cuddling, again—and not necessarily orgasms, that's something she
could probably say to her partner without fear of insulting or accusing him.

Reframing

*It really is okay to have sexual needs, and to express them to my partner in
a long-term relationship.*

If you wish a more active or a more satisfying sex life with your partner, that's what's normal for you. It can be one of your priorities.

Having sexual thoughts about other men does not make me a bad person.
Linda felt guilty about kissing another man; she wondered why she was entertaining thoughts of having sex with him; she was "a cheater."

It is not always easy for a woman to take a clear reading of her internal compass, and decide what's okay and not okay, or when something has crossed a boundary (of trust, integrity, or moral or religious values). These are highly individual responses. But it's important to consider that women can experience a sequence of events involving sex and clamp the lid on themselves early on. To some women's minds, a sexual thought or fantasy becomes as evil as the deed; lust after another man, and they feel as guilty as if they had the affair.

So often in our practices we have heard, "I'm married and I'm attracted to this other man, so I must not really love my husband," or "I've got a serious boyfriend, but I'll start having sexual thoughts about some guy I see walking down the street. What's the matter with me?" Rather than trusting her feelings—which might be expressed, "I'm married [I have a boyfriend], I'm having some fantasies about this other man, I love my husband [boyfriend]"—she believes that the fantasy erases the feeling. Which, of course, ties in to the ancient lessons that told us sexual thoughts are wrong and shameful.

Lustful thoughts aren't evil. Sometimes they're just fun, a way to let the imagination roam over some intriguing but safe possibilities. An essayist in the book *The Bitch in the House*, a married woman and mother fantasizing about other men, says, "It wasn't even sex that I wanted from a lover. It was the intoxication of being newly known."

If I do decide to press for my greater sexual needs, what might happen?
In the best-case scenario, of course, the couple together figures out ways to talk about and achieve a better match between their sexual appetites. It may take a while to get there, it may stir up uncomfortable emotions, but they work it out. What's most impor-tant in reframing, however, is considering the worst-case scenarios, which might include the possibility that the relationship really will

not survive. Or one that's perhaps more likely: She will bring up her sexual needs to her partner, and they still remain unmet.

Think through your own "what might happen?" scenarios, what you're willing to risk and what you're not and whether you can or cannot be satisfied living with the discomfort and sadness of unmet needs.

Movement Strategies

I can satisfy myself sexually.

For the woman who decides she really is missing orgasm, there are ways other than intercourse to obtain the satisfaction she wants. Buy a vibrator. Take shower massages.

Work on the "we" part of the equation.

If you've decided, as Linda did, to remain in your monogamous relationship and try to improve the sexual aspect of it, it's time to invite your partner along.

It's said that the five most dangerous "relationship" words in the English language are "Honey, we need to talk." Most liberated, younger women will insist that it's absolutely appropriate and critical for a woman to ask a man for what she would like sexually, but in fact even they find that difficult to do in real life.

Consider ways to start to begin to address your unsatisfying sex life without it sounding like your partner is in for an attack. A man may be anxious over the pop cultural expectations he hears about male sexual performance. He may be deleting from his e-mail six spam messages a day that shout: "Size matters! Buy this penile enlargement breakthrough and increase your length from 6 inches to 8 inches in just two months!"

Here are some ideas:

- Say: "I was thinking about our sexual relationship and how I feel about it. It's wonderful to be together with you and to love you in that way." That's a nonblaming opening that might ease you both into a further discussion.

- Take an article you've read or a movie you've seen that's sexually oriented, and use it as a starting point: "You know, this made me think about us and how we are together, like some of the times we used to make love."
- Try to have a pleasant sexual interlude, and then tell him how much you liked it: "That was delicious. I wonder why we don't do this more often!" Tell him the two or three aspects you most enjoyed.

All these ideas focus not so much on what's not there, but on the positives, on what you have had or can have.

Women and sex: It's an immensely rich, intriguing, and complex issue with many realities, only a few of which we've touched on through the preceding stories. Mainly we hope we have challenged the assumption that if your sex life is nonexistent, uncomfortable, or unsatisfying, there's something fundamentally wrong with you. The self-talk you've read has its own simple message about this unsimple matter: It really is worth the effort to figure out what you think and feel about your sexual self. It really is possible, and sometimes an excellent idea, to reveal those thoughts, experiences, needs, or worries—to your partner, to a trusted friend, or to a trained professional if necessary.

5

The Marriage Expectation: "I Can Achieve the Marriage I Want (but If I Don't, I'll Just End the Marriage)"

Here's the image of marriage as we assume it should exist: The contemporary couple is casual, communicative, sexual, and friendly, growing together and growing separately, unfettered (relatively, anyway) by the gender roles of another generation—partners in what sociologist Pepper Schwartz has termed "peer marriage." Implicit in the expectation of the peer marriage is the notion that "working at it," being willing to discuss issues and thrash out compromises, is not only appropriate but is all that's needed for success, and we've been inundated with advice on that score. In an egalitarian relationship, all is up for negotiation, and each partner gets his or her way at least 50 percent of the time. If working at it fails to work, however, a woman has the option and the power to leave, to pursue the marriage expectation elsewhere or to live an honest life alone—and she probably should.

This "companionate marriage" is what most of us, men and women both, claim we're after. And it certainly *sounds* good. It seems to make sense, or to be eminently achievable, since the old barriers that dictated the rationale and the shape of marriage have largely evaporated. Most women no longer need to be wives in order to gain respectability and a roof over their head. Many are supporting themselves adequately; at the least, they assume that responsibility and are working to make a living, despite the fact that women still earn less than men overall. In addition, a woman no longer has to marry either because she's pregnant or in order to have a child. Women can become mothers when and if they want, thanks to birth control.

Cohabitation without marriage is an increasingly acceptable phenomenon, even to aging parents who are willing to acknowledge an adult child's boyfriend or girlfriend as a "significant other"—the very parents who in an earlier age would have been shocked at the notion that visiting young lovers might share a bedroom. Mothers and fathers still hope their kids will find love and marriage, but there's no big rush. Said one client, "I was at a wedding recently where the bride was about twenty-three, pretty young. And one woman guest at our table said, 'My kids better not get married until they're thirty. Let them spend some time knowing what they're getting into and what they want.' Another woman in the group said, 'Amen to that.'"

Once, the woman who knew her husband was having an affair might have looked the other way; now she's ready and able to confront. She may start out intending that marriage is for better or for worse, 'til death do us part, but she knows she can end it if and when the time comes ('til death or divorce do us part). For one thing, that gives her the strength to forge the kind of marriage she wants and needs.

So isn't the modern husband's main value just being a loving, likeable partner in a companionate, egalitarian relationship? Isn't that what we want? And yet today, despite our independence and freedom of choice—maybe partly because of it—marriage for so many women doesn't seem to be all it's cracked up to be. According to some surveys, the majority of women say being a wife is not high on their list of the enjoyable aspects of femaleness. In our practices, married women who report being depressed and anxious most often—either at once or eventually—point to their marriages as the source of their discontent. The majority of divorces are initiated by women.

In a later chapter, we talk about some of the realities that can make a basically happy marriage often feel not so great to the wife who's living it (such as how come all this equality has added up to more work and less time for me?). Here, we spotlight several stories that center on disappointing marriages, and the issues they present:

- To leave or not to leave
- Needs fulfillment, or unfulfillment
- When one partner, and only one, grows

They tell us, among other hard truths, that divorce, although obtainable and no longer shameful, isn't so easy to go through at all; that the peer marriage is harder to achieve than we think; and that often, life moves on—for her, not for him.

Lily's Story

"I married right out of school, and I don't want to be married anymore. But what's out there for me?"

Lily, fifty-three, described herself as "a terrified-to-divorce home-maker." Her children were adults. The marriage was "dead." She felt stuck in a relationship and a household that gave her little plea-sure. "To tell you the truth," she said, "if I could start over, maybe I'd skip getting married entirely. My women friends are the best. I'm thinking now, the thing is to stay single, have the occasional affair with a man, maybe adopt a kid, spend your free time enjoying your girlfriends." She wondered if it was normal to fantasize about a romantic relationship with a woman she knew. Actually, she said, that little fantasy didn't really bother her; it was just a sign of "a lot of confusion in my brain."

She was a woman on the cusp of change. If she'd been born fif-teen or twenty years earlier, chances are Lily would have assumed that a less-than-great marriage was something to grin and bear. She would have met her emotional needs by spending a lot of time with her children, maybe with her mother or other female relatives. Since divorce has become an option, the playing field has changed. Grin-ning and bearing it no longer seems an admirable path for the woman who has had a vision, perhaps among contemporaries, of a happier life, a life that seems within reach if only one has the guts and gump-tion to go for it (*everybody gets divorced these days, doesn't seem so hard*).

And now, life is long. Once, any couple who stayed alive together for thirty years had a really good run of it. Today, the fifty-year marriage and even the sixty-year marriage is not at all uncommon, when both men and women are more able to survive the health crises of late middle age and sail into old age still relatively hale. With all that time ahead to anticipate, isn't it right to cut short a bad marriage and aim for another chance at happiness? Conversely, we have also talked with the midlife woman who's gone through breast cancer or another serious health problem and decided life was entirely too short to remain unhappily in a relationship that's no longer working.

Lily didn't particularly want to talk about the details of her marriage, or why she believed it had fallen apart over the years. She was past the point of investing herself in efforts to improve it; she felt she'd done everything she could. Now she wanted to sort out issues in her own mind and in terms of her own future. When she thought about that future, "I'm a blank. I guess the devil you know is not so scary as the devil you don't know."

She needed to explore and understand feelings that were clouding attempts to figure out what she really did want to do, and what was possible.

Voice Mapping

"Women my age shouldn't venture out into new arenas."

Lily felt stuck. She did have specific concerns about economic security. She'd worked only in temp and volunteer jobs over the years, and looking back she rued the fact that she'd never made an effort to establish herself in a field of work. However, women with solid incomes also tell us they think they can't afford to leave their marriages; despite personal accomplishments, they somehow have little faith in their ability to make it on their own. For some, those feelings tie in to a larger sense of self. Divorce may no longer be a social stigma, but a woman can still have the uncomfortable suspicion that she'd be a failure as a female if she pursued one: if you're a good woman and you chose well, the expectation tells us, you'll have a good marriage.

The point is, as long as you think you're stuck, you can see no options. Before you can begin to perceive what options may actually exist, you need to define why you consider yourself stuck.

"Wife and mother are the only valuable roles for women."
Am I clinging to an old self-image that I haven't revised with the passage of time?

Lily called herself a wife and mother: "That's basically all I've been." Give those up and she wasn't sure what would be left. But for one thing, the old roles in a real sense were part of the past.

We sometimes ask a client to complete the phrase: "I am a _____," telling her to come up with at least five or six roles she maintains or names by which she would describe herself. Then maybe with some effort, she'll move beyond wife, mother, librarian, and name herself a loyal friend, a good cook, a needlepointer, a Catholic, a pet lover, a seashore lover, an amateur genealogist.

The more ways by which you can identify yourself, the more personal strengths you may recognize. And personal strengths may hint at some options you hadn't considered. At least, they remind you that the sum of your parts presents an image much greater than being somebody's wife and somebody's mother.

Reframing

If I make the choice of leaving, would I enjoy the single life?

Do a "what if?" Without worrying for the moment whether you'll have enough money to live comfortably, picture yourself in an unmarried life:

- What does it look like?
- What will I be doing that I'm not doing now?
- How do I think it will feel without: my current daily small routines, like preparing dinner? A man to live with? Somebody to help with the kids?
- Where are my ideas about the single life coming from?

Feeling stuck in an unhappy marriage makes it easy to assume that once you get unstuck and leave, you'll be happy; you'll come into your own at last and be yourself. Which may turn out to be the case, but any woman trying to reach a hard decision will help herself by filling in the "after" picture with some details. Lily said she didn't imagine many specifics; she had no idea if she would enjoy being single. But she thought about her female friends, and a couple of them were divorced and seemed okay.

If she does make the move, she may do just fine. Studies confirm what we see in our practices: The deeply unhappily married woman, even past the age of forty, who initiates a change often turns out remarkably well. Economically she may struggle after divorce; emotionally and psychologically she's likely to soar, feeling more competent, self-sufficient, and in control, once the anxiety of change has settled down.

If I make the choice of staying, what are my reasons?
Whom am I trying to please by staying married?

A woman may elect to remain in an unsatisfying marriage for reasons that are important to her. Most typically, it's out of a belief that keeping the family intact is best for the children. But she may also feel a sense of loyalty to the individual she once freely chose as her life's partner. She may come from a cultural or religious background that values continuity and family ties over personal happiness. There is the history of the couple, too, many small connections, the memory of love shared and the beginning of it. If the marriage isn't genuinely toxic, any or all of this can be a powerful pull, even for the woman who has the financial independence to leave. The following are a couple of examples of other reasons that tap into a woman's psychological core.

One woman, married to a man who subtly undermined her, belittled her aspirations, and made her feel bad about herself, said, "The rest of the world sees him as generous, attractive, witty, kind. A wonderful guy and a great catch." He was entirely desirable, as her friends had let her know. "No one would understand if I pushed for a separation," she said, "I'd have no support from anybody, including my own parents." There were other issues besides lack of social approval tying her to him. She asked herself: If I leave, somebody else will snatch him up in five minutes, and how would I feel about that? If I leave, am I going to walk into the same situation with somebody else, because maybe I have a history of attaching to difficult men?

Another woman experienced deep shame—and, for a long time, denial—about the fact that she was married to a man with a substance abuse disorder. Her story was a common one, and one that rarely fits the picture of the wildly out of control, physically nasty drunk. Rather, her husband regularly drank after work with people from his business, came home to more drinks before dinner, and passed out after that. He was essentially a functioning alcoholic. Most men, interestingly, do not stay with an alcoholic or drug abusing spouse; many women do remain, for various reasons (becoming, perhaps, "enablers"). And, as was true for this client, they come to therapy tending to hide or deny what's going on, or not to recognize it at all. She felt she needed to keep the marriage together, and the only way to do that was by ignoring her husband's alcohol problem.

The point is that it is important to acknowledge, at least to yourself, your reasons for maintaining the marriage. That is a reframing step that can lead you from "I'm stuck" to "I'm making the choice to stay (at least for now)"—which is a better place to be, and gives you a sense of greater control over your life.

Movement Strategies

I need to take a good, realistic look at the financial side of the picture.
Can I, in fact, earn a decent enough living on my own?
This is a solid starting point, a clear-eyed analysis of the resources available, for any woman weighing her options about staying or leaving an unhappy marriage. Lily spent one long day "writing it all down, what we have, what I could expect to have if we divorced, just looking at the facts and figures." Another long day, she got on the phone and made a series of cold calls and some to people she knew regarding possible jobs. The picture was fairly grim, "but not an outright disaster, because I don't think I'd need a big income, and I'm not fussy about what kind of work I'd do."

Although nothing in her immediate picture had changed, these specific strategies started her thinking: "Maybe saying I can't afford to leave has been an excuse, my way out from having to make a decision."

If I stay, what behaviors do I need to adopt? And if I leave?

You can't make the dramatic choice of staying or leaving while you're totally caught up in desperation mode, overcome by feelings—of anger, disappointment, fear—that seem to have you pointing in one direction one day, in the opposite the next. To get out of desperation mode, ignore the feelings or at least try not to act on them so often (because acting on them only perpetuates the unhappy status quo). Remind yourself that you always have choices. Ask yourself: If I choose to stay, what behaviors *in me*, not in my partner, will make that tolerable? If I choose to go, what behaviors *in me* will make that possible?

Make a list of these alternatives and practice them. Perhaps you'll find yourself trying out a somewhat different persona; see how it works and how you like it. Don't assume that the minute you adopt some new movement strategies, you will have your answer. Give it a month or half a year. Then decide whether you do indeed want to stay.

Jerrell's Story

"He's a good guy, a good father. But I expected more."

"I'm bored," said Jerrell, thirty-nine, "and I feel oddly alone sometimes, like I'm on my own here." That was how she first described her feelings about her marriage of fifteen years when she came to therapy.

At the beginning, she admired the strong work ethic of her husband, Nick, and she still did. She had been drawn to him in part because of his ambition, the vision he had for himself and the two of them, and they shared the same sense of family. He'd build his business—Nick had his own company in the computer field—and she'd be a mother and homemaker. Now, the youngest of their three daughters had started first grade, and although Jerrell did occasional substitute teaching in the local school system, she had more unstructured time than previously.

She realized, "I'd better get more of a life going for myself," and joined a morning gym class and made a greater effort to meet a couple of friends for lunch. It helped, but not that much. "With the kids out of the house most of the time now, it's kind of like the quality of my marriage has been thrown into sharp focus. And what I see is, one, with Nick, the business is his preoccupation, he's hardly ever home. It's his obsession, really. Two, when he is home, he doesn't talk much. The sex is fine, when it happens. A lot of the time he's too tired. There's just not much going on between us." Jerrell had considered having another baby, "but I got over that idea fast, because obviously I wanted another kid for some not so good reasons and it made me feel sad about myself."

She had started taking golf lessons once a week at the community club, and struck up a friendship with the pro who was teaching her. He was an older man, long married. "He's just good to talk to. After the lesson, sometimes we sit around in the coffee shop for a while, just chatting. He brought me a book he knew I'd like. I told him about some of my frustrations, not feeling I was doing anything terrific with my life, aside from raising nice kids. I told him about some spiritual stuff I was going through. He's a great listener."

Connecting with the golf instructor ("It's just a friendship, nothing sexual between us") had been a little unsettling, however. Jerrell was buoyed up, looking forward to their meetings. She felt "less blah." And that contributed to the "sharp focus" in which she was seeing her marriage. One morning she toyed with the idea of a temporary separation from her husband, wondering how that would feel. But the thought upset her. "All the complications of a separation just don't make any sense. It's too awful to think about what that would mean to the kids. And for Nick, it would just devastate him. We both were in this for the long haul. I'd feel terrible."

Before Jerrell or a woman in her circumstances can decide whether or how her less-than-great marriage might be improved, she needs to define her individual good-enough standards.

Voice Mapping

"My husband is my best friend, and that means he should meet all my needs."

Looking at what she did have in her marriage, there was much Jerrell could point to as solid plusses. She'd chosen an excellent breadwinner, and that, she had believed from the start, was one of the keys to a successful marriage. Maybe *the* key. She had elected to be a homemaker, and they had the resources for her to do so. The children were great, the sex was at least "fine." But as she grew into new stages of her life, both external and internal, and other needs gained in importance, she perceived what was absent from the picture. And the good breadwinner husband didn't seem capable of satisfying them.

Reframing

Why did I pick him as my husband?

An excellent place to start reframing is by figuring out why she married the man in the first place: Aside from the fact that she loved him, what was good about him at the time? Jerrell chose Nick largely because she admired his drive; she knew he'd be a success. He came from a fairly well-to-do family and had a good business sense. "He was a man I knew would always be responsible and reliable," she said, "and I thought of him as really macho. We'd make a great team."

She remembered how they often went out to dinner and to the movies. Sometimes they went for long walks in the park. "We liked hanging out with each other, although in all honesty I don't think we ever had a very intellectual relationship, if that's what you'd call it." After the children arrived, the pleasant hanging out times disappeared.

But a woman may settle on a future husband for all kinds of reasons, including some that from the start hold the seeds of letdown or worse in the future. One woman, who grew up in a household with an alcoholic father, determinedly set out to marry a man who was anything but similar to her father—which meant, most importantly in her mind, a professional man, not a blue-collar worker. She found him, a successful lawyer. She paid little attention to any factors other than his professional status, such as what his family was like or how he acted with coworkers and others. In fact, there was much evidence that he was a harsh, controlling, and psychologically demeaning man, but—as is typical in abusive marriages—it became visible to her only in hindsight. (Partly, the woman in such a situation may not want to know. Partly, the abusive man is often a

Dr. Jekyll and Mr. Hyde, an individual with the ability to present a front that is not an accurate reflection of his true personality.)

Did he meet my needs before? If so, what's different now?
These are two questions we find useful with the client who comes to talk about her disappointing marriage. Usually, the answer to the first one is "Yes, he did fulfill my needs, he was what I was looking for, that's why I married him." The obvious follow-up question is what happened after that? What changed between then and now? Have your needs shifted, and does he seem oblivious to or unable to meet your new needs?

You may find it helpful to take a needs-and-wishes inventory. Make a list indicating what you want more of, right now, at this stage of your life:

- Time together?
- Playing, more fun?
- Involvement with the children?
- Intellectual stimulation?
- Financial security?
- Planning for the future?
- Shared interests?
- Hugs and kisses?

Rate your needs list. Ask yourself how critical are your most important, currently unmet needs. Is some degree of boredom or lack of intellectual stimulation tolerable or is it becoming truly unbearable? What can you let go of, or not?

Many women realize that what they didn't miss before, or didn't much think about, they now want. For one woman, as it did in part for Jerrell, it might come about when the children no longer absorb so much of her time and energy. It might be when she suddenly, surprisingly meets someone new and emotionally she's thrown for a loop. It might be a big birthday, turning forty or fifty, and doing a life reassessment. Maybe at forty-five she needs more passion. By sixty-five, companionship may head the list.

At the same time, nothing may have changed for the man. Said Jerrell, "He's not doing anything different than he has for the last fifteen years. He works incredibly hard, he comes home, he has dinner, maybe watches TV with the kids a little, goes to sleep. Then he wakes up the next morning, works hard, comes home. He doesn't think anything's wrong. He's held up his end of the bargain. So why would I have any complaints?"

It's a common progression. Initially, the man and woman are building toward marriage, then they're building a home and a family. As the years go on, the sense of building something together evaporates. They begin leading emotionally parallel lives. For many women in Jerrell's situation, there's no real desire for divorce or separation. What Jerrell wanted, she realized, was simply, or not so simply, more zest in the relationship, and especially better communication. "Just talking more about thoughts and feelings," she said, "being able to tell him when I'm down and discouraged. As trite as this sounds maybe, I want him to understand me better."

Do I value his "good qualities"?

Put aside the "me" part of the equation (what are my needs?) for the moment and consider the "him" part. Ask yourself what value you place on the areas in which he *does* come through or *does* shine? Is there enough there to outweigh what's missing for you?

One client, taking the measure of her husband, had come to think of him as ineffectual, a limited man in many regards; she didn't see him so much anymore as a husband and lover, and was trying to decide if she could find enough satisfaction in a "friendly" relationship with him. Like some women who view their marriages with disappointment, she chose to focus on his good qualities. "He's a wonderful father. He's the one who takes the kids to the playground or the museum on the weekends, reads to them every night. He's the playful one, you know, the fun one, much more so than I am. They adore spending time with him." Then she asked herself, was she pumping up the good qualities in her mind to make herself feel like less of a failure?

Describing her husband's interactions with their children, she reached this understanding of herself: "Actually, the way he is with our kids is the way I wish my father had been with me." She had grown to adulthood somewhat fearful of men, she believed, largely because of a chilly, undemonstrative, and harshly critical father—which probably had at least something to do with her choice of a mate: "Maybe this sounds strange, but I feel like I'm redeeming the past. My daughters are going to grow up very different than I did, much more secure and happier. And that's terrific." This line of self-talk helped bring her full circle, in a sense—less depressed, more at peace.

Can I hope or expect to get more of what I want from him?
Let's say you know what you'd like to change. You're thinking of some ways to press for more of your needs, and you're wondering what kind of reception you can anticipate from your partner or whether it's worth making the effort in the first place. Cast back and consider:

- Was he ever good at sharing ideas?
- Does he listen?
- Was there any point in the past when things were going badly between us, and we did turn it around and get on a better track?
- Does he have the potential to change, which starts with communicating differently?
- Is he willing to try? Is he interested in learning and growing?

A "yes" answer to any of these is a hopeful sign.

Changing my expectations—would that be a good idea? Am I overreacting, for example?
Do I want to reframe my own responses to his behaviors?
For one woman, reviewing her needs inventory led to a reality check on her perceptions of her husband's flaws. She had described him as "abusive." When we asked for illustrations of his abusiveness, she ran down a list: he had a quick temper, with everybody; he cursed in traffic; he often sounded annoyed when she called him at his business. Extremely sensitive to emotionality and anger, she hated the loud voice; to her it felt like an attack. He was a difficult

man, it seemed, but in a way that happened to be a particularly bad fit with her views and needs. In time she was able to reframe like this: "Am I reacting too strongly to his being short-tempered? What am I afraid of, actually? Is he going to hurt me or push me around? No, of course not, he never has and I know he never would. He raises his voice a lot, and I don't like it, but that's the way he is. So, should I—and do I want to—work on myself to have a little thicker skin? Tell myself people get cranky, it's not personal, and maybe I can diffuse that and handle it differently?"

Movement Strategies

I need to find ways to be more tolerant.

Unhappy wives so often report a persistent amount of bickering between themselves and their husbands. The woman who, let's say, needs more affection from her mate finds multiple other, smaller issues to challenge him on. But if you've decided to address what you need more or less of—and you really want him to hear you—it helps to first pay some attention to lowering any general atmosphere of hostility or fault-finding.

Consider a strategy from a child-raising practice, geared to reducing nagging. This technique advises a parent to keep a list for a week of all the minor battles that erupt between her and her child. Then she is to review the list; decide what *really* matters (maybe punching out his little brother or using curse words is not in any way acceptable to her) and what *somewhat* matters (soggy towels on the bathroom floor or toys not put away). Push for changes over the big-ticket items and practice greater tolerance of the rest, and not only is daily life more pleasant but compliance from the child is more likely. It might work with husbands.

Try making a list of the issues that precipitate bickering. Decide what you can tolerate, if not with a glad heart then at least without judging your partner negatively and picking a fight. Learn to identify trigger points—those moments just before you lose patience. Practice distancing yourself right before the blowup, maybe by taking a walk or simply by leaving the room.

I can learn to communicate better about what I'd like and need.

Most women think their husbands should "see" what's wrong; they believe the man should "get it," because it seems so obvious (*we don't talk about things, we don't spend enough time together, I'm depressed*). It's necessary to convey the message—in a friendly atmosphere, in a calm and relatively private moment, without laying blame—that you need something more or something new. You might start out talking a little about what you both wanted back when the marriage started, and what you both want now.

Here's how it went with Jerrell, after a period of reframing in which she defined her needs and thought through things on her own: She'd never previously brought up with Nick her "blah" feelings, her dismay over what felt to her like a lack of emotional substance and true connection in their relationship. She did start to talk to him about all this, especially how she wanted to improve the communication between the two of them, and he was surprised. He had no idea. But Nick loved his wife and his family, and he was willing to try. So they arranged to have some dinners out, away from the children, just to talk. It was, she reported, "a start, no big overnight success."

Countless magazine articles and books offer suggestions on how to turn around a listless marriage—the romantic weekend away, the importance of "I need . . . " rather than "you never . . . " dialogue. What we would stress here are two realities to keep in mind. First, the overnight success is rare. Life may slip back into its accustomed pattern, and continued effort may be necessary. Second, as willing and accommodating as he may be, the noncommunicator husband may simply have less need for interdependence in a relationship. Not only is he not dissatisfied with their joint life, he is capable of fulfilling his own emotional requirements. He may never come around very much.

Consider couples therapy, without the other half of the couple.
He won't go—does it matter?

Many women considering therapy to address issues in the marriage think they must attend couples therapy, with both partners in there understanding that things have to be thrashed out one way or another. But often therapy can be hugely helpful even when one partner wants no part of it.

If you do decide to seek further help, consider what you're looking for. Are you trying to save the marriage? To have someone tell you there's no way to save the marriage? To find a way out with the least pain and shame for all?

I can do more for myself to get more of what I'm missing.

If it looks like communication isn't going to improve dramatically, if she still wants more for herself, a wife may have to conclude that her changing needs may not be met within the marriage. Jerrell started several things going. She sent for catalogs for graduate school, and considered going back for an advanced degree with the idea of improving her job possibilities and also putting herself in an intellectual community for part of her time. She revitalized her network of friends, which had skewed far toward only other mothers. She reestablished contact with some old college friends. With each step, she was hoping to build a more satisfying life.

I can tell myself that although I wish things were otherwise, I can and will still be happy.

This is a big one. We could also put it this way: Can you change your mindset from settling to accepting? Consider it a mental movement strategy.

If working at having more of your needs met hasn't succeeded very well, or after some initial improvements everything went back to "normal," you may come to the uneasy understanding that this is as good as it's going to get. You really would prefer him to be different, yet you have reached a resolution of some sort.

Here's the problem, however: If you *settle* for a situation that you cannot change, you'll probably continue to feel dissatisfied, perhaps angry, perhaps miserable, and sense that you've abandoned all hopes and dreams. But there's another goal: Rather than settle, *accept*, and aim at feeling actually happy and satisfied. Not everyone will attain that level, but it's one to strive for: This is the path I'm on, and it's not ideal, but overall, I have a good life.

For a marriage partnership to work over the long haul, both partners need to be grown-ups who are able to give and take, compromise, and flexibly weather life's inevitable ups and downs.

Diane's Story

"In some ways, my marriage has become irrelevant to who I am."

Diana, forty-eight, worked as a guidance counselor during the early years of her marriage, stopped for a while to stay home with her son and daughter, and returned to part-time work midway through their youth. Meanwhile, her husband, Bob, a senior manager in an international chemicals corporation, followed a steady job path and did well. A couple of years before coming for therapy, Diana had joined forces with a friend in opening a small antiques store in their town. The friend put up the money; Diana had always had an interest in furniture and decorating. The venture started as something of a lark. Then Diana surprised herself. "I loved running a business. And I was good at it!" Nervously, she'd gone on a buying trip to London and Paris, and now couldn't wait to do more of it. Suddenly fired up, she decided to quit counseling, which she had never much loved, and began courses at night in interior and graphic design. Bob didn't object to any of this; neither did he seem very interested.

Her main problem, as she perceived it and began to talk about it in our sessions: "I discovered I'm more ambitious and more competitive than I thought I was. More so than my husband. It's like I'm passing him by." She suspected, too, that his saying little about it all meant he was disapproving, or maybe angry or threatened. So she played down her accomplishments, or didn't mention a sale she'd made or something good that happened in class. "I'm constantly stifling myself," she said, "so as not to make him feel bad." And that made her angry, this need she felt to suppress her enthusiasm around him.

All this had come to a head over the past half a year, after Bob—who was twelve years older than she—took early retirement. "I don't want him around all the time. I got used to coming and going when I want," Diana said. "Or actually, it's not him being there that gets on my nerves. It's more that he's turned into an empty vessel. When he was still working, at least he had his work friends and he had stories to tell about the office." Now that was gone. In addition, she felt she was expected to be his source of stimulation and direction. "He wants us to do things together all the time, and I don't always want to or I can't. And then I'm guilty about going off for classes and working in the shop."

Diana cared about Bob and she didn't want to hurt him in any way. But she was frustrated and sometimes found herself viewing him with disgust. That's what most disturbed her, and what she wanted to think her way through.

Voice Mapping

"Good wives take their lead from their husbands."

As excited as Diana was about her new business and studies, as annoyed and impatient as she was with her husband's seeming passivity or disinterest, it still felt uncomfortable—wrong, somehow—to be the partner who was taking actions, going places, seeing new horizons, and finding new challenges. It undercut the unspoken agreement of the beginnings of the marriage and the pattern it had followed for many years: Bob—his career, his schedule—determined the broad outlines of their daily lives; Diana fit herself to them.

"Good wives make husbands feel good about themselves."

The emotional well-being of the husband is the wife's responsibility, says this common cultural voice. If he seems at loose ends, or a little insecure or a little threatened, she should do what is in her power to relieve his discomfort. And that may be, as it was for Diana, making herself seem *less* so that he will seem *more*.

But stifling her enthusiasm and newly discovered competitiveness and ambition—her own voice—didn't pay off, she realized. It made her annoyed with herself, and maybe was doing him and the marriage a disservice in the long run. That was where Diana began her reframing.

Reframing

I'm getting more satisfaction now from my personal pursuits than from my marriage.
Does that really mean the marriage is irrelevant?

For Diana, along with the excitement and absorption of her new activities came a large dose of anxiety. She looked at her burgeoning career and her somewhat stalled marriage, and tended to see black and white: go down one road and that means the other road isn't important anymore.

But any woman torn by such ambivalent feelings can help herself by considering a broader context. For one thing, a wife's and a husband's work and career paths often differ. During the years he's plowing his energies and ambitions into a job, she may be putting her own career desires on the back burner or not even experiencing them, as she focuses on the children and the family. For another, couples don't always grow in tandem. It's entirely possible, and very common, for her to be discovering new interests that put her out in the world in different ways, just as he's ready to kick back and relax, or maybe struggling through a personally hard transition from work into retirement.

I've decided my husband is annoyed about my career ambitions, but is what's really going on here that I'm afraid to grow and change?
Was Diana making assumptions about her partner that might not be true? Was growing and changing a threat to the marriage? Gradually she came to accept the fact that people do change, and change isn't bad, and that she didn't owe it to her husband *not* to change. Also, maybe he really did have no problem with her new ventures. She admitted that she hadn't received any signs from him to the contrary.

Movement Strategies

I shouldn't try to solve all his problems for him.
The questions leading a woman to this strategy might be: If he seems bored or at a loss as to how to fill his days, is it up to me to fix it? If I do think it's up to me to fix it, or I do want to try, what does that mean to me? Pushing him to get out more, make new friends, join a club? Is giving up what I want to do what he wants?

In surveys, the majority of husbands say they think couples should do things together, but wives often don't agree. One client, a woman in her early sixties, said, ruefully, "One of my big pleasures is going to a movie all by myself. My husband could not in a hundred years conceive of going to a movie all by himself, without me."

Diana, however, had to give some more thought to her description of her husband as "an empty vessel," a piece of furniture who was constantly looking to her to arrange his life for him. Yes, Bob had sometimes suggested they go out for dinner at a nice restaurant, just on an evening she had a class. Once he had wanted to take a weekend at a country inn they had both liked in the past, just when she was getting ready for the busy holiday shopping season at her store. Her feelings—maybe in this order of severity—were guilt that she had to let him down, anger that he didn't appreciate the new demands on her time, disgust that he didn't have "a life" of his own, and pressure to make things better. Then she tended to overcompensate for all that, urging him ("nagging at him, actually") to call an old office friend of his and make a lunch date, lining up a few household chores he could see to, sending for seed catalogs to try to promote a gardening hobby for him, and bringing home a flyer for a course in woodworking at the university extension.

Diana chose to try to put a strategy into practice. "Maybe Bob is feeling a little at loose ends at this stage of his life. A lot has changed for him over the past year, the biggest thing being his early retirement. But he doesn't seem depressed or wildly unhappy. I think he needs to be left to his own devices a little, to let him figure out some new interests gradually. He's a smart man and a strong man. I'm going to do less pushing and prodding and thinking I need to solve his 'problems,' which maybe he doesn't even see as problems. Just let him know I'm sympathetic and supportive of whatever he does decide to do next."

I need to bring my partner into my changing life experiences.

It was, perhaps, time for Diana to take the lead somewhat, and to find ways to let Bob share in her new ventures and accomplishments. Maybe he might actually get a kick out of spending an afternoon in her shop during the busy season, or might wish to look over some of her design assignments. She wasn't sure, but seeing ahead, she could imagine that her marriage might actually be enriched by her own added independence and ambition, that she might be bringing into it people, experiences, and information that would enhance the solid commitment they did have.

At the heart of this strategy was a resolve to shift out of her negative take on their situation (she was "passing him by," he probably felt "threatened" by her success, she was forced to "stifle" her enthusiasm) and to place greater trust in the overall resiliency of the partnership.

I can find at least one new activity we can pursue together.

Earlier, we mentioned that often within a marriage the sense of building something jointly dissipates as years pass. Despite the popular images in TV ads and elsewhere of the after-the-children-are-grown couple—the husband and wife, finally, having the freedom and resources to go sailing or open a bed-and-breakfast or enjoy other happy adventures together—it is not at all uncommon for the older man and woman to find themselves leading somewhat parallel lives. And they neglect their need to sustain their closeness as a couple, even while wishing for closeness.

There is a pointed strategy that can help. Settle on one brand new, common interest to develop together, a pursuit each might find pleasant and neither knows much about. Diana gave this some thought, and came up with a bold stroke. "Tango lessons! There's a dance studio in town near my store, and to tell you the truth, I've always thought that would be a lot of fun." She suggested it to Bob, who also thought it would be fun, and they decided to sign up for an introductory class one night a week. She was still busy, pressed for time, but she determined to make this Diana-and-Bob hour a priority.

Sharing the pleasure of discovery can be a powerful way to reinvigorate an aging marriage—learning while together.

The very strictures that once kept marriage in its place—social convention, children, religious persuasions, the difficulty or stigma of divorce, the woman's economic need—made the institution simpler to maintain, if not necessarily more content. Former generations of couples, and not that long ago, may not always have believed in happily ever after, but married life was *there,* not to be everlastingly questioned. Once vows were said, the line was crossed, the thing was done. "Working at it" wasn't part of the picture, or rather, working at marriage meant he did what husbands/ fathers do and she did what wives/mothers do, and everybody knew what that was.

Today, the playing field has changed, largely because the very freedoms and opportunities women now enjoy make it more incumbent on the individual to find her own voice and shape her own marital path. But along with that necessity comes the greater possibility of achieving a true and satisfying life, within or outside of a marriage.

6

The Child-Rearing Expectation: "I'm Raising a Perfect Child, and Loving Every Minute of It"

We choose to have our children (and we have them when we choose), and so—according to a popular image of the modern parent—we're ready, willing, and able to raise them happily and well. Informed by several decades of child-raising advice, we're psychologically sharper than previous generations of mothers. And if we're looking better, doing more, feeling greater confidence than ever, so are our kids.

Under that image lie troublesome realities, some that spring from the complex culture within which today's families chart a course over the years of child-raising. One client, a woman who felt that overall she and her husband were doing a pretty decent job with their children, talked about what she perceived as the difficulties of twenty-first-century parenting: "When I had my kids and I was learning about being a mother, my mom used to say to me sometimes, 'It's not a big deal, I did it, your grandmother did it, just use your common sense, kids are kids, things don't change.' Now I have a fourteen-, an eleven-, and an eight-year-old, and you know what? My mother was wrong! Just about everything has changed from when she was raising young kids. It's another landscape entirely."

She sketched out that landscape: "My children watch TV sit-coms and cartoons that portray parents as idiots who deserve to be insulted. They are exposed to God only knows what over the Internet, although we try to monitor computer use. Some boys and girls in my eleven-year-old's class have already hooked up and are recognized by the other kids as 'boyfriend' and 'girlfriend.' A couple of my eight-year-old's classmates I know are taking Ritalin and Prozac just to help them be good, sit still, and concentrate in school. My sister's teenagers go to a huge city high school where they walk through metal detectors every morning. Half of my kids' friends have divorced parents."

She was keenly aware of incidences of school violence, aggressive bullying, drug use, and other modern-day worries that parents face just by sending a child out the door. It seems "harder to get things right these days," she believed. "At the same time, I think in some ways we're doing a better job of it than our parents did."

Many mothers we talk to do consciously look back at the way they were brought up and wish for something better for their children. Even within a loving family, they remember a "do it because I say so" atmosphere—or, for some adult children of 1960s parents, a "do whatever you want" atmosphere—and so they make efforts to explain the wisdom or the "whys" behind their own parenting rules. Many of them feel that their worries or concerns were brushed off when they were children, so they believe their children should be listened to and respected as individuals with their own points of view. Besides the usual responsibilities—clothing, housing, feeding, and educating—these modern mothers also take on the burden of their children's psychological well-being (*if my child is unhappy, it's up to me to fix it*). All this, in so many ways, is to the good. But all this also presents women with choices and decisions that complicate their lives.

The client who talked about the changed landscape described her family of origin as traditional. "My dad worked, my mom was a homemaker. She also had three children, my two kid brothers and me. And I don't remember her ever looking at a book about how to be a parent. Maybe she had Dr. Spock, I don't even know that." She herself, on the other hand, owned a shelf full. "Spock, of course, and Brazleton and White and Penelope Leach and the things from the Gesell Institute. Books about the preschool years, the elementary years, the scary teen years. Books about how boys develop, how girls develop."

Our intention in this chapter is not to add to the abundance of child-raising advice, but to focus on a particular quality of modern parenting. Among the stresses that we identify throughout this book are troubled marriages, single parenthood, and the expectations of and about high-achieving women. When those stresses are combined with today's democratic parenting style, blurred adult/child boundaries and skewed relationships between a mother and her child can be the result.

In this chapter, we look at three stories:

- The child as confidant to the parent
- Mother and child tensions during the onset of divorce
- The drive to produce the perfect child

Each essentially concerns how a woman's needs may conflict with those of her child.

Jackie's Story

*"Now that I'm dating again, my daughter has
become hostile toward me."*

Jackie, a forty-three-year-old single mother, had always been close with her daughter, until lately. "When we're both home, most of the time she's in her room with the door shut, TV going, on the phone. Then she emerges and announces, 'I'm going to Jen's house, bye,' and that's it. No conversation." Amanda was fifteen; Jackie was thinking this was "typical teenage stuff." But it was especially hurtful to her, because she and Amanda were "best friends," Jackie said, "since she was a little kid. We go shopping together, we both love baseball, we both love to cook and eat." To Jackie, it was even more significant that she'd tried hard to be available to her daughter. "Nothing was ever off limits to talk about. She's always known what's going on in my life. And she knows she can come to me if she's having problems, and I'll listen and try to help."

The "typical teenage" behavior seemed especially hostile now, however, and Jackie thought she knew the reason: "Maybe Amanda feels we're sort of in competition, since we both have boyfriends."

Jackie had been seeing Stan, her first serious involvement in many years. Amanda had no strong objections to him, Jackie believed. "She's met Stan, and she knows he's a good guy." But Jackie apparently felt girlishly nervous about dating—over things like what to wear or what kind of eye makeup to use—and she asked her daughter for advice. Amanda didn't seem very interested, although she would offer her opinion.

One evening, the two had an uncomfortable conversation. "I wanted to know how you give a man a blow job. Specifically, you know, how do you do it without gagging. I thought maybe it was a little weird to be talking to her about something like that, but I wanted information. She'd know, kids these days talk about all kinds of things, and I've always been candid with her about sex." Her daughter started to say something about oral sex, then the talk turned awkward and the two drifted from the subject. Since then, Amanda had been keeping a greater distance; she answered her mother with a curt yes or no, and spent almost all her free time at the home of one friend or another.

We asked Jackie to describe her earlier years with Amanda, how their relationship had evolved, and it seemed that mother and daughter had been a family of two for virtually all of Amanda's life. Jackie and her husband divorced shortly after their daughter was born, he'd moved to another state, and she'd been supporting her child adequately on her income over the years.

Jackie's was a common modern-day family constellation. Perhaps as many as one-third of American families with children are headed by single parents; in addition, the largest group of young, divorced mothers are women raising an only child. Much of the societal attention paid to this population focuses on the economic difficulties and the time constraints facing a woman bringing up a child on her own. Much of what we observe has to do with the emotional and psychological connections between mother and child, and how easy it can be for the parent to view the child as comforter, confidant, or pal.

For Jackie, reframing meant taking a closer look at the "best friends" relationship with her daughter, including how the conversation about oral sex might have sounded to each of them.

Voice Mapping

"My child and I should be friends."

Like many mothers, Jackie wanted to have a relaxed, affectionate relationship with her child, unlike the one she had had with her parents. They would communicate, they would share things, they would enjoy each other's company.

And Amanda was a terrific girl. "She always seemed to be more mature than other kids her age. Maybe she just knew she had to grow up a little fast, because for a lot of years I was frazzled, working two jobs. And she was so smart, wise beyond her years, I'd say." Starting when Amanda got to be around nine or ten, "she was better to talk to than any guys I knew at the time. I could confide in her, and she appreciated what was going on with me. She had real empathy."

"Sex is no big taboo."

From her own mother, Jackie had heard virtually nothing about sex, other than, as she described it, "the old-fashioned stuff about not doing it until you're married, because otherwise the guy is just going to use you and then walk. You know, why should he buy the cow if he gets the milk for free? But there was no information, just rules. Plus, my mom was so uptight about the whole thing, she was the last person I'd go to with any questions."

She thought all this was a bad idea, and found support for her thinking at school-organized parent meetings and studies she read elsewhere. "It's not only okay to talk to your kids about sex, but you should, because the kids whose parents don't are the ones who get into trouble. They have sex too early. If there's a pregnancy or a disease, they don't tell their parents about it." When Amanda was younger Jackie had initiated talks "not just about how babies are made, but that you need to feel close to someone and like him before you think about having sex."

Reframing

Do I want to be my child's friend or be a friendly parent to my child?

This was a way for Jackie to start considering the issue of boundaries, and how—or if—that might be affecting the shutout she was getting from her daughter. We suggested that Jackie ask herself what she would define as an appropriate friendship role, and what she would define as an appropriate parent role.

"A friend's role," she said, "is to be there for the other person. Friends talk about what's going on in their lives—the good, the bad, and the ugly—and they give each other support. Friends are the people you can turn to when everything's falling apart. They genuinely care about each other and they want what's best for each other. They're not necessarily absolutely alike, but they're on the same wavelength. And they have fun, they just like being around each other.

"For me, a parenting role means letting my daughter know that I love her, I'm looking out for her, I'm available to her. I want her to grow up strong and make good choices, and I think one of the ways I'm doing that is by encouraging communication between us. Always keeping the lines open. And yeah, having fun together too."

The two roles were clearly somewhat different in terms of reciprocity. Her daughter had many friends from school. "I know the way she talks to them isn't the way she talks to me now. They can spend hours on the phone or the computer. She always tells me where she's going, who she'll be with, but she doesn't let me in on all the details about what's happening in the group." Realistically, she couldn't be—she wasn't—a friend to her child in the same way as a peer, Jackie realized. But she could be a friendly parent. That's really what she wanted to achieve.

Am I expecting an adult-adult or peer-peer relationship rather than a parent-child relationship?

Jackie had to give some thought to what it was she was asking from her teenage daughter. She had focused on the boyfriend issue, and maybe she wasn't entirely wrong about that. Some competitiveness might have motivated her decision to involve Amanda in aspects of her own love life; she was uncertain and anxious about getting it right with men, something new for her. But in the larger sense, Jackie seemed to be seeking female intimacy, a girlfriend and a confidant—a kind of relationship that she might have done better looking for elsewhere at this stage of their lives.

The challenge is that a child needs to maintain connectedness with parents while also going about the developmentally necessary task of separating from parents and investing in peers. A parent needs to maintain connectedness with her child while allowing the child to develop in those separate ways.

Closeness between a mother and child can be a lovely thing, of course. And it's understandable that an unattached single woman might overlook her only child's need to separate and individuate, because it's a pleasure to have such delightful company right there at home. But the girl who's made privy to her mother's emotional ups and downs, and especially her romantic relationships, may not feel free to break away, rebel a little, and put her energy into forming her own trusting and intimate commitments with her peers. She may feel happy and gratified that her parent seems to need and value her so much; she may think there's no one else as great as Mom to talk to. And that's not such a good thing.

In the "hostile behavior," the turning away, Amanda probably was cluing her mother in to the fact that the lines needed to be redrawn or defined in some other way. In a few years, mother and her young-adult daughter might well enjoy a "best friends" relationship. For now, Amanda was saying that she needed distance.

Movement Strategies

I need to restore some parent-child boundaries.

Appropriate boundaries can be hard to discern. Each parent-and-child pair will develop its own way of talking and sharing and being together that reflects family history, culture, personality, sense of humor, life circumstances, and many other factors. One observation, however, is safe to make across the board: while the sex-is-no-taboo voice has its merits, it can lead to difficulties. For one thing, information may be conveyed in a manner that's inappropriate. One mother, for example, showed her daughter and daughter's friends a dildo in an effort to demystify some of the mechanics of intercourse and get across the idea that sexual pleasure was nothing to be ashamed of. The girls looked embarrassed.

That was probably an unusual lapse in good judgment. But it's critical for any parent to know that a child of any age really does not want to think of her mother or father as a sexual being. At some level, every kid prefers to believe that her parents had sex as many times as the number of children they produced, and no more often than that. It is still as true as ever that children don't want any visual—or auditory—evidence of their parents' love lives. The archetype of the virgin mother lies deep in our psyches.

Taking off from there, some appropriate boundaries for Jackie might be these: "I'll be available to answer questions and ensure that my kid doesn't take in a lot of misinformation, but I'm not going to talk to her about my own sexual needs, worries, or experiences." "We can enjoy the shopping trips and baseball games together, but I'm not going to discuss my boyfriends or engage in peerlike exchanges about how to carry on an adult romantic relationship."

There's also the matter of physical boundaries. Single mothers we've counseled described living conditions or habits in which there was not much separation between what's-mine and what's-my-child's. Sometimes finances made it necessary to live in a very close space. But small strategies that ensure a little more privacy are probably a good idea for both mother and child—setting up a folding screen to mark off sleeping areas, making sure clothes don't get mixed up together and shared without permission, remembering to knock before opening a closed bedroom door.

I will make a conscious effort to spend more time with adult companions.

Working a full-time job, raising a child on her own, meant that for years Jackie was booked full. She had a couple of good female friends whom she didn't see too often, but she was thinking now that those were the people to talk to about personal issues, such as the new boyfriend in her life.

Sheila's Story

"I'm trying to help my children understand what's going on between their father and me."

Sheila, thirty-five, divorcing and the mother of two sons, had been telling her boys, eight and ten, "It takes two people to make a marriage work, and Daddy didn't want it to work anymore," and "Daddy doesn't care about our family so much right now, but he says he still loves you." She didn't see anything too wrong with this. "I'm not trying to turn them against him. But he is the one who wants the divorce, and our kids should understand that." Sometimes she "lost it" in front of the children, either starting to cry or banging around pots and pans in a fit of anger. To her mind, however, she was just being herself. "This is a very difficult and sad and painful time for me, and they know that. They're not stupid. I don't think it's good for any of us for me to pretend that nothing so terrible is going on." Her children needed the truth, she thought, and she was providing it.

The truth was something they weren't getting from their father, Sheila said. He initiated the separation to pursue a romance with another woman, but he hadn't told his sons about her. In fact, he hadn't mentioned the word "divorce," and said only, "Mom and I aren't getting along so well," and "I'm going to have my own apartment for a while and you can come and stay with me whenever you want." Sheila told them the rest of the story. "Your dad found someone else. He loves her, he's been spending a lot of time with her over the past year, and he wants to be with her. This is his decision and there's nothing we can do about it." When the older boy asked his father about this "someone else," the father became furious at their mother because he had wanted to ease the children into the new reality gradually. Believing that she and their father should both "be on the same page" when talking to the kids, Sheila suggested to him that he join her for counseling. He said no; she was furious.

The atmosphere between the two parents wasn't improving. Sheila gave these examples: "He comes by to pick up the boys on Saturday mornings. I'm supposed to have them ready and waiting out on the porch, because he won't come in the house. Sometimes he's a little late and I wait out there with them. Then last weekend he drove up, the kids got in the car, I leaned through the window to give my little boy a kiss, and my husband said I was on his property and I should get out. This is the kind of nastiness that's coming from him."

Another time, the children were with their father for an extended weekend, Friday evening to Sunday evening, because their father had made big plans—a drive to visit their paternal grandparents and a day at an amusement park. When they got home late Sunday, Sheila was enraged to learn they hadn't done homework, although this had been part of the arrangement with their father. "I told the kids I wasn't blaming them. I said Dad always wants to be the fun person, but he's the parent too, and it's his responsibility to make sure you get your work done." The boys' father was there while she expressed these thoughts, and he left in anger.

Sheila was genuinely hoping to help her children through a confusing life passage. But she felt they weren't doing terribly well; her younger son was clingy, her older son was unusually quiet and preoccupied. A couple of friends had told her she needed to let it all go a little; she was dumping too much of her own turmoil on her kids. It seemed she didn't want to hear that advice, however, or perceive what was apparent to a number of adults around her.

Further changes were coming up for the family, and Sheila came to therapy to talk about them. She was considering moving to a smaller house that would be easier for her to maintain, she wanted to switch from a part-time job to a full-time job, and her husband's girlfriend would probably be moving in with him shortly. All these were very grown-up issues, she acknowledged, but she wanted to see that her kids understood and were prepared. And she insisted that children suffer more when they're kept in the dark—which is how she started reframing her perceptions of the choices she was making in dealing with her sons.

Voice Mapping

"It's good to be honest with children."

To Sheila, that meant that children survive divorce better when they know everything that's going on. She was another woman who found in her family of origin a model she did not want to repeat. Her parents had separated when she was a teenager. "This was after years of constant war," she said. "We kids didn't have a clue what was going on. There was just a noisy, shouting argument every so often, followed by days of the deep freeze between them. My sister and I would be walking around on eggshells, trying to keep them from getting mad at us or getting mad at each other again. Then one day our parents sat us down and said Dad was moving out, they were getting a divorce. That was it." She never learned many details. She rarely saw her father for years; only in adulthood and after having children herself did she reestablish a reasonably satisfactory relationship with him.

This experience of her parents' disintegrating marriage and then divorce left a deep and negative impression, and now that she, her husband, and their children were going through something similar, Sheila was determined to see that her kids came out of it less scarred than she felt she had been. "It's wrong for parents to say nothing," she believed; "kids have even more fears and worries that way."

Reframing

Am I rationalizing my behavior with my children?

"I should be honest with my kids" is an instance, again, of a complex issue couched in a positive virtue. It's when the positive voice is distorted and rationalized that trouble starts. Any woman in Sheila's position needs to ask herself what the motivation is behind the way she's chosen to talk to her children. Is it really all about being open and honest, because she believes that's best for them?

We asked Sheila to bring to the front burner some of her thoughts and feelings about the dissolution of the marriage, and what that meant to her. The more she talked, the clearer it became that she was tremendously upset about the social benefits she was losing. It wasn't because of the end of love, it wasn't the new girlfriend; rather, she was loath to give up the status she enjoyed as the wife of a successful professional man. Recognizing this embarrassed her; she felt greedy and self-centered to be worrying about matters she thought were shallow. But the fears were real, and were fueling the anxiety and rage directed at this man who had elected to end a life in which she liked to see herself.

With some difficulty, Sheila began to consider whether under the guise of honesty, she was actually diminishing their father to her kids, painting him as the bad guy, and perhaps hoping to get them on her side. And then she was able to ask if she was expecting from her children a level of understanding that was not only unrealistic but hurtful. In this situation, a woman needs to ask herself:

- Where's a better place to draw the line between pretending all is well (when obviously it isn't) and revealing more than necessary to my kids?
- What are my children going to think or feel or do when they're teenagers?
- How are they going to perceive this whole sad time in our lives once they reach the age of greater mobility and greater understanding of adult realities?
- If I'm intent on making him the bad guy and me the good guy now, could there be a backlash for me in the future?

It's a useful exercise to look ahead, trying to imagine how the seeds planted by today's child-raising choices might affect family affections and loyalties later on. The woman going through a divorce may be in great pain, feeling angry and wounded and betrayed. In the midst of all that, however, she needs somehow to maintain awareness of possibly disastrous consequences if she sinks into a state of permanent victimization or bitterness.

See the world from the child's point of view.

It's not news that divorce is hard for children, even when the mother and father are working well together and not using the kids as pawns. They experience a loss, they mourn, they may entertain the fantasy of getting their parents back together. When a woman is caught up in her own emotional upheaval, it's difficult to put herself in her child's head and make sensitive parenting choices in terms of talk and behavior. Two fairly simple questions help: What does my child probably most want to know right now? What does my child probably most need right now?

For most women at Sheila's stage of the end of a marriage and the breaking up of a family home, the answer to those questions is probably something like this: My kid wants to know that the divorce isn't his fault, that Mom and Dad aren't separating because of anything he's done. He wants to know that both his parents are still going to be in his life, he'll see his dad and he'll have a safe home to live in and he's not going to have to leave his friends. And what he needs right now is affection, reassurance, a stable routine, small familiar gestures to relieve his anxiety and worry.

Movement Strategies

I need to figure out how to get support for myself in this difficult time. Are my own needs for allies and understanding actually spilling over to how I interact with my children? And where's a better place to look for allies and understanding?

An angry, scared woman going through a hostile divorce feels a little crazed; to friends and others around her she may even look irrational. She may be emotionally unready or unable to perceive herself clearly, and to recognize that her feelings are running away with her good judgment. But if the feelings can't be changed, they can be vented in relatively safe ways—specifically, not to or in front of the children, who are somewhat hapless bystanders. When a parent is so emotionally needy, kids react badly: one may withdraw into angry silence; one may act out in school or with peers; another may take on the inappropriate role of comforter and caretaker to the parent, wanting to make everything right again. Not good.

Sheila started practicing a wise strategy: When she felt herself in one of those "losing it" moods, she settled her kids down with a video to watch and then called a close and sympathetic friend who was willing to listen. And she took another action that proved to be a real help over the months to come, starting up a regular e-mail contact with an old college dormmate, Elena, whose situation was almost identical—divorcing, two young kids, ex-husband's girlfriend in the picture. Together, they talked out some thorny issues.

"For one thing," Sheila said, "once my sons started spending week-ends with their father and Janice, his girlfriend, I had an irresistible urge to grill the boys about Janice. What was she like? How did she act with their dad? Elena knew exactly what I was talking about. We both realized this kind of thing wasn't doing us any good, and obviously the kids were uncomfortable."

So many women going through divorce tell us they're talking to their lawyers, they're talking to their divorced friends about their lawyers, all focused on how to get the thing done faster, more equitably, or more harmoniously. But it's good to remember that a woman needs support around issues of child rearing too.

I can do some better nuts-and-bolts problem solving.

It certainly did seem that Sheila and her children's father were not "on the same page" regarding the child-raising issues of the moment, and they'd probably do well to seek out some objective advice through joint counseling. But there wasn't much she could do to arm-twist him into taking that action. It was within her power to reduce the general air of tension, partly by identifying the times when her children seemed most stressed.

Typically, that was right before their father came to pick up the children and after he brought them back home. Sheila adopted some simple strategies to make those transfers take place more peacefully. She sometimes arranged for a babysitter to be on hand for the pickup, while she left the house for an hour and ran errands. When the boys returned from a visit, she gave them all some time to decompress and allowed herself to be "the fun person" for a while, playing a board game with her kids or watching TV together.

Separating parents often report such moments of transition as especially hard on children. In the bigger picture, the periods immediately before, during, and immediately after the dissolution of the marriage—when the adults may be experiencing a range of emotions, such as sadness, anger, depression, and loneliness—are usually identified as particularly troublesome for kids. But there's good news: Studies suggest that a year to a year and a half after the onset of separation, things have calmed down and the children have adjusted; some even prefer the new configuration of the family.

Olivia's Story

"I've given my children every advantage. What went wrong?"

Olivia had big ambitions for her children, as well as big fears: "Getting started in a career or just adult life in general is not easy for young people these days. I want them to be prepared." That was part of the rationale for the fact that she and her husband had loaded their two children, from preschool on, with a long list of activities. "Like any parents, I guess we thought our kids were special," she said. "They were quick and bright, early walkers, early talkers. They're also very good-looking children. We wanted to give them every chance to develop their strengths and interests, whatever those were." They'd gone about it in a determined and methodical way.

The two children had taken beginning lessons in various musical instruments, and in swimming, dance, karate, skating, and art. As they developed, it seemed both were athletically adept. So it was decided that Tyrone, Olivia's son, would focus on swimming and ice hockey, and Jade, her daughter, would study ballet. For the past several years, they had attended summer camps designed around those specialties, and both took afterschool classes during the rest of the year. In addition, they were encouraged to continue with music lessons—Tyrone in classical guitar and Jade in piano—because their father, said Olivia, "believes being able to play an instrument is a great social plus."

All this required outstanding organizational skills on Olivia's part. She had them. The family had always employed a nanny/housekeeper, but still the logistics of scheduling and shepherding both kids among their various appointments took up a lot of their mother's attention. She was happy to fill that role; it was doing what was best for her children.

When Tyrone, fourteen, announced that he was dropping out of competitive swimming, his mother was crushed. "I'd hate to add up all the hours we've spent over the years getting him to lessons and meets. But that's not even the point. He's really a strong swimmer, he used to love it. I feel he's throwing away a golden opportunity to excel." Adding to her concern, Jade, now eleven, had been getting careless about schoolwork and her grades for the first time had slipped. She had missed some recent piano lessons, saying she didn't feel well.

What brought Olivia to therapy was an upsetting incident. Tyrone had gotten into a fight at school; the school suspended him from classes for three days and informed his parents that Tyrone would finish out the year on probation. Olivia was so ashamed that she didn't mention the episode to any of her friends. Now she wanted to talk about getting her children into counseling. They were so smart, she said, so talented in many ways; she was genuinely worried that they were slipping out of her control and also damaging their chances for future success.

Besides that, she was disappointed and even bitterly angry. By no means totally insensitive or unaware, she realized that her children had been kept enormously busy, and that probably they needed to ease up—or have their parents ease up on them, at least for now. But Olivia explained her feelings this way: "When kids are very young, parents have to have drive and ambition for them. By the time they get to Tyrone's age and Jade's age, that drive and determination should be internalized, the children should understand the value of all this. Frankly, I think my kids should thank their lucky stars that we've given them the best. They should be grateful to us for setting goals for them."

Beyond the anger, there was sadness. This well-intentioned parent had a glowing vision of her children, and the vision was fading before her eyes. After working so hard to get it right, she wondered what was going wrong. Before involving her son and daughter in counseling, or deciding if that was in fact something they'd benefit from, she was willing to reexamine her own needs and choices.

Voice Mapping

"If I do the right things, I'll have the right kids."

Olivia—although she didn't see it quite this way—wanted perfect children and thought it should be within her power to produce them. In the non-child-raising aspects of life, this was a woman unused to being stymied. She picked her challenges carefully, analyzed what was necessary to meet them, and generally triumphed. Justifiably proud of her accomplishments, she described establishing her own highly profitable interior design firm. Her husband was an admired architect. They expected an equal degree of success with their children.

"Keep up with the neighbors."
     Olivia acknowledged that she was indeed influenced by a wish to keep up, or rather to keep her children up with what almost all their peers were doing. "From when the kids were little," she said, "everybody in our circle of friends was enrolling the children in all kinds of early enrichment programs—infant swim classes, toddler gymnastics classes, music appreciation. One mother I knew used flash cards with her one-and-a-half-year-old to get him started reading at an early age."
     The school her son and daughter attended was academically demanding; some of Tyrone's classmates were already taking extracurricular preparation courses for the exams that would help determine the colleges they would go to. Olivia didn't want her kids left behind in any way. She remembered, also, the lessons of her own childhood, and how as an African American it was necessary to work hard to be seen as just as good as others.

Reframing

About my children, what's in my control and what isn't?
In other words, how much of how those kids turn out is entirely up to me?
     Olivia held high expectations for her children, just as she did for herself, and believed that with the right opportunities and parental encouragement, they would soar to the top. This was her nature. This was also the cultural message that probably she, like so many modern parents, had absorbed: the ideal child is an attainable goal.
     For one thing, parenting advice over the past several decades has "granted" us enormous power. Employ the proper techniques—bolster a child's self-esteem, validate his or her efforts, be authoritative but not authoritarian, and so on—and you'll shape the proper child. In addition, there exists a specialist or program for any problem, and all a parent needs to do is hunt up the particular tutor, doctor, after-school workshop, or other resource with a solution to what's going on with her kid.

It doesn't end there. Many mothers and fathers are encouraged to believe that with the right medication, a child's quite possibly routine emotional "growing pains" will be eliminated. (The number of children taking psychiatric drugs more than doubled from 1987 to 1996.) Increasing understanding of the human genome suggests that at some future date not only will prospective parents be able to receive information about potential genetically determined diseases; they may see the markers for a child's height, intelligence, sexual orientation, and other characteristics as well. (An editorial cartoon entitled "Your Perfect Baby® Check List" proposed the options of finger length, mouth shape, and ticklishness.)

All this, in combination with busy and highly structured family lives and the pressure of all those seemingly overachieving other parents and other kids, can cause mothers like Olivia to feel they should be in control of all possible outcomes for their children. In fact—and this is something we all do know intellectually—a lot of what a child turns out to be or do is not entirely the result of what a parent is or does. A child is shaped also by biology and temperament, by the quality of the friendships he or she forms with peers, by siblings, and by the influences of teachers and the other adults in his or her life. It's not all up to Mom and Dad.

Am I judging myself by my child's perceived failures?

Parents always have hopes and dreams for their children. It's impossible not to. When we ask a woman what she wishes for her child, the typical answer is "I want him to be happy, to have a good life." Sometimes the expectations are more specific and pointed ("I've always wanted her to become a doctor"), and the disappointment acute when it seems those goals will not be reached. But there can be more subtle disappointments too, and a lot of self-blame, because the drive to produce the perfect child reflects the drive to be the perfect mother. Which, of course, no one is, although that's hard to remember when so much in our culture tells a woman that if a child is having any kind of difficulty, not only is it up to her to fix it, it's because of something she did wrong.

One client mentioned watching her three-year-old at a birthday party hovering around the edges, apparently feeling not confident enough to join in. This mom was concerned that her daughter was growing up terribly shy and she thought she knew the reason. "I went back to my job when she was five months old, and she didn't get enough time to bond with me." Another client talked about her son's fearfulness—he didn't like new places and loud noises. "I've always worried that because I got sick and had to quit breast feeding suddenly when he was three months old," she said, "that's made him insecure."

To see your child clearly, to take an accurate reading of what's really in his best interests—what he needs and what you want for him, and how the two might differ—start by reducing the self-blaming and self-pressuring. Ask yourself: Overall, have I been and am I now a good enough mother? Are most of my choices for my child motivated by love? In the presence of love, there's room for mistakes.

Is my child truly in danger of going downhill?

What are those perceived failures in my child? And how bad are they really?

For Olivia, focusing so intently on her children's achievements, their somewhat less than stellar performance felt like the beginning of the end. She looked at several immediate events—a couple of Bs instead of all As; a couple of missed piano lessons; a scuffle among classmates; a teenage boy's decision to drop out of a sport (which, after all, was his perogative)—and saw looming disaster.

A woman often has a tendency to "awfulize" a situation that's probably not so terrible at all, or at least one for which there is insufficient evidence to point her down that road. To reframe her thinking and decide if her concerns are being awfulized or are in fact reasonable, she can help herself by shifting her focus a bit and thinking about what's going on in a child's life in general. Some questions might be:

- Does he have friends with whom he enjoys spending time?
- Do she and her friends engage in constructive activities together?
- Does he seem like a basically happy individual?

- Does she usually like going to school?
- Can he learn to soothe himself by finding a quiet space when he's tired and cranky?

Looking at the bigger picture, Olivia said her kids were really doing okay. They were still bright, decent children; the relative slacking off was something new; and everybody would probably feel better if she stopped anticipating the worst for them.

Maybe I need to rethink the goals I've set for my child.
Am I doing things for my child that I wished for myself?
Am I laying out a path based entirely on what I believe is best for the child, and not taking into consideration what he or she wants?

For Olivia, a turning point in her reframing came when she started hearing her own complaints. "I've been frustrated and angry because I see my kids as ungrateful. They have successful professional parents. Their father and I have overcome the prejudices and barriers that often still stand in the way of African American families in our culture. It's important that people understand who we are, not like the poor black dysfunctional families so often portrayed in the media." But she added, "I've been thinking they don't appreciate what their father and I have done for them, instead of thinking about what it is we are doing, and whether it's making them happy and feeling good about themselves." Their actions seemed to be giving her a message: we need to back off, take some time out, maybe do less.

Children who may be feeling overburdened by parent-oriented rather than child-oriented goals get that message across in various ways. They may seem sleepy, bored, resistant, going through the motions rather than actually enjoying all the activities Mom and Dad have arranged for them.

To make good choices, it helps to remember that one of the ways children learn, and grow into their unique selves, is by being left to their own devices sometimes: to play, test and explore, and participate with other kids in activities that haven't been structured by adults and around adult agendas.

Movement Strategies

We asked Olivia to describe a typical day or week of family life, and what emerged was a picture of a household running along like a well-oiled machine. There were detailed schedules to follow; Tyrone and Jade were expected to give their parents a daily accounting of homework assignments, how they had done on tests, what the coach or instructor had said about the swimming workout or the piano lesson. There was no lack of love and affection; what seemed to be missing was any time to relax and just be together. Olivia decided to adopt for herself two strategies that might feel relatively new for everybody.

I need to listen better.

For many parents, the drive to produce the ideal child interferes with really hearing what's on a child's mind or in her heart. It takes practice to learn to listen better. Consider these questions: Can I try harder to put myself in my children's place, to "be them" briefly as I listen? Can I seek to understand, not to control? To understand what they're communicating, do I need to clarify and inquire gently, at once or later?

Listening better can mean not bombarding a child with a barrage of questions every time she comes home. It can mean not focusing with laser intensity on how well she is or isn't mastering a sport or performing in school. It can mean just allowing her time to tell the story she feels like telling, which might be about something funny that happened in school or an argument with a friend. Olivia gave her children "a little breathing room," she said, and avoided grilling them for the usual progress reports and leaning on them to practice and study. And a couple of days after putting this strategy into practice, her daughter said something about a clique of girls in school who were excluding her. Mother and daughter had a little talk about how Jade might handle the situation; Jade seemed calmer after that.

Toward the end of her first week of listening better, Olivia said to her children, "You know, I think Dad and I have been doing too much nagging and prodding and pushing. I'm sorry about that. We're going to listen a little better to what you kids want to do, and we'll make some decisions together." This was a brave admission and probably of value to her kids. There's something to be said for realizing that in your parenting mistakes, you give your child a small gift. That's what helps build a child's strength and resiliency and preparation for the world.

I need to enjoy more.

Focused as we are on doing right for and by our children, sometimes we forget simply to enjoy them and have fun with them. A little more fun is usually good for everybody.

Make a list of past, current, and potential future enjoyable activities. Post the list on your refrigerator or bathroom mirror, as a reminder to include at least one of those pleasurable interludes each week. Ask your child or teen what are her favorite top five activities. See if you can stand to learn more about one of them to share with her—if she wants you to. (If she doesn't, forget it immediately.)

Olivia had prided herself on not letting her work life cut into her home life, and she'd been careful over the years never to schedule evening or weekend meetings with clients, because that was her family's time. Now she was determined to allow some of that time to be less programmed, more relaxed, and not so focused on getting things done. "Nothing too big. Now sometimes we take a walk after dinner and buy some ice cream. I'll watch a TV show with the children. I'm trying to have a little more kicking back and hanging out time with them."

The payoff, she said, was something of a surprise: "I'm enjoying them more. I'm enjoying being a parent more."

"Bringing up kids is the most important thing I'm doing with my life," said one client, echoing the feelings of so many mothers we meet. Happily, despite the challenges of twenty-first-century parenting, many also believe, as did the woman we mentioned at the start of this chapter that they're doing a decent job of it. Remembering the perspectives and strategies outlined here—maintaining appropriate parent/child boundaries, for example, and being sensitive to what children need during a time of adult difficulties—will reenforce the sense of what it takes to be a good enough mother. There's also this: Engaging in enjoyable activities for and by yourself and taking care of yourself helps you to be a good parent, because it makes you healthier, happier, and more available to your child.

Perhaps the most important gift you can give your child is the encouragement to talk to you about whatever is bothering him or her, even if what's most troubling at the moment is the relationship you share.

7

The Work Expectation: "I'm Happy with My Career (or Happy without One)"

Women make up about half the workforce in the United States. We have critical mass. Jobs and careers once closed to us are there for the taking. Women are matching men in numbers entering law school and business school. What's more, according to the modern-woman expectation, we *like* working. Its rewards—money, independence, and recognition—provide us with a degree of freedom and a sense of self that's worth the hard effort. Even women who work without pay, volunteering to help support a favorite cause or charity, find pleasure in what they are doing.

On the other hand, if a woman with young children elects not to work outside the home because she wants to be with her kids, that's fine too. She is respected and supported. Fifty years ago a mother who valued her career role as much as her parent role was frowned upon. Twenty-five years ago a mother who *didn't* pursue a career was letting down the side. Today we've evolved to a higher stage of enlightenment, which includes mutual acceptance. Personal, informed choice is what matters.

When it comes to women and work, in other words, we've supposedly made a lot of progress (we've come a long way, baby). Conversations with our clients—both younger and older women—tell a different story: Both the working mother and the stay-at-home mother often experience a deep and disturbing lack of surety and contentment about their choices, and disapproval from others as well. Women who are not raising children, and thus are relieved of many of the work-time/family-time struggles, are as often disappointed in as delighted by their job realities. Women in corporate positions discover what Gail Evans, a corporate executive and author of *Play Like a Man, Win Like a Woman,* calls the still-unlevel playing field. "Business is a game created by men," said Evans, "and nobody handed women the rule book."

Some facts and figures: Apparently most people, men and women both, don't love their jobs. According to a *Wall Street Journal* poll, only 14 percent of individuals say they work for personal satisfaction. According to another poll, this one conducted by Youth Intelligence, a research firm in New York, two-thirds of young single and married women (ages eighteen to thirty-four) would prefer *not to work outside the home at all* if they didn't have to. That preference may reflect a number of realities: To a post-feminist-era woman who views employment not as a hard-won gain but as a birthright, it matters that many jobs aren't all that interesting or rewarding. Establishing a home and having a child and working turns out to be more of a burden than imagined, and a pressuring expectation. (Said one thirty-two-year-old client: "Screw you and your whole generation. You said we can do it all, and now we *have* to!")

And, it's still a gender-biased work world we live in. Unfortunately, to pursue a career seriously a woman cannot opt for the "mommy track." Women seen as serious about their careers put in ten-, twelve-, fourteen-hour or longer days, travel when the men do, and still must run their households. The bottom line is that career women have to give up their leisure time while trying to get it all.

Whatever an individual woman's reasons may be, the possibility that two out of three would opt *not* to work if they didn't need the money casts doubt on one of our cherished notions about the modern world of women and work.

In this chapter, we consider some lines of self-talk that might help a woman reach a happier accommodation with her choices. We'll concentrate on these issues:

- Women, children, and careers
- Job discontent
- Women as second-class citizens in the workplace

Lynne's Story

*"Whether you're a working mom or a stay-at-home mom,
you can't win."*

Even friends, said Lynne, thirty-five, the mother of two young boys, made casual remarks about her careerless life that caused her to feel both annoyed and guilty. "They'll say something like, 'Boy, I really admire you, I couldn't be around little kids all day without going insane.'" Although she had elected not to work outside the home and felt fortunate that she was able to make that choice, Lynne was often on the defensive. "I heard myself telling someone the other evening that I'm not working right now because my husband is often out of town on business for a week or two at a time, and somebody has to be on call for the kids." But she wondered why she felt the need to explain herself at all. An account executive in an ad agency "in my former life," she said, Lynne planned to get back to a job, "but probably not for a few years."

At the same time, Lynne's sister, Ann, with whom she's close, remembered being made to feel uncomfortable about *her* decision to put her own child in full-time daycare when he was six months old and return to her job with a nonprofit organization. Once her son, Julian, was in elementary school, life became less stressful for Ann. "I only need babysitting for part of the day, so the money issue is not so acute, for one thing. But working full-time, I'm left out of things going on with my kid." She felt distant from some of the other mothers in her child's school. "We have points of connection, obviously—the birthday parties and so on. But I take Julian to school in the morning, drop him off and then literally run out of there to get to work. I'm never around when school lets out. I feel out of the loop, not being able to hang around and talk to the other mothers. Occasionally, they seem to be in on something I don't know, like about the different teachers, who's good and not so good."

Ann and Lynne agreed: "If you have young children, you can't win. You're damned if you do and damned if you don't, as far as careers go." Each sister had made a conscious decision to do what she was doing. Neither was entirely happy with it. Both said they actively continued to question themselves, and they wished they could feel more certain, settled, and content.

Mostly, each woman had talked about two contrasting choices, and the emotions they aroused: being at home with the kids and being in the world at work. But those, in turn, encompass a range of other goals and needs that make up a complex picture. They may include intellectual nourishment, admiration, feeling in sync with one's contemporaries, being the best mother, or not relying economically on a husband or a partner. All reflect different parts of the self.

An announcement advertising an upcoming talk by two recently published authors read: "Can Women Have It All? Two experts reveal whether women can climb the corporate ladder and still rock the cradle." We women, it seems, are still brooding and debating about career versus kids, work versus family. "Having it all" is still a buzzword, all these years later. The challenge for Lynne and Ann and any woman who has a career life (or has put one on hold) and a mothering life is to weigh the parts of the self, and maybe do it again and again as circumstances and feelings shift.

Voice Mapping

"Of course you should stay home after the children come."

Because nobody but a mother can raise her kids right, this voice from the culture (and sometimes closer to home) tells us. We hear it from many corners. Child-care experts (some of them) warn us that mother-child bonding during the first minutes and weeks and months of a child's life determines all that comes later—and if you're not there, how can you bond? More child-care experts tell us that the first three years are make-or-break time in terms of a child's emotional, psychological, and intellectual development—so you'd better be around. Sometimes the voice comes from men who still, in their hearts of hearts, think the wife's job is to be home taking care of the kids. (On the other hand, we hear from clients about the husband who gripes about his wife's lack of earning. For some, it seems, we may have gone from "no wife of mine is going to work" to "get a job and bring in some money.")

"Of course you should keep on working after the children come."

Because that's what a thoroughly modern, ambitious, and extremely well-educated woman does these days. Some women who have dropped out of the workforce to be home with their children tell us they feel on the defensive, self-conscious, or like slackers. Many of them—this was true of Lynne—are in their late twenties or thirties and grew up with their own working mothers, the women who were proud of their combined roles and "proved" that it's possible to have a successful career and be a successful mother. It's a very modern iteration, that a woman can achieve as much as a man—produce children and work a job—and that therefore she should *want* to; her priorities should be his.

There can also be subtle pressure brought to bear once a woman's children are no longer very young. It seems to be socially acceptable for her to be home with toddlers and preschoolers. Once those kids are well launched into the school years, Mom may be frowned on for not finding a "real job" for herself (despite widely publicized studies showing the benefits to teenagers of having a parent at home after school).

Either message—quit your job to stay home with the kids, keep your job even with the kids—muffles a woman's ability to hear her own voice and perhaps make better peace with her choices, and with other women as well. The bottom line, of course, is that these issues are never absolutely resolvable. There are always tradeoffs; there may always be conflicted feelings. But because our society places so much value on what we're *paid* to do—the male standard of success—caregiving can feel like the lesser choice. This was how Lynne started reframing.

Reframing

How and why did I make the choice to keep working, or to stay home? Was it a choice at all?

Obviously, if keeping a job was a clear financial necessity, a woman may feel resentful, annoyed, or unhappy about it, but she's unlikely to blame herself for not being home. The greater the element of choice, however, the more useful it is to focus on the reasons for her decision.

Lynne said, "We could afford for me not to work. I liked my job, I liked the whole field, and I left it with some reluctance. I do have worries about losing seniority, or if I can ever get back to where I was.

But I really felt it was important to be with my son when he was still a baby, and then the second one came along a year and a half later. Staying home was my decision, and my husband supported me in it. That remark I made, that I'm not working because he's out of town so much, that really isn't it. I wanted to be there."

Sometimes, even aside from economic considerations, the choice can feel out of a woman's hands, as if it's fated to be. A number of women have told us about enjoying their jobs, working up their career ladders, making the decision to have a child, arranging for the nanny, planning to pop back to work—and then coming face to face, stunningly, with their previously unanticipated need to be with their infants. Said one, "Before my child was born, I had it all figured out. I arranged for a six-week maternity leave. More than enough time, I thought. In fact, I scheduled a business meeting at my office for the Monday morning of the seventh week!" Then her daughter was born, "and it all went out the window." She extended her leave, then she quit her job.

What did I give up?

It may be easier for the working mother to name what she is missing or has given up, because it revolves around time with her child—less of it, and perhaps the kinds of opportunities that Lynne's sister Ann mentioned, to "hang around" with other parents and feel more "in the loop" in some ways. But despite the strains of working and parenting, and the sometimes awful feeling of being pulled in opposite directions, she does maintain aspects of the self in both worlds.

The stay-at-home mother may be certain of the wisdom of her choice; she may derive enormous satisfaction and self-esteem from her parenting role. And still there is a longing for what she's missing.

Typically, a woman fears losing her professional identity. ("I felt pleased with myself being an ad exec, just being able to call myself that," Lynne said. "Now I can't say that anymore.") She may worry about skills growing rusty, or the real concern of not being able to land a new job when she elects to return. Those fears may subconciously prompt her to defend her choice of being a stay-at-home mother. But jobs give us many other payoffs as well, some of them highly personal, even idiosyncratic.

If you're in the position of having dropped out of the work world and you're missing it, write down the parts you most valued or enjoyed back then. For example, I liked:

- Earning my own money and spending some of it however I wanted
- Doing good in the world, having the sense of making a wider difference
- Getting a commendation every now and then for a job well done
- I'm competitive, so I liked the challenge of being up against coworkers
- Intellectual stimulation, learning new things
- The rhythm to the week, Monday to Friday and then the delicious weekend
- The sense of getting ahead, a feeling of progression—the raise every year, the promotion
- The image of being the opposite of the woman at home who never gets out of sneakers
- The idea of being "successful"

One woman missed her morning job routine, which involved getting to her office early and having a coffee and a cinnamon bagel before everybody else arrived.

What do I dislike—or what's surprised me—about my choice?

Ann Richards, former governor of Texas, addressed a group of high school senior girls: "When I was your age, my God—the only thing I could think of was gettin' married, havin' a family, havin' a little house with a dog and a cat. It worked that way. But it's not what I thought it was gonna be. And I want you to know, I love children— I've got four of 'em, and seven grandchildren now. But I also have a life other than raising children. Those babies are cute as they can be, but they are booooooooring. You know, it just consists of spoonin' the applesauce in the mouth. Spoonin' the cereal in the mouth. Cha-ange the diaper. Pa-at the back. Pray that it will sleep for a little while."

It's tough to say out loud, that it's not always great fun being around little kids all day! It can be terribly difficult to acknowledge ambivalent feelings about child-raising. Said one client: "The best time of being a mother for me was after my daughter got to be about twenty-two or twenty-three. And not just because she's no longer costing us thousands of bucks a year. We meet for a glass of wine after work. We shop. We have a lot of laughs. Being adults together is just so satisfying." Said another client: "I only started to really enjoy being with my children once they were talking, and we could discuss things and I could answer their questions."

Does any of this have to do with not loving them? Of course not. Given that you adore your child and would cut off an arm for him or her, name what else may be going on in your thoughts and feelings. Is being home with your kids sometimes lonely? Tedious? Unrewarding? Frustrating?

Lynne described two dislikes or surprises. For one thing, her mother wasn't as available as Lynne had expected her to be. Her mom was a fifty-eight-year-old woman in the thick of her own working career, and in only limited ways able or willing to play helpful grandma. Lynne admitted she felt slightly abandoned by this woman who had encouraged her along her career path and mothering path, and then couldn't be there to help her.

Her second complaint: "I took the boys to a new playground recently, and it was like walking into homeroom on the first day when you're just starting in a new middle school and you don't know anybody. Not for my kids, for me. Nobody talks to you. There's a clique. Then your child shoves another child, and some mother or nanny comes over to you and complains. The mothers do it fake-sweetly, the nannies get a little hostile. Then, although you've been teaching your kid about how it's nice to share and take turns, you see him getting his pail taken away or nobody's giving him a chance on the tire swing, and you suddenly want him to get in there and be assertive, show what he's made of." Going to client meetings back in her old job, she said, was easier.

How do I feel about the women who made a different choice from mine?

Social comparison—marking where she is vis-à-vis the mothers she sees around her—can make a woman feel vulnerable, discontent, or insecure. Give this some thought:

- If you're a working mom, what do you think about the stay-at-home moms?

- If you're at home, how do you view the mother who's out at a job everyday?
- Do you feel critical of another woman's choices? Somewhat superior?

If you view your counterparts negatively, are you projecting onto other people, perhaps thinking another parent is judging you when she isn't?

As she reframed her thoughts, Lynne recognized that she was sometimes admired in small ways by her career-women associates: "One former coworker of mine, who's a pal, tells me I've got really great, sweet kids, and I must be doing a good job." There was something to the "damned if you do, damned if you don't" argument, she still thought, but maybe she was hypersensitive and even assumed some innocent remarks were intended as digs.

But negative feelings about the counterpart woman may be based in something a lot more concrete. One client, a stay-at-home mother, resented the fact that her working-mother neighbor frequently asked her to do an emergency pickup at their children's school or take a playdate on an afternoon when the school announced only half-day classes because of teacher conferences. Office surveys have shown that both parent and nonparent employees harbor suspicions of unfair treatment. Childless women feel they're called on to pick up the slack when their coworkers with young children come in late because of a sick child at home or head out on the dot at five o'clock to attend a school event. Parents are perceived to get a break in scheduling vacations or work responsibilities. On the other side of the fence, parents think their nonparent coworkers have the edge in terms of pay, promotions, and plum assignments. We have more progress to make, it seems, it terms of mutual understanding and responsiveness.

Would I make another choice knowing what I know now?
The answer may not be a clear-cut yes or no. For example, Lynne didn't think she'd made a mistake in her stay-at-home decision. What she did regret was not getting further along her career path. "I had a particular job in mind and a particular time line for getting there. So I do feel sad that I didn't make it." She went on, "At some

deep level, I'm sorry we had kids when we did," she said, and this was a difficult admission. She felt guilty sometimes thinking about the career successes she might have enjoyed if she'd waited longer before having children. And maybe she was a little envious of her sister Ann's path.

If your answer is not so clear, that's normal. You'd hardly be human without some second thoughts.

Movement Strategies

I can learn to find elsewhere some of what I've been missing.

Which part of the self is being neglected at the moment? If your mothering role is taking precedence for now, look over that list of "what I'm missing" or "what I gave up," pick your top-rated two or three items, and think about how to reintroduce them into your life from another angle. That might mean determining to spend more time in adult company by joining a reading group. Or getting back some of the sorely missed kick-back Friday afternoon feeling by hiring a college student for a few hours of babysitting.

One at-home mother deeply regretted not earning her own money, for the first time in her life. She said that feeling made no sense, because her husband was successful, generous, and unquestioning about the family's expenses. But there it was anyway, the need to be paid for work she accomplished; it was an important piece of her self-definition, an identity stemming from her adolescence and her earliest years of working. She started a "mini-mini-mail-order business" out of her basement, and found great satisfaction in the effort.

I need to get more outcome in my days, to balance the process.

Child-raising is all about *process*; never does a woman reach the point at which it's possible to say, "There, that's done." Working at a job, on the other hand, involves at least a much better chance of a woman's efforts being about *outcome*—having a task, doing it, finishing it. On the job, too, she can recognize when a thing has been accomplished properly. As a mother, she's always wondering whether she's good or good enough, whether she's getting things right.

In another chapter, we note the observation of a personal trainer who had as clients many young mothers, "tiny little things" pursuing intense fitness regimens. For some of them, said the trainer, "working out is like a career." Perhaps the push for the buff body is about competition (I'm fitter than all those other mothers), or about control, which may be an antidote to the reality that there's a lot a woman *can't* control in raising children. It may also be about outcome, having a measureable achievement in one's life (the lean body, the size 4 jeans).

Whether or not aiming for the size 4 is for you (and maybe it shouldn't be), it's good to recognize the huge distinction between process and outcome, and try to incorporate more of the latter in your days—through a hobby, a personal passion, an activity that leads to a clear-cut result.

Make a point of getting to know my counterpart (working mom, stay-at-home mom).

Lynne felt that aside from her sister Ann, her social life was largely confined to other mothers like herself, and sometimes it seemed like a kind of self-induced isolation. She decided to befriend a couple of the working mothers she knew slightly from her kids' groups, and extended herself to set up coffee dates. Talking with them, she discovered they all had more in common than she might have expected, especially that each in her own way was trying hard to be a good mother.

It's still the case that women who work and women who are home with children are—or *feel* they are—somewhat pitted against one another, and that one may be valued more than the other. And what we need, as a society and as individuals, is respect for both choices.

I must adopt a realistic long-term perspective.

According to figures from the U.S. Census Bureau, increasing numbers of mothers are opting to quit work in order to stay home with their young children. For the first time in twenty-five years, labor force participation among new mothers has dropped to 55 percent. It is likely, however, that the majority of those women will reenter the work world in the future. In a survey of stay-at-home moms, Mothers and More, which describes itself as "a nonprofit organization that cares for the caregiver," found that about three out of four mothers intended to return to the workforce eventually. These numbers reflect the fact that women's career trajectories often differ from men's. The author Arlene Rossen Cardozo used the term *sequencing*, in her book of the same title, to describe the three-stage path taken by many mothers—from full-time career woman, to full-time mothering, to reentry into paid or volunteer work, in ways that are satisfying for the needs of both herself and her family.

This is all to the good, but not necessarily as smooth sailing as it may sound. Any woman who envisions returning to the work world after a child-raising hiatus needs to consider:

- Is part-time work a realistic option? Where is it to be found?
- Am I willing to accept a part-time position for which I'm overqualified and may be underpaid?
- Will it be impossible for me—because I've lost seniority, a helpful network of mentors, or a client base—to return to an equivalent position?
- Is moving down the ladder to a lesser position in my former field something I can consider without feeling like a failure?

Helen's Story

"Why don't I enjoy my job more?"

Helen, forty-two, was a speech therapist who had come to hate going to work every day. She was seeking help for depression, which she traced to her feelings about her job: "I think I'm good at it. It's just become harder emotionally, and not satisfying anymore." She wondered if she'd get out of her rut by switching careers, but didn't see a way to do so, and that was deepening her gloomy mood and feelings of being in a life that was on hold.

We asked her what exactly was happening on a daily basis that made the job so unpleasant. The clients were okay, she said. But she'd had difficulties with two office mates; she and the coworkers had recently argued about Helen's involvement with a young woman, Jenna, who was the secretary and receptionist in the learning center where they had their offices. "Jenna graduated from college a couple of years ago," Helen said. "This job is just for paying the rent. She wants to be a writer, and she's finished a screenplay that she's trying to get read by some agent. I feel so sorry for her. She comes from a really dysfunctional family, she doesn't talk to her mother at all, she's always hard up for money. A few months ago, she got mixed up with a dreadful boyfriend."

It seemed that Jenna was emotionally, visibly needy much of the time. Some mornings she arrived late and weepy. Some afternoons she made hour-long, agitated phone calls. When Helen was in between her client appointments, Jenna usually piled into her office to talk and unload. "She's just a confused kid, but really very sweet and very bright," Helen said. "I've been trying to give her advice about this guy she's with and about careers." On two occasions, Jenna had spent the weekend with Helen and her family, when the young woman was avoiding her bad-news boyfriend.

The coworkers wanted to let Jenna go. They found her a distracting presence and not very good at her job—she let work accumulate, she didn't pass along phone messages promptly, and she'd already been advised, nicely, that she needed to improve her performance. Helen was opposed: "I just think it would be devastating to Jenna. It would feel like her second family was abandoning her."

The office friction was part of what caused Helen to start rethinking her career. "I got a degree and training in this field, but it was something I sort of backed into, mainly because I couldn't come up with anything better," she said. "I wanted to have a profession. That was important to me. But I expected it to be a lot more rewarding than it's turned out. I probably should have done something else."

She needed to think through matters on two fronts—the meaning of work and the meaning of family.

Voice Mapping

"I should have a career (and love it)."

A woman around Helen's age is often an individual with her foot, mentally and emotionally, in two worlds. In her mother's day, a woman wasn't encouraged to pursue a work life or educated for one, except possibly with the message "Get a teaching degree in case, God forbid, you have to support yourself." On the other hand, Helen charged into a profession, married, had a child, kept working, and discovered the career wasn't especially satisfying. She thought she *should* be getting more out of it in terms of personal meaning; since she wasn't, she'd decided maybe she was just in the wrong line of work.

"I should take care of people."
Many women do impose the traditional view of home and relationships on the workplace (these people are my family). Many women also lack the often useful male talent for compartmentalizing: work interactions and connections go in one mental box, emotions go in another.

With Helen, the special circumstances of a rather unusual childhood almost certainly had something to do with her excessive involvement with the "mixed-up" office assistant. From the time she was about eight or nine, Helen was often a surrogate mother to her younger brothers as their parents went through a drawn-out divorce and their mother was emotionally unavailable. Helen felt that her mother never really got back on her feet, and through her teens Helen believed she needed to be "the acting grown-up in the house, not just for my brothers but for my mom too."

Reframing

Maybe I'm expecting to have feelings about my job that are just not there.
To sort out what job unhappiness or boredom is really all about, here's a place to start. The idea that working gives such personal satisfaction is something of a myth. In reality, for many women having a career is simply never going to be terribly fulfilling. Helen began to think her expectations about what the job should mean to her—or give to her—were too high.

If I started from the beginning, what would I do differently?
Another way to come at this "what if?" line of reframing is to ask, "If I won the lottery, and money was no longer and would never again be a worry, what would I do?" The answer may go a long way

toward clarifying whether it's working in general or a job in particular that's at the root of discontent—and whether a career change might solve things or not. For example, Helen came away from her "what if?" mental exercise thinking she'd still "back into" a career, because she didn't feel particularly drawn to any other line of work. Her passions and interests, her real satisfactions and her sense of self lay elsewhere—as a homemaker, as a serious gardener, and in her many involvements in her church's outreach activities.

Movement Strategies

It's important to remind myself: The people I work with are not my family.

It's business. Coworkers may become friends, even close friends, but life in the workplace really isn't the same as life with the family.

This is a hard lesson to learn for the woman who feels let down by a coworker (she was like my sister!); who assumes a motherly role with a needy associate; who finds it next to impossible to deal with an incompetent or troubled assistant in a way that's both kind and businesslike; or in some other way has allowed the lines between family and work to become blurred. Helen's parenting, caretaking instinct was stirred up by a young woman who wanted, among other things, a shoulder to cry on. But the fallout didn't help Helen in her own position as a professional—or Jenna, for that matter.

Separating work and family instincts may call for specific strategies, depending on what's going on. They may include limiting after-hours contacts, refraining from offering advice on personal matters, or getting past feelings of hurt and betrayal.

Victoria's Story

"The men in my office don't include me."

"Managers go to other people for answers when I'm the one who has them," said Victoria, thirty-eight, an officer in a financial services corporation. She thought somehow she failed to "project a leader image." Or she couldn't figure out the "unwritten rules. I know they exist, but I don't seem to get them. I don't feel any bonds with the guys I work with."

She had expected to move into an upper management level in the corporation by the time she came to talk about being "stalled." It hadn't happened, and now Victoria was wondering if it ever would. A career adviser and a headhunter were helping her figure out her likely or possible next moves, although she didn't particularly wish to leave her present company. As an Asian American woman, she had incorporated many of the cultural values of loyalty to both family and the company that she had learned while growing up.

In short-term therapy, she was hoping to get some insight into what else might be going on that was holding her back. She believed she had "missed out on the competitive gene." In certain situations, such as staff meetings and "think-tank" sessions, she suffered flare-ups of insecurity, which annoyed her.

Mostly, however, Victoria first tended to focus on the unfairness of corporate life. "It's just a lot harder for women to get ahead than for men." As an example, she described the recent promotion of a male colleague whom she perceived as less qualified for the job than she was. "There's a lot of an 'old boys' club' feeling about the place," she said. "Given the same credentials and achievements, a man and a woman still aren't on equal ground. The man is going to get the move up and the woman isn't."

Victoria was a familiar figure—a bright, educated, and hard-working woman with ambition. And her arguments regarding the unlevel playing field surely held water. The "glass ceiling," as the *Wall Street Journal* named the corporate environment that stops women from moving past a certain level, is still up there, rumors to the contrary. Fewer than 12 percent of the top jobs in the largest five hundred firms are held by women. Women still aren't pulling down the huge salaries. While about one in two American workers earning in the $25,000 to $30,000 salary range are women, less than one in ten earning half a million or more are women. Many of our clients—MBAs and all—tell us they feel stuck, victims of double standards that supposedly have crumbled, or at least lessened dramatically. The old boys' club Victoria talked about incorporates the notion of collegiality, too, or shared power among equals, and yet the aggressive, determined woman can be judged as not collegial enough—not one of the boys. This is especially true for nonwhite women. Women who are highly attractive have their own set of problems too, as they may be sought after for their exotic qualities but not respected for their knowledge or intellectual abilities.

But that's only half the story, the external half. Victoria needed to explore the internal part, starting with the messages that got her as far as she was, but then left her "stalled." She was wise to begin to distinguish the *them* (men, corporate life, the glass ceiling) from the *me*. If there was a limit to what could be done about *them*, what about herself might be changed to make her more productive, satisfied, and successful?

Voice Mapping

"You can do or be anything you want to do or be."

This was what Victoria learned from her parents. They told her, "I could be anything I wanted to be. Just what girls should hear!" And yet, while her two brothers were encouraged to hold high aspirations (demanding courses of study, the best colleges, and useful summer internships), she, in subtle ways, was not. For example, when she was thinking of majoring in economics and maybe going on for a graduate degree, her parents—especially her father—were less than enthusiastic: "He thought a career in the business world was too chancy, too many long hours. Between the lines—they didn't say it in so many words—I think they were both worrying I wasn't going to get married and have kids and live a 'safe' life. Or I was going to have to be hard and tough if I was going to get anywhere."

Here's a curious paradox about the "you can do anything you want" voice many women heard from their families and from the wider culture as well. For so many, it turns out to have been both empowering and burdensome. More accurately, the message might be read, or was heard as: "You *can* do anything, but don't aim too high, don't dream too big, and don't act like a man." So while a postfeminist era has provided a woman societal support for moving out in the world and moving ahead, she may charge forth with only a thin veneer of confidence in herself.

Reframing

What is the overall atmosphere of the work system I'm in?
Coming up with a good analysis to that question may begin, as it did for Victoria, with a clear assessment of just how traditionally male the environment is. She had many illustrations that her company was, in fact, traditionally male—coworkers at her level were almost all men, the men often went out for lunches or drinks after work, male camaraderie was evident in many daily exchanges, the men got the best office furniture, and so on.

If that's the story of your office, how uncomfortable does it make you? Reframing your dissatisfaction calls for accepting the environment you're working in, and then deciding if it's for you. Assess how traditionally male the system is, assess your own values, and see if the two can mesh. Ask yourself if there is a serious lack of fit between what you're expecting and the reality. If you are relying on your talents for affiliation and connection with others, and it looks like those talents aren't especially rewarded in a certain company, are you going to feel forever underappreciated, unhappy, or like a misfit? Or can you say, "Okay, those are not the skills that are going to get the job done and I'll have to adopt some additional ones"?

In the environment I'm in, what's my goal and what will it take to reach it?
There may be conflicting goals: "I want to make a lot of money, I like making a lot of money, I want to do anything the guys do, and I know I'm as smart as they are. But I also want to be female in the sense of connectedness, nurturing, and support, and I dislike being in a place where that's not valued and respected." The woman who articulates her goals in that way may experience not constant overt conflict with her work environment, but a sense of ongoing tension, as there so often is between work and home. She may need to decide if she's willing to live with the reality that she's never going to realize both goals.

This is the conclusion Victoria came to: "I want to stay where I am, for a number of reasons. I want to get over feeling resentful, and that probably means learning how to play the game better in some ways." She wanted to figure out how to be strategic.

Exactly when, where, and how do I feel I'm overlooked or ineffective? What situations or requirements make me most uncomfortable or most annoyed? Challenging a coworker? Asking for help? Making myself heard?

Victoria recognized that she felt deeply uncomfortable when she needed to disagree with a coworker's point of view or piece of information. "I think it's that old notion about being a *nice girl*, not seeming to attack other people." She had difficulty being assertive, which is a huge bugaboo for so many women, especially those who come from a culture that still frowns on assertive women. We are still socialized to be *nice*, to say what we deem to be appropriate to the situation and the people present, not necessarily what we think. It is still the case that strong men are perceived as assertive, and strong women are perceived as strident.

Speaking up, asking for more information, and disagreeing with an associate all sound *not nice*, and we feel distress, or anticipate some kind of "punishment," such as another's anger.

Movement Strategies

I can learn some male tricks.

To be strategic and to develop what it takes to get to the goal, it can help to adopt some of what men know and practice, including the following:

- Don't take it personally when someone criticizes your work.
- Don't let liking someone get in the way of disagreeing with that person.
- Don't wait to be asked to give your opinion.

It's time to start taking more small risks.

Many women feel reluctant to go out on a limb and take a risk; they feel satisfied achieving what are called low-cost goals (like just being noticed). To get ahead in a traditionally male environment, it may be necessary to get a little riskier.

Victoria asked herself if she felt she needed to know *everything* before she said *anything*, and answered, "That's me!" In fact, during meetings she often found herself quietly seething over what she

believed to be the ill-thought-out contributions of her male coworkers. "It always amazes me that some guy will just blurt out whatever comes to his mind, and everybody listens and nods. Actually,
it makes me mad at myself, because I know I've got the better idea,
but I feel I should refine it before I bring it up."

She needed to focus not so much on being more competitive or
"projecting a leader image," she thought, as simply on starting to
take small risks, like stating her piece without worrying endlessly
about how it sounded.

Another woman who worked in an environment she found not
especially welcoming described her typical behavior as "loitering
around the edges of things. Like the school kid who always sits in
the back row so she won't get called on, I'll park myself in the most
remote chair when we have a staff meeting." She resolved to move
more front and center, make herself more visible, which for her
meant actually taking a significant risk.

I can change some simple speech patterns.

"When I'm about to question someone," Victoria said, "I always
start off by qualifying what I'm going to say—'Well, that's a good
idea too,' or 'I don't know if I'm on the right track here, but...'" She
thought she probably came across as uncertain. She decided to
change that.

At the same time, here's a rude fact: many men in the workplace
don't listen to women in the workplace. The evidence comes
through loud and clear from much research. If a woman speaks
directly and assertively in a meeting, the men simply stare at her
and say nothing. Within a few minutes, a man may say essentially
the same thing, and everybody responds, What a great idea!

Nevertheless, eliminating unnecessary qualifiers, disclaimers,
and excuses when putting forth her certainly well-considered, possibly excellent observations and suggestions does a woman good.
It's one of the steps that builds real self-confidence.

While women now enjoy previously unequaled job opportunities,
it is still the case—as the experiences in this chapter demonstrate—
that a woman can face unsettling tradeoffs and uneasy accommo-

dations: merging work life and family life, and sometimes making the hard decision to bow out of the first in order to devote herself fully to her mothering role; the difficulty of managing a balance between being tough enough and nurturing in a work environment; the feeling of being unwanted or excluded by male peers as part of the team. Many women also struggle with the disconnect between old messages and new possibilities; they have the green light now, but grew up with the red light that discouraged them from aspiring too high.

Clearly, many of the changes that will create a truly level playing field are beyond the power of the individual to bring about. But by following some of the reframing and movement strategies we have outlined, you may find a greater degree of confidence and satisfaction in the choices you do elect.

8

The Money Expectation:
"I Have My Financial Life Well in Hand"

Here's the popular notion about women and money in this day and age: Any woman can and should earn an income at some time. Any woman who puts her mind to it can maneuver her way, on her own if necessary, through a financially secure life and into an adequate if not lavish retirement. Money is only money, the wherewithal for living decently, and nothing unknowable or to be avoided. Within marriages and committed partnerships, gone are the bad old days when he made the money and the money decisions, while she remained clueless or at least willfully naive. In addition, it's not only within her right and abilities to be financially astute about whatever resources she and her family have, it is her responsibility, a sign of adulthood, and she's meeting it very well.

There's an identifiable, societal basis behind some of that modern notion. Obviously, much has changed in terms of women and money over the past couple of generations. Women today can obtain credit in their own names. We own and operate successful, multi-million-dollar companies. We can buy homes without a cosigner.

Nevertheless, money remains a major source of anxiety in the lives of a surprising number of women. What we hear from our clients are the realities that belie the expectation. In the stories that follow, problems around money surface along several lines:

- Investing it
- Earning it
- Discussing it

147

In each case, self-talk focuses on a woman's ability to deal with money realistically, which means different things to different people. For one, it may be a matter of saying, "This is what I need to do in order to make more and plan better." For another, "I need to talk candidly to my partner about our financial situation."

Interestingly, people rarely come to therapy with the stated intention of tackling money issues. As we begin to talk and explore, however, it is not unusual to find that money is at the heart of what's troubling them, and a factor that is having a destructive effect on other areas of life. A woman's inability to get a reality take on money may express itself in various ways—spending money that isn't there, for example, harboring simmering resentments *about* the money that isn't there, or breaking into a cold sweat at the sight of an investment statement. Money-and-women is still a freighted issue, mixed up with security needs, power needs, gender identification, division of labor, and societal and cultural realities. For example, in some ways it is easier for an African American woman to earn more money than an African American man. All these are potent forces that shape our relationships and our lives.

In addition, money is one of the last great taboos. We don't want to talk about it. Consider this: Do you know anything about your elderly parents' financial situation? Can you speak to your partner about what you consider your partner's impulsive spending or unnecessary miserliness, without sounding enraged or defensive? Research tells us, maybe not so surprisingly, that the issue couples fight about most often is money.

One of our goals in this chapter is to offer questions and suggestions that help eliminate the money taboo. In the process, we look at what may be the psychological obstacles to acting wisely and realistically about this critical resource in your life.

Maggie's Story

"Thinking about money, investments, and all that makes me anxious."

After twenty-two years as a copywriter on a national magazine, Maggie, forty-five, suddenly lost her job. She walked away with a packet of papers giving information about the IRA she had amassed during her years on the staff, and vaguely thought she ought to see what options were available to her regarding this nest egg, her only savings for the future. Not long afterward, she found a new job and was again contentedly employed. Maggie signed a form that rolled over her IRA, and soon fell into her old habit of planning no further than the next paycheck.

She came to therapy, she said, because of generally "antsy, unsettled" feelings; she worried a lot of the time these days, for no clear reason. The job loss had shaken her badly, and heading into middle age she sensed she was not genuinely in control of her life. "I've always worked, starting when I was in high school," she said. "Getting fired was a blow to my self-esteem. I sort of haven't recovered from it."

Gradually, Maggie zeroed in on financial security as possibly the most concrete source of her anxiety, and the one that at least theoretically she ought to be able to do something about. She made an interesting observation. "You can't read a newspaper or a magazine without running into an article about what you should be doing with your money. But I skip over things like 'Ten Steps to a Financially Secure Future.' Or sometimes I'll save the article, telling myself I'll read it tomorrow, and I never do. I find it on my desk a couple of weeks later, and I toss it. It just makes me incredibly nervous for some reason." Now, she started to explore what might account for her head-in-the-sand approach to money.

Voice Mapping

"I'm not capable of being really smart about money."

That's a voice that has so often been internalized by the woman who's resistant to informing herself about money matters, the woman who becomes anxious or depressed thinking about "investments and all that." It's a message she may have picked up in various ways, often in childhood.

When we start talking to a client about money issues, we ask her to tell us a little about her family's financial situation as she was growing up. What did she learn back then? Typically, we'll hear, "Oh, nothing much in particular." Or, "Well, we never had a lot, but we made out okay, we never wanted for the important things."

When we dig a little deeper, however, frequently our client starts discovering some old messages that linger on into adulthood in the form of entrenched lessons.

What Maggie learned was this: Don't get into debt; pay your bills on time; be frugal. "We were comfortably middle class, I'd say, but the family setup was very traditional," she said. "Mom raised us kids, Dad went to work. My mother was super cautious about spending. She made most of our clothes and curtains and things for the house. I picked up the idea early on that you should never owe anybody. One day—I was maybe about ten years old—Dad gave me some envelopes, bills he was paying, to take to the mailbox. He followed me to the door, saying, 'Don't drop those! This is important!' The mailbox was on the corner, half a block away, but you'd think I was being entrusted with a major, perilous mission." He never had a credit card throughout his long life.

Don't run up debt, don't pay your bills late, was a perfectly good message. It was also a limiting and somewhat fearful one, telling Maggie that being smart about money meant only not getting into money troubles. Anything more than that she somehow understood was beyond her.

"Men are in charge of money matters."

Some women learned from the family that men are the ones who see to the money matters. Here's an example. One woman grew up in a home with unhappily married parents, including her self-made businessman father. Her father, possibly as a way of compensating for the lack of love elsewhere in his life, lavished his daughter with all the comforts. She was never required to stick to an allowance as a child, and had all her college expenses covered by a check from her father. Now a young woman off on her own, she was determined to start taking care of herself—but didn't have a clue how to go about it. She bought what she wanted, never comparison shopped, and spent a large chunk of her monthly income paying off the interest on her credit cards. She was—and she knew it—handicapped in a very real sense, influenced by a voice that's not so unusual (from a father, from a husband): "I'll give you money, honey, all you want, but I'm not going to take the time to help you understand it, because that's my job, not yours."

Our older clients tell us they've received invitations to financial planning seminars and the like, hosted by investment services corporations, and they never attend. Thinking about sitting around with a group of men, they say, makes them feel sheepish or intimidated, fearful of asking a "dumb" question. They were never any good in math, they say. The fact is, the typical boy grew up knowing he was expected to play sports and repair things and handle money. The one who didn't take to any of that naturally worked hard at figuring it out as best he could (maybe not all that well), because therein lay the source of his self-esteem: you can't be a man if you don't deal with money. A girl's self-esteem, on the other hand, and what it meant to be a woman, did not require the same.

In fact, "you can't be a man if you don't deal with money" is true in almost every culture. Even in Orthodox Jewish communities where studying is supposed to be the man's primary role, the woman is not meant to have to earn money; others in the community will support the family.

Reframing

How real are my fears about money?
Why did thinking about investments cause something close to panic in this employed, accomplished magazine editor? It's helpful to realize that money really can be the lightning rod for so many of our vulnerabilities as women. We fear losing it or having it taken from us; we think we're too inadequate to manage it. Women who are doing perfectly fine supporting themselves confess to fears that somehow they'll end up as "bag ladies," regardless of their recognizable successes or the size of their bank accounts. We have counseled married women who stay in relationships they might otherwise leave, solely because of financial fears. The sense of being stuck and essentially controlled by outside forces doesn't necessarily end when the marriage does, either. We see divorced mothers who are tremendously anxious about managing alimony and child support, because they perceive it as an unreliable, unpredictable source of income.

Thinking about money can bring these terrors, even the irrational ones, to the surface in an instant. But acknowledging that the fears exist—and recognizing that "bag lady" status is probably not a likelihood for the future—is the beginning of good change. Develop a new mindset: Instead of working for your money, think in terms of making your money work for you.

Many women still have limited knowledge about how to make money *do something* for them. More than a few remain strongly in the sway of those ancient patterns and messages. Taking aggressive and informed charge of their finances means declaring true independence, and perhaps that seems lonely or unseemly. Or they camouflage the reality: "I work, I pay my bills, I've got a 401K, so I'm doing okay." All the while the broader picture of their financial positions never gets evaluated in a clear-eyed and determined manner.

To Maggie, "managing money" meant just not spending it foolishly, which was pretty much her mother's role and attitude in the family's financial life. However, she had never graduated to thinking of her income as not only a means of paying bills, but as a resource she could manipulate to increase her feelings of control. She was proud of the work she did. "I feel competent," she said, "it gives me a sense of power and self-esteem." Figuring out how to *manage* her money could enhance her self-esteem as much as earning it did. It starts with a new way of thinking: It is right, proper, powerful, and might even be exciting to find a job for my money, to put my money to work.

Should I be thinking about earning more?

This wasn't an issue for Maggie, but for many women it might be: If I want to get smarter about money, have I been aggressive enough about making more of it? A recent college graduate said, "Almost all the guys I knew in college majored in economics or business, and now three years later, they're bond traders or whatever, making four times as much as I am. But I think what really matters is doing something that has redeeming social value, something you love." She expressed a common feeling, that emotionally rewarding work is what's most important. Women, more than men, tend to put the monetary rewards behind the emotional, psychological, or spiritual rewards of their chosen work—which is a splendid attitude, except when it allows a woman to convince herself that acquiring financial smarts isn't so important.

If you have decided to make greater financial security a bigger priority in your life, should you be considering a career change? Or are you undervaluing yourself in your present career? Many women cling to a notion of the workplace as meritocracy: do your job, don't make waves, achieve the assigned goals, and the financial rewards will follow. Not necessarily, as anyone who has seen a less diligent, less qualified coworker get the promotion and the perks has come to learn. But believing that doing a good job should be all that's necessary keeps many women from stepping up to the plate and asking to be paid appropriately (and as the men are).

How do I define my goal regarding the money in my life?

What Maggie most wanted, she realized, was to feel mentally freer of the ups and downs of the job market in her field, which were more and more volatile. She wanted to know that another layoff, if it happened, wouldn't be such a blow to her ego and wouldn't stir up all that free-floating anxiety.

If you've been avoiding taking actions that can start making your money work for you, this is a good place to begin. Identify a specific goal, or several:

- Do you want to be able to retire by age 55?
- Do you seek to feel more secure by building up a certain amount of money that you know you don't need for expenses?
- Would you like to enjoy dinners out and attend the theater without worrying about the extra expense?

Movement Strategies

I need to start reading some of those money articles.

Maggie was right about the ubiquitousness of money advice. Some individuals can't resist it; in fact, the columnist Jane Bryant Quinn coined the term "financial porn" to describe the act of people almost addictively reading all the latest money news. While financial information was once confined to the business pages, now it's right in our face. The largest selling daily newspaper in the United States includes, along with "Entertainment" and "Sports," a separate, color-identified section called "Money."

At the same time, open any paper and there's the article about buying stocks, switching to bonds, balancing your portfolio, the benefits of one kind of account over another, or the future of social security. And maybe on the next page you'll see the bank ad showing a competent-looking woman, smiling out and waiting for you to give her a call. She's an investment adviser who specializes in dealing with women. "We have the woman for you!" says the ad copy. The hidden message there might be something like this: Not only do women need unique help with their finances (because unlike men, they don't know anything about money), but that help should come from another woman.

Put it all together, and it can feel overwhelming. The reality we learn from our clients is that many women are aware money information is available; indeed, they can hardly escape it. But they're not reading it, learning from it, and using it.

Starting small, simply familiarizing herself with financial lingo, could help Maggie, or any woman who's somewhat terrified by money matters, gradually feel less threatened—and realize also that the world of investments and savings isn't such an impenetrable mystery.

The key word is "gradually." Take a concrete step or two by reading up on money information, start to get it on your radar screen, accept the emotional discomfort that that will probably entail at the beginning, discover that investing is not inevitably a high-risk and complicated activity, and ease your way in to becoming better informed. Small positive actions feed bigger positive actions: When you compel yourself to become somewhat more current and informed, you feel more confident; because you feel more confident, you are less hesitant about taking greater charge of your financial reality, or at least engaging with its details.

I can find a pleasant and knowledgeable coach to help me get smarter about finances.

Often intimidated about asking for advice, women tend to be hesitant to use readily available aides. But they're out there, and they're all to the good. Maggie at once thought of a woman she knew from her yoga class, a friendly associate who also happened to be an investment counselor. She thought that with this individual, rather than with a formal "financial adviser," she'd find it easier to ask for some ideas.

We have at times suggested to a client that she set up a co-coaching arrangement with someone she trusts and who has money expertise, and with whom she can swap skills and information. Each person then brings something to the table that will benefit the other. One successful coaching partnership developed between a savvy real estate lawyer and a speech therapist. The lawyer coached the speech therapist on breaking through her money resistance issues and guided her in her investments. The speech therapist coached the lawyer in dealing more effectively with the challenges of being the only female partner in her company and supported her in exploring ways to achieve greater balance in her life—a win-win arrangement.

Actually, there's nothing wrong with calling up that "woman for you" in the ad, if indeed you sense you would feel more comfortable talking to and getting help from another woman. Many such professionals, particularly those trained recently, are supportive of those who are unfamiliar with the lingo of money management. Women-only investment clubs and groups also aren't that difficult to hunt up, and may provide an encouraging or inviting atmosphere. If you decide to seek out a financially knowledgeable coach, try to find one who speaks your native language or understands your particular cultural background.

Megan's Story

"My husband makes about one-third as much as I do.
We're pretending this isn't a problem, but it is."

Megan, thirty-five, was married, with two children. A lawyer, the primary breadwinner in the family, she came into treatment because she was exhausted and angry. She resented the pressure of working all the time, and after the second child was born things had turned harder. "I have a feeling the difference between having one and two kids could be the difference between one and five." Her husband, Hank, took care of many of the child-raising duties. But she still had little of her own time; "more Megan comfort," was what she thought she needed, but it wasn't happening.

Megan ran down a list of the things she did in the family, and it was a very long list. In the too-familiar working mother's story, even when it came to the activities that Hank "took care of," she was the one who arranged them: Hank had a flexible schedule, he was home during many of the daytime hours, and so he got the kids to the pediatrician, but she made the appointments, reminded him, and did the follow-up. He might drop off seven-year-old Madison for her playdate with her friend Kayla, but Megan made the phone calls to Kayla's mom to set up the afternoon, arrange for pickup, and plan for a reciprocal date.

As we talked, it also became clear that Megan was aware of a cloud of bitterness hovering in the atmosphere over the fact that she out-earned her husband. During a recent argument—having nothing to do with finances, actually—Hank suddenly said, "Well, of course you make more money than I do, as you are perpetually reminding me." She was both infuriated and hurt. "I've never accused him of not earning enough, or held it over him that I brought in more."

The tension between husband and wife pointed to underlying power issues, for one thing. If Megan resented the pressures she felt herself under, her husband resented the power apparently associated with his wife's income. And then, what was preventing this smart woman from claiming for herself more "Megan comfort"?

Voice Mapping

"Outearning my husband makes him seem not so manly and me feel not so feminine."

"Before we were married," Megan said, "we talked about this. This did not sneak up on us out of the blue. We knew it was likely I'd always earn the most, but I would be doing what I wanted to do and he would be doing what he wanted to do, which was to compose music and teach classes in a music school or take in students for private lessons." Over the years, however, and especially recently, she thought she was starting to look at him as not aggressive or competitive.

Where did that voice come from? Partly, Megan thought, from her family, especially her parents. "There was a lot of silent but real opposition to us as a couple. Hank and I were together for five years before we finally did get married, and during all that time, it was obvious to both of us that my mom and dad thought Hank wasn't quite good enough for me. They liked him and knew he was a fine person, but I was the one with the law degree. My father in particular was bothered. He still asks me every so often, privately, how Hank is doing, what his 'long-range goals' are." That's a voice that pervades the culture. Some of Megan's friends, for example, made off-hand, probably good-natured remarks about the couple and their arrangement. ("Megan brings home the bacon, and Hank cooks it.")

Our societal expectation and the implicit contract between many couples remains, as ever: Being a man means supporting your family; he *should* earn more than she earns. Even when a woman is making a sizable income herself and finances aren't strained, she might struggle with thoughts or angry accusations that he's not doing "his job" or not "working hard enough." While a woman might have no problem with equality in earnings (and studies show that women feel happier or less depressed the *closer* their earnings are to their husbands'), it feels uncomfortable being one-up on her man. This is where Megan found herself. "I guess I do see him now as not very manly."

"Mothers are supposed to arrange the playdates."
The picture Megan described of her home scene was virtually identical to the stories we hear from countless mothers who report that working a job outside the home doesn't mean they're in any real way relieved from working as much as ever inside the home.

In the more common scenario, however—working dad brings in the major paycheck and thus accepts primary responsibility for the financial well-being of the family—the quid pro quo might go a long way toward alleviating a woman's feelings of being put-upon:

"Okay, you're the main hunter/gatherer so I'll be the main nurturer/caretaker." When she's the leading player in both roles, the resentment grows. This lawyer/wife/mother was supplying the bulk of the income and getting the least of the time and the personal benefits (which of course also had a lot to do with the old voice that says Mom is supposed to arrange playdates and Dad is not supposed to).

"Money buys things for other people, not for me."

Megan had no particular "spending issues"; she described herself as having "no hangups about money per se." But she didn't buy personal things, other than the decent wardrobe she needed for work. Aside from very occasional lunches with a couple of girlfriends, she didn't treat herself to much of anything, although she had ideas about what she'd enjoy. "I've always wanted to take tennis lessons. I'd like to go away by myself for a weekend to a spa and just relax and get pampered." Megan had never done any of that, however. She had one or two big-ticket items in mind, too, including possibly starting graduate study in art history, one of her old passions. Like huge numbers of married women—well-off and not so well-off, all ensconced in the crowded life of husbands and kids and homes—she put herself last on the list to reap some personal pleasures.

Here's the voice a man in our culture often hears: "Money gives me the right to do what I want when I'm not working." The successful man feels a powerful sense of entitlement to his leisure and his toys—play golf on Saturday, buy the wall-sized projection TV. Here's the voice a woman in our culture often hears: "Money buys things for other people, not for me."

Reframing

Develop a new mindset: I'm entitled to spend money on myself.

The core difference between male and female attitudes about discretionary spending goes deep in the bone. We observe it in our clients. Although men might seek out psychotherapy later and more reluctantly, for example, they rarely argue or worry about fees. But even when they are equally comfortable financially, our women clients are fretful about spending their money on therapy and anxious about insurance coverage. It's a reflection of that notion that it's not okay to spend for yourself, on things that matter to you. Even an understanding of financial partnership between husband and wife often doesn't translate into real equality. Men, generally, feel more empowered to spend; women, generally, are still more likely to seek agreement, or even to ask for permission.

So reframing for Megan meant, for one thing, making the connection that so many women find difficult or uncomfortable: Having money or earning money buys *me* something; I'm entitled to use some of our money for my own comfort.

Would I be happy, right now, with less income but more time?

Not every working mother has this option, of course, but Megan considered for the first time whether to rethink her job track, and move into an area that would enable her to cut back on her hours at work. She decided that was a choice she didn't want to make at the moment. But here is a question we pose to many of our clients: Look ahead three, five, six years, and what do you see? How will things be different?

The point is that if you are highly stressed over your time-and-money equation, one way to reframe the current problem is by focusing less on what can be changed tomorrow or next month, and more on the developmental flow of life circumstances. It's enormously encouraging, and goes a long way toward feeling less "stuck," to be able to say: "Okay, xyz is not going to be a priority for me right now, but later it can be and I intend to see that it is a priority when the time comes."

Do I want to push my partner to earn more?

There can be a vast gap between a couple's articulated, intellectual embrace of gender-neutral roles in terms of jobs and incomes, and the reality of how that man and woman actually behave and actually feel. Lip service (although it's often something nobler than that, a genuine conviction that it really shouldn't matter whom the money comes from) isn't nearly as convincing as deeply embedded, culturally encouraged messages, such as that being a man means hustling to make a buck. (These days, we hear the other side of the story too: the husband who thinks it's about time his wife got out there and found a job.)

This was one Megan struggled with; she knew that she was seeing Hank as not very "manly." But she also admired his talent and his passion for his music; they weren't hurting for money; she decided not to confront him about his income, and try to forge some other changes—muting some of the outside disparaging voices, arranging more time for herself, dreaming up some long-range plans that might satisfy her passions. For another woman, expressing her need for him to earn more might turn out to be the *right* thing to do— because resentments in the form of verbal sniper attacks, sarcastic comments, or cooly polite silences are poisoning the relationship.

Saying in so many words "I want you to contribute more here" can be hard, maybe impossible. It's a highly personal decision that inevitably goes right to the heart of the relationship and that can be reached only after a woman thinks her way through all the variables in the picture: Is he truly capable of providing more or is he doing the best he can? Is there enough good in the relationship that I can live with my disappointment in this one area?

Movement Strategies

I need to stop accusing my partner of failure, or sounding like I am.

Megan did not want the simmering hostilities between herself and Hank to reach the boiling point. This was a priority for her, the emotional starting point to getting unstuck. Taking off from there, with some difficulty she was able to put her finger on small ways she might be stirring up the pot, accusing her husband of failure even if she didn't say it in so many words. She made remarks to Hank ("It's nice Madison can go to camp this summer, isn't it?) that might have an accusatory subtext ("Isn't it good I make all this money so Madison can go to camp this summer?"). She found it irritating that she might need to be more conscious of Hank's feelings in this tiny way, but it was an irritation she thought she could stand for the greater good.

Getting rid of accusations and "holding it over him" obviously makes life a lot more pleasant. Just as important, it also means that any legitimate argument for a new way of doing things is more likely to be heard and heeded.

I can spend more on my own needs and wishes.

The working woman with children probably needs to do something about her "mothers are supposed to arrange the playdates" voice (more about that in a later chapter). Here, we're talking about money, and the wisdom of acquiring the mindset that says "money buys *me* something, too, it's okay to put *my* needs or wishes further up on the list." From there, she is able to start considering what it is she wants, and how she can get it. Megan thought she would sign up for a tennis lesson every other week, and she'd look up some information about a nearby spa. That was a start.

She also might consider paying for more outside help. The women we talk to often have a tough time asking others to do things for them—that is, paying for services they can perform themselves, like laundry or marketing. The last items typically included in most family budgets are household support, meals cooked by others, home office help, and so on. If money *is* an object and there's not much to go around, spending more for you can mean taking a closer look at what might be traded off. Is all the discretionary money going for name-brand clothes, music lessons, and sports classes for the kids? Is it time to divert some of that toward the goal of destressing yourself and/or supporting your own creative desires?

It's time to recast the agreement we have about money.

Couples make all kinds of agreements, or come to all kinds of understandings, concerning the money in their lives. Some agreements have been talked over (even written down) in detail; more simply have taken on the nature of a governing law within the relationship over time, although neither partner ever spelled them out. The thoroughly modern egalitarian couple might be in absolute accord at one stage—maybe, who earns the bigger paycheck doesn't matter, "you'll do what you love, I'll do what I love."

But life goes on. There might come a time when the past understanding goes sour in the present reality. What made sense for two twenty-seven-year-olds just starting a marriage can be a source of irritation or disappointment ten years and a couple of children later.

What worked for two fifty-year-olds earning equal salaries and splitting the home chores down the middle isn't such a happy arrangement anymore when one retires at fifty-eight and the other is still putting in sixty-hour weeks in the office. So many couples, however, never address these shifts in a concrete way. Think of your own, possibly unspoken agreement, whether you feel a new one is in order, and how you can talk about what's on your mind. Maybe, instead of his-and-her money going into one bank account, do you want to start a checking, savings, or investment account in your own name? Instead of leasing a new car every two years as he's always insisted on, do you want to earmark some of that money for other purposes? If you always did the housework because you couldn't afford a cleaning service and now you can, is it time to budget that as a necessary expense?

Emily's Story

"We're in big debt, but my partner and I don't talk about it."

Money was the topic right up front when Emily came in for therapy. And it turned out to be a can of worms, because Emily, twenty-six, a social worker, and Janice, her partner, were sinking into a lot of trouble, very fast. Janice worked on a freelance basis (she was a post-production film editor), and her income was erratic and sporadic. She might be paid $10,000 for one job, then not receive another check for four or five months. Emily's earnings picture was more stable, but her salary was small, not enough to cover all their expenses.

One thing Emily always liked about her partner was that Janice was "a happy go lucky, what-me-worry? sort of person," while Emily saw herself as "sort of staid and boring." But Janice's live-for-the-moment behavior might be ordering a dozen DVDs from Amazon or buying the latest digital camera. All this went on the credit cards, and meeting her minimum payments meant that some months Janice had to ask Emily to pick up both halves of the rent ("I'll pay you back in a couple of weeks"). Occasionally, Emily made vague observations about her partner's purchases, like, "Whoa, that must have set you back a bundle!"—a remark that she thought somehow would open up a discussion about all the spending and a remark that Janice ignored.

Once the money started really running dry, however, Janice might suddenly blow up at Emily, getting angry about *her* spending, although both knew that Emily was pretty frugal. There might follow a couple of days of storming and fuming over minor stuff, such as who mopped the kitchen floor last. Then, ideally, a paycheck arrived for Janice. Then Emily thought (vaguely) that things would certainly turn around after this latest close call, and meanwhile, she'd find ways to cut corners a little more. She felt buoyed up when she bought economy-sized packages of paper towels or decided not to run the air conditioner that day.

Voice Mapping

"Somone or something will turn up to save me."

These two were *not* working together as a unit, and money was the commodity they were not working together over. A big part of the picture seemed to be that neither was terribly grown up, and each subconsciously wished some adult would step in and take charge.

Many women who are locked into denial mode concerning their finances hope or sense that some caretaking force is waiting just over the horizon, like magical realism. One of our clients was admittedly searching for a rich husband. Another mentioned a well-to-do, childless aunt in her eighties, on whom she was pinning her hopes for a little inheritance. Nothing wrong with that—except if such notions make it easy to ignore the need to get realistic about debt.

Reframing

Accept the fact that talking about our money problems is hard to do.

The silence, the bite-my-lip attitude, Emily's vague and ineffectual swipes at "talking tough," the blow-ups she described, were far from uncommon.

When our female clients tell us about their money issues, the wish we most often hear expressed is that they could sit down with their partners (husbands, fiancés, lovers), and communicate more openly. In most relationships, money seems to be a commodity that one handles or the other handles, but seldom something that both handle and discuss as a couple—and this last, of course, is critical for any pair sinking into the morass Emily worried about. Most couples find this hard to do. Realizing that taking the bull by the horns will probably be unpleasant, however, is a critical step in reframing the picture.

What am I doing instead of talking to my partner about our money problems?
After some thought, Emily decided her minor cost-cutting was not so terrific. Not only did these economies make no perceptible dent in their overall bleak financial picture, but they somewhat sugar-coated it, allowing her to avoid what *really* needed doing.

This is another common story. When faced with large debt, many women adopt short-sighted strategies, clipping coupons to save $5 and telling themselves they can wait until tomorrow to confront the reality of a bad situation head-on. Here are several other going-nowhere kinds of self-talk:

- Well, it's not all that serious, another month or two and things should be looking better.
- There's nothing I can do about this, it's all too far gone.
- I'll get the mail before he does and pay the utility bill and the phone bill and the credit card, so he won't see them and get angry and upset.

All such denials delay the inevitable, which might mean talking to a recklessly spending partner about problems with mounting debt.

Movement Strategies

It helps to break down this huge money thing into smaller pieces that might be easier to talk about.
However the talk gets started—and an advisable approach is a cool-headed, nonconfrontational "I'm concerned about our bills, I'd like us to sit down together tomorrow evening and go over some

ideas"—one initial step toward responsible budgeting can be to discuss money broadly in terms of three categories: survival, essential, and luxury.

Survival is bare-bones stuff, such as paying your rent or mortgage, buying food and electricity, and so on. Essentials are items or experiences that are excellent for your mental health and sanity, like seeing a movie or an occasional dinner out, although you're not going to die if you don't have them. Luxury encompasses everything else. Categorizing expenses this way can be especially helpful for young people without a lot of experience living within a budget. For one thing, it underscores the reality that things some of us consider essentials (like the ten latest DVDs) are, in fact, luxuries.

I can get help in the form of credit counseling.

For Emily and Janice, it seemed getting their feet on the ground through some credit counseling was the immediate move that might reduce their anxieties and tensions. Emily brought up the idea; Janice was against it, shrugging off the suggestion. "She's very embarrassed, very ashamed really," Emily said, "about getting herself or the two of us in such a place that we have to consider credit counseling." In therapy, we will work with a client or couple on feelings of shame or embarrassment, but the fact is, when the reality of their situation is so perilous, they're unlikely to feel much better until they get some practical advice from a financial expert. Emily persisted, and Janice finally, grudgingly agreed.

Credit counseling can be a major step in turning things around, not only in terms of meeting immediate bills, but in establishing a framework for the future. Such outside services can offer practical, valuable assistance in:

- Consolidating credit card payments
- Making installment payments to the Internal Revenue Service
- Creating a realistic budget
- Reducing interest rates
- Rebuilding and reestablishing credit
- Ending embarrassing creditor calls
- Learning how to better manage money in general

The Consumer Credit Counseling Service is a wonderful resource available to help people under financial duress deal with their circumstances in more productive ways. It's offered at low cost or no cost in many communities throughout the United States by agencies with membership in the National Foundation for Consumer Credit (NFCC). The services are funded by groups like the United Way and are usually listed in the Yellow Pages under "Credit." If you can't find a local listing, call the national toll-free NFCC at 1-800-388-2227.

During most American women's adult lifetimes, they will have been single, married, divorced, remarried, and perhaps widowed. You may have been, at different times, childless, a mother, a grandmother. You may have been flat broke, comfortable, or financially well-off. You may have been anxious about money, relaxed about money, or naive about money. Like countless others, you may have felt inadequate about money and also had great times spending money.

The point is, you'll almost surely find that your relationship to money changes, and more than once, during your lifetime. But as the issues discussed in this chapter underscore, the human emotions swirling about this finite resource—Who gets it? What do I do about it? How is it spent? How do we talk about it?—can be complex, and tap into a woman's psychology in powerful ways. Indeed, money is such a significant issue that ignoring it or avoiding conversations about it drains our power more than almost anything else we can do to hurt ourselves.

Avoidance never gets us far. Whatever you've done, or not done, isn't nearly as important as what you choose to do from this point forward. Bite the bullet, educate yourself, and learn to make the decisions that are right for you.

9

The Balancing Act Expectation: "I'm Running My Life, It's Not Running Me"

We may charge through our days booked full, but the modern woman image suggests someone who has, finally, got everything under control. Thanks to recent decades of social change, we are expecting the men in our lives to share equally in home responsibilities (just as we're expected to work outside the home), and we're asking them to do so. We are aware of the need to nurture ourselves; we're heeding the advice of popular media personalities to "live your best life now" and "take time for you!" We're not caught off guard by the demands of our multiple roles; we anticipated them and we're ready. Said a publisher of a woman's magazine describing its thirty-something audience, "Women are not trying to do it all. They're picking and choosing and doing it well. They're more empowered."

This "she's on top of her game" image is pervasive. As proof, consider the reaction whenever revelations or data come out to the contrary: working wives and mothers say they are in fact exhausted and often furious; the woman who delays having a baby in order to pursue a career may never, to her sadness, get the baby; an elected state official announces that it's just too hard thinking about the job and about her children at the same time, and resigns. And social commentators of all sorts treat it as surprising news. What? Wasn't all that settled already?

The balancing act refers to a woman's efforts to fulfill all the responsibilities and enjoy all the pleasures of the various hats she wears—individual, wife, mother, daughter, career woman, home-maker, and so on. It's a misguided term, implying as it does a satis-fying state that will be achieved if only a woman *acts* in certain ways; it may take work, but as long as she keeps trying, she'll bring all the pieces of her life into an alignment that feels perfectly comfortable. This is a myth, but one many women find easy to buy into. In the opening chapter, we mentioned that so many of our clients suspect every other woman out there is *getting it right*. Every other woman is calmly, competently, and with good cheer pulling off the balanc-ing act. And she, our client, is not. So what's wrong with her?

In truth, of course, picking and choosing—among chores, re-sponsibilities, the focus of attention—is no doubt an excellent idea, and would help ease the worry, anger, or self-blame so many women struggle with, not to mention the exhaustion. But two fac-tors interfere. First, she knows that maybe she can't do it all, but it all does have to get done and who else is going to see to that? Or who better than she? Anyway, she's tried to explain what's needed, what *she* needs, and that hasn't worked. *He* doesn't get it.

Second, she knows that choosing to pick up ABC at any point in time almost always requires sloughing off XYZ. She believes that the choices she makes, even if difficult, are sensible, or necessary, or motivated by the right stuff. And yet emotionally, she can't give her-self a break. Like poking at a sore tooth with a tongue, she worries away about the XYZs in her life.

Concerning the balancing act, more so than with several of the other subjects we discuss in this book, it may be productive to separate out the *them* from the *me*. To ask, in other words: What do they (husband, partner, children, parents, bosses, colleagues) expect from me? What do I expect of myself? (And why is that?) The stories we describe in this chapter reflect several *them* and *me* issues, and how they are experienced by two women in two differ-ent ways:

- Overloaded and anxious about it
- Overloaded and angry about it

Today, women have equal access to education and to many jobs. As any working wife/mother knows, family responsibilities constitute the piece of equality that still hasn't been accomplished. Specifically, the working wife operates from the assumption that she will manage the household and the children; the working husband, from the assumption that he will help her in those efforts. She's the CEO. He is her assistant. Any woman who resents that state of affairs has almost certainly picked up much advice in the popular press on how to promote a better deal for herself: draw up lists, make chore-sharing agreements. Here, we focus more on some voices that can make a woman one of her own worst enemies in her balancing act efforts.

Margaret's Story

"Who has the luxury of getting a cold?"

Margaret, thirty-five, is a production manager for a publisher of industrial trade magazines, married to a lawyer, and the mother of four children—ten-year-old twin boys, a nine-year-old daughter, and six-year-old Sam, who has a developmental disorder that requires special tutoring and other resources. Her family's needs are complicated; Margaret said with a small laugh, "The reason I never get sick is because I don't have time to."

Sam's disorder had been correctly diagnosed only a year earlier, and "finally knowing what we're dealing with," she said, had eased some pressures. "From the time he was about two up until age five, I remember that as a long endless stretch of seeing one specialist after another, trying out one preschool program after another. And just total frustration." She also remembered taking great care to insure that her older children never felt overlooked because of their kid brother's special needs. That was still of paramount importance to her, and Margaret conscientiously blocked out segments in the evenings and over the weekends to spend time with the twins and with her daughter. Their father was a loving and willing partner in these parenting efforts. "But his work schedule is backbreaking, and it's just not possible for him to be always on tap. He and I joke that we're probably going to be in our eighties before we have time to get back to the marriage."

Between the two of them, they brought in a nice income; raising four children was an expensive proposition, however, and Margaret described the family as "comfortably middle class. Money isn't piling up but it isn't a huge worry either." She came for a few therapy sessions "not because I'm falling apart, but because I need to get a better handle on what's going on with me."

She described her thoughts this way. "I give off an impression of being superwoman, nothing fazes this girl. I know, because people tell me it's terrific how I keep everything running so smoothly. Before Sam came along things were pretty hectic. After he was born, and then when we suspected he had a disorder of some sort, that started the real crunch time. Remember the movie *Star Wars* and Han Solo navigating the *Millennium Falcon*? When the bad guys are gaining on them, he shifts into hyperdrive. The last few years I've been in hyperdrive, I can't get out of it, and nobody knows it."

Her mind was never at rest, she said. She woke up at four every morning, "mentally running over the checklist of two dozen things coming up that day." She didn't eat right—"If my husband isn't home, usually I just finish off something from the kids' plates." It was a blessing having a sturdy constitution, she said, although she was adding pounds at an alarming rate and disliked how her body looked and felt. She was occasionally irritable and short-tempered.

There was a growing and disturbing disconnect, she thought, between her inner life and the superwoman impression. "That's not really me, that just *looks* like me! I'm constantly jittery. When I've got Sam on stable ground and he's doing okay for the moment, one of the other kids seems needy or unhappy. I never feel I'm really up to speed in my work at the office."

She'd been toying with one possibility. "I'm wondering if I should quit my job and just concentrate on the kids and the family for a couple of years, so I don't feel stretched so thin. We could manage it financially, with some adjustments." But it was a choice she didn't really want to make. She liked her job, her coworkers, the whole field. Plus, she wasn't sure she could jump back into it at a later date.

Talking it all over, Margaret started to explore other options, other ways she might be able to ease herself out of hyperdrive, and also feel more satisfied that she was actually doing well with all the demands on her time and emotions.

Voice Mapping

"First come the children, the husband, the job. Then me . . . maybe."

Margaret couldn't remember when she last took any extended time just for herself. But there *wasn't* time, she believed, "except maybe for reading in bed a few minutes before I fall out for the night." It was okay, though; she felt that everything else had to take priority for now. That's a familiar voice. Women have been so acclimated and acculturated to tune in to the needs of children, husband, elderly parents, in-laws, and others that they rarely think about what they'd like for themselves. Often, they don't have a clue what that might be.

Margaret made a distinction between the impression she gave out and the "real" Margaret inside. But actually, many women truly are superwomen. A woman's capacity for multitasking is immense, and may in fact have something to do with the way her brain is made—capable of focusing on a number of things at a time. Typically, however, everyone else gets the benefit of the multitasking woman; she's at the bottom of her own list.

"It's selfish to put my needs out there."

When a woman *does* ask for what she wants or needs, it often sounds to her own ears like "whining." Somehow, the idea of *healthy,* appropriate selfishness gets lost in the shuffle; rather, the message that being a little selfish is always a bad trait takes precedence.

Reframing

At this pace, what's my life going to be like five or ten years from now?

She really hadn't looked ahead. When she did, like most women Margaret fixed on a vague point in the future when her children would be more independent. Well, we said, assuming that will be seven or eight years from today, do you think your stamina and sturdy constitution will still be going strong? Will you be paying a price? Margaret pinpointed one aspect of her current lifestyle that did concern her. "This never getting a decent night's sleep is hard. I'm so wound up from the day, sometimes I take medication."

Am I taking the signs of overload seriously?

The bad sleep, the wound-up feeling, and a mind always racing were signals that her system was overloaded. But that's just the inescapable fallout from too much work and too little rest, she told herself, nothing fatal. Yet ignoring signs of emotionally induced tension is unwise. Some questions to consider:

- Am I constantly worrying because something didn't get done or didn't get done well enough?
- Am I persistently disappointed in or angry with my partner, my kids, my coworkers?
- Do I berate myself for not managing my time more productively?
- Do I often feel tense, never fully relaxing and giving myself over to moments of mental and physical serenity or enjoyment? Have I forgotten *how* to relax?
- Do I feel isolated or depressed in the midst of all this busyness, as if no one else understands what I'm up against?

Typically, a woman will answer: "Yes, I'm a worrier; no, I never take time for myself, but all that will change when [the kids are older, we get more money in the bank, my parents are settled into their retirement community, I switch jobs, the cows come home]." Less pressure is a feeling she might wish for, but actively seeking it is put on hold, future indefinite, until some event is reached or accomplished. And everything we know about women and stress tells us this is a bad, bad idea. According to the findings of much research, including the studies conducted by Dr. Alice Domar, director of the Mind/Body Center for Women's Health at the Beth Israel Deaconess Medical Center in Boston, relieving tension and stress is critical to good health. When *not* relieved over time, that state can promote or exacerbate all manner of physical problems: high blood pressure, cardiovascular disease, chronic fatigue, infertility, even susceptibility to common colds.

Reframing for Margaret and any woman feeling overloaded and on hyperdrive—which means many of us—really must start there: take seriously the need to reduce stress, and start now. In a sense, it's making a determined, conscious effort to develop a degree of healthy selfishness. This may be especially difficult for the woman—and we have counseled many of them—who found it necessary to assume a caretaking role early on in life, perhaps looking out for younger siblings or dealing with a sick or alcoholic parent. She tended others well, but never became very good at taking care of herself.

Movement Strategies

I'm going to reset some priorities.

There will never be enough time to do it all, or all at once. Accepting that as a given, consider reallocating some of the time there is, with the specific intention of putting yourself on your list of priorities.

To start, here's a useful exercise we sometimes suggest to the client who doesn't see even a sliver of an opening in her day. Keep a log of every last little thing you do in the course of one twenty-four-hour period. This takes some time (which, as we know, there is too little of), but if you carry a pad of paper with you and jot down a quick note on the run, it's not impossible. The results can be revealing in terms of practical choices.

For one thing, a number of activities will fall in the "must do" category (driving the kids to school), similar to the fixed expenses on a budget list (rent and utilities). Others will at once seem more clearly discretionary, of less value or lower priority, and maybe they can be eliminated or at least not included in every day's schedule. For another thing, small pockets of time that can be put to better use—in other words, reclaimed for *you*—may become apparent. For example, Margaret said, "In the mornings, after breakfast and getting dressed and all, there's about twenty minutes or so when I'm waiting for the kids to be ready to leave the house. They're good about pulling their stuff together, I don't have to do a lot of nagging." What she *did* do during those interludes was "straightening up, just general household things that really don't have to get taken care of right then." But she didn't like "sitting still." Sitting still might have been the best thing for her—possibly putting into practice some techniques to untense herself for the day ahead.

The point is, stop thinking about the future-indefinite point at which life circumstances will have conveniently rearranged themselves, or the next likely opportunity for a whole weekend on your own. Instead, use the fifteen-minute or half-hour window of time to do something kind for yourself, your mind, and your body.

I need to adopt some relaxation strategies.

Margaret had actually made stabs at relaxing more, "such as coming home and taking a bath before getting into all the evening stuff. Terrible idea for me. It didn't work." But there are various stress-relieving techniques that take little time and no special skills, equipment, or strength. Just a walk around the block, some deep breathing, or simple yoga moves can make a large difference. In addition, much research in the areas of health, caretaking, and coping shows that individuals who possess personal faith find it helpful to turn to sustaining religious and spiritual activities. Another positive stress reducer, also supported by research, is humor. Take the time to buffer yourself from stressful difficulties, and find comedy, laughter, and fun.

We do know what constitute *inadvisible* methods of stress reduction: drinking more than one drink; overeating or bingeing; excessive amounts of passive activity, such as TV watching; using recreational drugs; Internet addiction; negative cycles of thinking that blame the self or others, and keep one from genuine support and problem-solving; risky behaviors, such as running away or signing over assets to proseletyzers who promise to cure all one's problems; and ignoring the signs of known past vulnerabilities, such as depression, that may be cropping up again.

I can decide to remove certain information from my personal radar screen.
Here are some ways to come at that notion. Consider:

- Would I feel less stressed if I could manage to turn over more of the reins to my partner? Or to my colleagues on the job?
- When I delegate, do I ever completely let go?
- Can anyone else in my office do what I think I have to do?

- How much do I need to know about and engage with every single aspect of my family's life? Or with what's going on at work?

We've observed a certain behavior in many of our overachieving, overloaded clients. Even when it's agreed between a woman and her partner that he will be in charge of one area of family business—let's say, sitting down once a month to pay the bills—and even when she's absolutely confident that he can be relied on to handle it, she still keeps bill-paying on her brain. And maybe she feels compelled to question him about details. Her issue is not really a need to control; it's a need to know, because that's what a good, responsible, caretaking woman does.

One client spoke about acting "like the ultimate custodian of my husband's mental state." As she described, "He was under pressures at work recently, and in the evenings he'd be tense, sometimes short with the kids. So I asked him to talk it over with me one night, and he told me a little about what was going on in the office. He said he was preoccupied, and he'd make an effort not to let his mood affect the kids. Which he did." She was reassured that nothing disastrous might happen; losing his job was not a possibility. Nevertheless, she watched each evening for clues to how he was feeling, she encouraged him to fill her in on what had happened that day, she worked at being a careful listener. Maybe this emotional caretaking was helping him, she said, "but it was actually making me feel more uptight." She finally decided it would be better for her own mental state to draw a line between reasonable demonstrations of empathy and support, and what amounted to an excessive involvement in all the details of his current difficulty. Letting go of the need to know doesn't come effortlessly, but it can be enormously freeing.

I might be able to make my time with the kids more fun for me.
Having fun is an excellent stress buster. That might come about from taking in a movie with a girlfriend or signing up for belly dancing lessons. But everyday parent-child activities sometimes can be more fun for the parent.

Once she was home from the office, Margaret was 100 percent mother—seeing to her children's needs, diligently ensuring that each of the four kids felt he or she was getting equal time with Mom. We asked if she enjoyed those moments, if she had some laughs and some fun. Of course, she said, she loved her children, she didn't want to be anywhere else or doing anything else. "But do you have fun?" we asked. "Are the activities, or some of them anyway, pleasurable to you, something you actually feel like doing?" "Well, no, I guess not entirely," she decided after reviewing how she'd spent some recent evenings with her children. They went over homework together. She made a point of engaging each in conversations designed to show her support for their friendships and school activities. After hunting up a couple of child-friendly recipes, she got her two oldest boys to help her make lentil soup, wanting them not to "grow up clueless about cooking and food." She set her daughter up with a box of cards and a pencil to write thank-you notes for birthday presents she'd received, and then Margaret addressed and stamped the envelopes.

All of this was fine. All of this also had the quality of an agenda, a good mother determined to do right by her children. To feel more relaxed and less stressed, Margaret might help herself by easing up on the agenda and being more simply playful, which is often the kind of time fathers share with their kids. Studies show that men tend to be more peerlike with their children. Fathers are the ones who engage the kids in fun—good-natured roughhousing, games, watching sports on TV, shooting baskets, or tossing a softball around in the backyard. On the other hand, even when mothers are having "down time" with their children, they're likely to be caught up in activities with an educational focus or purpose—reading books together, doing craft activities.

I need to take stock of what's going right.
Overloaded women like Margaret tend to ruminate about everything that isn't getting accomplished—about the XYZs that are being overlooked because of the ABCs taking precedence at the moment. One simple-sounding strategy we use with our clients is to get in the habit of seeing the glass half full and not half empty. Call it cognitive restructuring. Call it accentuating the positive (even if you can't entirely eliminate the negative).

Consider the good news. Write it down if you wish. Make an index card collection of what you see as troublesome about the choices you have made, one to a card—what's bothering you and why you think it's your fault. On the reverse side, write down what's right:

Side A: My thirteen-year-old is just a so-so student, and if I'd been home more instead of working ten-hour days he'd be doing better in school. Side B: He's a good kid. He has nice friends. People find him pleasant.

Side A: I've got my job, my marriage, my kids, my home, and I'm not doing a great job at any of them, because you really can't have it all. Side B: Actually, I do have it all, a little of everything, and if I'm not doing a great job, it's a good enough job.

This exercise can help you see that there really are two sides to every story, or two ways of perceiving the same reality.

Kate's Story

"I have to do everything around here!"

Kate, forty-two, was angry. "I get no help from my husband with the kids, no help around the house." Her resentment had grown over the past year, as her parents suddenly became more infirm and needed her regular assistance in their home, about a half hour's drive away. Kate had become one of the seven million Americans— 80 percent of them women—who spend many unpaid hours a week caring for older family members. All this was in addition to maintaining a full-time job in the services department of a major personal-computing manufacturer.

In fact, Kate was more than angry; she was bitter. "Sometimes I think I got a raw deal. My mother had it easy—married to a strong, traditional, protective man, cooking meals and taking care of the kids and never having to worry about making a buck. I don't blame her for that, I envy her. I do everything she did at home, and then I earn a damn good living too."

There were flareups between her husband and herself, usually about household chores and sometimes about child-rearing. She gave this example: "He's terrible at dishes. He doesn't rinse them properly before loading the washer, and when he cleans a pot, it's still greasy. I've pointed this out to him several times, but he refuses to get the idea, which isn't that hard to get. This is not rocket science, as they say. So I finally said it would be better if he didn't do any dishes, leave them for me. Last weekend we had some family over for an early supper, and then I went out shopping with my sister-in-law. I got back that evening to an untouched mess. I said to Bob, you know, it would have been nice if you had cleaned up the kitchen a little, and he said, you told me I should never do the dishes." It was "classic passive-aggressive behavior," she thought. "Don't learn how to do the thing right so he doesn't have to do it, and then he can just aggravate me."

They'd been married for fifteen years. During the early years, neither had paid much attention to how things got done or who did them. "Once Annie was born," said Kate, "the whole burden of parenting fell on me." Annie was now eight; her sister Jennifer was six. "Bob takes the girls to the playground on weekends. He'll help Annie with her homework. He thinks that makes him a wonderful father." Kate and her husband were having more disagreements than usual about their respective approaches to dealing with the kids: she thought he was "way too easy-going and laidback"; he called her "obsessive" and "the sergeant."

One development had brought to the surface these resentments that Kate—and, apparently, her husband too—had been harboring just below the surface for some time. Her need and wish to be of aid to her elderly parents—shopping for them, accompanying them to doctor appointments—had added several hours of caretaking work to Kate's week. As it happened, the beginning of all that effort coincided with some changes her company put in place as part of an internal "work redesign" project. In a stated attempt to help them achieve a happier balance between job and family roles, many employees were offered opportunities to work from home and software and training to facilitate telecommuting. Kate was one of them. The problem, as she soon discovered, was that making the job more flexible didn't mean there was less work to accomplish. Like huge numbers of American workers, Kate—Bob too—carried an ever-increasing workload. But he believed that relative to his situation, she had it easy, and they argued about it. "He thinks that because my actual in-the-office hours are now a lot less than his, I have no right to complain. But I'm still doing a full-time job, *and* taking care of the house, the kids, my folks. Because it all falls on the woman."

Kate really did want to bring about improvements, and they were big ones—to reduce the marital arguing, to reach a better agreement with her husband about what was best for the children (who were learning to play Mom and Dad off against each other), to share the home work more equitably. She needed to think about what factors got her to this point in the first place, and then maybe start reframing some of her assumptions.

Voice Mapping

"I'm the one who does everything best."

This was no doubt true. Kate *was* best at loading the diswasher properly and degreasing the pots and pans. She was the one who kept their daughters to a schedule, because Bob was more casual about bedtimes, for example, and unaware of the fact that the children were often tired the next day. She made lists of needed household supplies, coordinated the babysitters, sent out the Christmas cards and bought the presents for the relatives, and did a hundred other things. She did them well, better than the other adult in the household, she thought—and those things needed to be done well. In fact, though this realization took her a while to reach, she went about it as her job, not his.

"Women are supposed to worry about the kids and the house."

Kate was angry and resentful. And yet, deep down she still believed it was up to her to be the exclusive caretaker, because "that's what women do." Firmly planted in Kate's psyche was a *should*, based largely on prior generations (her mother, the happy homemaker) and old messages—the very thing that, at least in part, was underlying her sense of getting a "raw deal."

Reframing

How greatly do I truly enjoy the caregiving role?

Put aside for the moment considerations of who does the brunt of the work and any resentments about that, and consider: What value do I place on—and how much pleasure do I derive from—maintaining a home and caring for the people I love?

Kate could recognize that under her anger was deep fatigue, and that deep fatigue was the result of shouldering a very large burden. But there was a payoff. "All this is important to me. It's not only that I consider it my job, I guess, but it's the best thing I'm doing with my life—seeing to my family, knowing that everybody's okay. Even the house." She laughed: "The cleaned-up kitchen, clean laundry, flowers on the coffee table in the living room, all this matters to me in a way I think it doesn't matter so much to Bob. Actually, I have a friend, my old college roommate, who could care less about the stuff she has around her. She could live out of a suitcase, and be perfectly satisfied and productive. But I care a lot." That self-insight was a critical piece of her reframing.

In her highly praised book *Home Comforts*, Cheryl Mendelson (who happens to hold a J.D. from Harvard Law School and a Ph.D. in philosophy) offers an exhaustive, fascinating rundown of advice on everything from dealing with dust mites to insuring the safety of electrical outlets. This impressive assemblage of information, she writes, grew out of her "passion for domesticity"—which had little relation to monogramming finger towels or weaving wreaths out of dried vines. Those activities, she notes, are "playing house instead of keeping house by a genuine desire for a home and its comforts."

Creating a home and its comforts is what many women do genuinely desire, and greatly value about themselves and their lives. One client spoke of the essential contradiction in her feelings about her role as "head of the universe," as she put it. She thought it was unjust that her husband—and to some extent, her teenage children, although she expected less of them—got to enjoy the reliability, coziness, and pleasure of their truly lovely and inviting house, while she almost single-handedly was the one who made it that way. And yet, she said, "Sometimes I'll be preparing dinner, and there's a beautiful evening light outside. I'm having a glass of wine, listening to music,

I'm hearing my son watching TV in the other room and my daughter on the phone. Maybe my husband is just getting home and he says how great dinner smells. And I just feel the deepest peace and contentment. I think, I've been able to create this for them. For us."

Is doing everything best the best thing for me and this family?
Kate was not reluctant to point out to her husband what needed to be accomplished. But there was always that feeling that she could do it better, even concerning their two daughters. "I spend more time with them, I just understand them more than he does." Being the one who did everything better, which usually meant she was the one who did it all, was her way of keeping control. And perhaps she harbored a secret fear that in giving up some of the "everything," she'd slide down a slippery slope and not be in charge of anything anymore. She resolved—and for Kate, this was a major step—to put into practice more mindful picking and choosing throughout the course of her time with the family, and to ask herself: What will suffer *least* if I'm not the one who does it? What would happen if I take no action right now? Why do I have to solve this particular issue?

She made one immediate decision. The house needed a thorough going-over, a fact that had been nagging at her, and she thought she'd hire a professional cleaning service for that.

Can I appreciate a little better how my partner might feel?
"Two generations ago," noted one social commentator, "men didn't have to be good husbands. One generation ago, they didn't have to be good fathers. Now, of course, they have to be everything." In recent years we are seeing some men wanting both paths available to them—work life and home life—and facing the conflicts women experience in filling those dual roles. These are the fathers who opt out of the high-pressure jobs or decline the promotional transfers, because the hours and the pressures will distance them from their children; these are the mostly young (in the twenty to thirty-nine age bracket) men who say they would even accept less pay for more family time.

Still, being a good father doesn't have the same meaning to a man as being a good mother does to a woman. When push comes to shove, Mom is still the one to find the babysitter, to stay home with a sick child, and so on. But it can benefit a woman like Kate to consider if and how she may be complicit in the fact that her partner isn't a fully involved participant in the lives of their children. Regarding the child-rearing, does he feel somewhat out of the loop? And am I, perhaps unintentionally, keeping him there?

Kate came to therapy; Bob did not, and therefore we didn't know his version of events. However, from another father, with children about the same ages as Annie and Jennifer, we heard about several experiences and the feelings they evoked that might have paralleled an atmosphere in Kate's family. He told us, "From the day our first kid was born, my wife just seemed to know what to do. I had a learning curve. Maybe she did too, but it didn't feel that way. She was the one in charge, I was looking on. Today, when the kids are upset about something—maybe something happened in school, or one of them has a bad dream—they go to her. When they're having a fight between themselves, they go to their mother to settle it. And she probably is better than me at handling all this. It's like all four of us have decided I'm the incompetent one. Sometimes I think she could kind of gently steer the kids a little more in my direction."

Movement Strategies

I would like greater acknowledgment and greater appreciation.

When women talk about "getting more cooperation" from their partners, they focus on the sharing of chores and tasks. That that division in most households typically overloads women and benefits men is without question. Studies show that both employed and unemployed wives perform at least three-quarters of the unpaid work within the home. Husbands with wives who maintain full-time jobs outside the home do no more work within the home than do the husbands of women who don't hold jobs. Talk about how we have *not* come a long way, baby!

How to bring about a more equitable division of labor is the subject of debate from the level of uniform policy initiatives concerning paid parental leave, corporate daycare facilities, and other advances, right down to the highly individual negotiations that happen between a man and woman. Here, we suggest this consideration: Do you want more cooperation (such as should be expected in the truly "collaborative couple") or more thanks? The answer is both, of course, but if you've having a hard time getting the cooperation, would you feel better if you asked for more appreciation, or at least recognition and understanding?

I can tell him what I do to maintain the smooth functioning of our children's lives. Probably he doesn't know.

In a survey by the Radcliffe Institute for Advanced Study, 96 percent of those polled, both men and women, believed parents should share *equally* in the caretaking of children. That it's not happening, lip service to the contrary, is no surprise to any woman. But our clients tell us that their partners have no idea what the caretaking of children involves. And this gets to the heart of what so many women find irritating. Not only is the common assumption that his role is to help her: the emotional and organizational responsibility of the home is in her lap; she maintains the executive function for the family and the household. Specifically, their anger and dismay (in happier situations, it might be bemused annoyance) is over the man's inability to *know* what's needed. Said Kate, "If I tell my husband, Jenny needs to bring six containers of apple juice to school tomorrow for the class picnic, would you stop on your way home and pick them up, he'll say, 'Sure, no problem.' But I'm the one who knows about the picnic and the apple juice."

Whether a woman is able to let go of that particular gripe and chooses to focus on trying to bring about a more equal sharing of tasks is up to the individual. But in a calm moment, not trying to stir up an argument, she might help him to understand the quality of the child caretaking she assumes, and how completing particular chores is only part of it. In his book *Why Parents Disagree*, family and child psychologist Dr. Ron Taffel proposes, "The 'who feels responsible for the kids?' quiz." His questions, pointedly, are not concerned with who *cares* more about the children, or even who *does* more, but rather, with which parent feels ultimately *responsible* for their daily welfare. Among the twenty questions are these:

- Who first notices the signs that one of your kids is getting sick?

- Who searched for and interviewed prospective pediatricians?
- Who bought the last small "thinking of you" present when your child seemed to be blue?
- Who first notices that your supply of "kid foods" is running low?
- Whose datebook contains the dates of the school concert, Little League sign-up, and other kids' birthday parties?
- Who thought to call the parents of your daughter's playmates after she came down with the chicken pox?

I can try a little rephrasing.

Here a conundrum. The woman, typically, is in charge of the "communication" within the relationship. She's the one who says, "You know dear, I'd like it if we did some things differently, and here's what and why," careful to use communication-enhancing "I" language and so on. She may feel she *has* communicated. But he has not really heard. In therapy, at the point things are starting to unravel in his marriage or relationship, a man will so often tell us, "I didn't think anything was wrong! I come home at a regular time every evening, I don't spring any surprises on her that way. I help with the kids, I help with the house. I take care of the yard. If she's got a business meeting or something, I drive carpool, I'm there for her. So what's going on? What's the matter?"

Communicating about the *division of labor* in the home, even when the relationship is under no threat of disintegrating, is a sore point for many women. Some try written contracts. Sometimes they work; often they produce no significant changes or changes that last for a week. Whatever negotiating tactics a woman elects to pursue, however, it is within her power to take small measures that might begin a new kind of discourse—or if not actual discourse, ideally at least a gradual shift in perceptions.

Don't automatically jump to assume responsibility for a task. For example, Kate mentioned that her husband often brought to her attention something that was needed. "He says, 'Do we have any 75-watt bulbs?' This is after looking in the closet where I, and only I, regularly stock up on bulbs, and seeing none there. So he already knows the answer to his question. My instinct is to say, 'I guess we're out, I'll pick up more tomorrow.' Now I am trying to reply instead, 'No, looks like we need some more.'" Recently, he observed that "some spots of mildew had formed on the shower curtain liner. I almost said, 'Yeah, I need to wipe that down with a little bleach.' What I did say was, 'Yeah, that liner needs to be wiped down with a little bleach.'"

Her husband also tended to lose track of his possessions. "He'll say, 'Have you seen my checkbook around anywhere?' 'Do you know where I left the car keys?' Typically, I'll get up and help him look. Now, I say, 'No, I haven't seen it,' and keep on watching my TV show or whatever. Then to everyone's surprise he's usually quite capable of finding his own stuff."

Kate said she was "taking some little baby steps here, to prove to both of us that I don't have to be the only one in charge of everything." This might be one of the best steps for an overloaded woman to take.

We've been talking in this chapter about the pressures on the overloaded woman, and how they can so easily lead to feelings of anxiety or anger. In fact, anxiety and anger are not mutually exclusive. Some women experience them in combination—and the more such emotions you're dealing with, the more exhausted you will be and the more elusive any semblance of achieving a "balanced" life may seem.

To ease the feelings, to gain a sense of greater control over the day and all that it requires, develop a good dose of healthy selfishness. Your needs and wants count.

10

The Appearance Expectation: "I Love My Body, Just as It Is"

After years—centuries—of conforming to one or another accepted notion of the ideal female form, women have supposedly arrived at a better place. We're confident in our own skins. We're proud of our wrinkles. We make no apologies. A noticeably heavy actress says, "So I'm fat, so what? I'm gorgeous and sexy and fat!"

We are also (so we hear and read) flaunting our body pride. An article in the *New York Times* titled "More of Less: Scantier Clothing Catches On" proclaims that women of all sizes and ages are happily showing off their breasts and legs and arms. Magazine fashion pages suggest we're wearing four-inch ankle-strap heels and plunging necklines with our business suits. A decade ago, notes a professor of human development, "the feminist ideal was to have a great career and a family. Now the ideal is to have a great career and a family and dress like a sex kitten too." Copy describing a fashion show for the next season's collections reads: "The bitch is back. She is strong. She is invincible. She is, well, superwoman!" Go ahead, we're told: wear pale gloss or vivid red on your lips; be girlish, be androgynous. It's all about one word: confidence.

As it turns out, in our therapy practices "I love my body, just as it is," is the last thing we ever hear from a woman. Any woman.

The message that women are "free" to look however we want has not, in fact, made us more accepting of the bodies and faces we do have. Rather, a woman may be simply less sheepish about going to great lengths and expense to pursue a more idealized image. The statistics are amazing: Between 1992 and 1998, the number of face-lifts performed in the United States increased by 77 percent; the number of breast lifts increased by 296 percent and the number of breast augmentations by 306 percent. Over one and one half million Botox injections were administered in 2001, smoothing out the wrinkles and frown lines that supposedly we're wearing with pride.

It seems that media images of attractive women don't help us feel better about ourselves. Even if we know in our highly intelligent minds that the wraithlike actress we're looking at has had the benefit of professional makeup artists, personal trainers, designer clothes, and photographic enhancement in the form of airbrushing and other flaw-eliminating techniques, we still think hers is a look that should be attainable. According to one study, three minutes spent leafing through a fashion magazine caused 70 percent of women to feel "depressed, guilty, or shameful." Said one client, a woman who'd been battling being overweight for most of her adult life, "This new plus-size model business is supposed to be so encouraging and supportive to us 'big girls.' But look at those women. They're really beautiful to start with. And they're a size 14, not a 22!"

Instead of women becoming more comfortable with their bodies, it may be that men are joining us in body craziness. Where once a man worried about whether he had enough hair, about whether he was tall enough, and perhaps about penis size, now he is expected to focus on obtaining the six-pack-abs look.

The social commentator Molly Haskell, writing about "the strains of trying to define oneself as a physical and spiritual woman in a feminist age," observed that once it was common for a woman to become self-conscious about her appearance sometime around April or May, just when she's starting to think of being out in shorts or on the beach in a bathing suit. Now, says Haskell, we've got "Image Awareness Month 12 times a year, siren calls to reshape the body through surgery or diet, and messianic fitness gurus beamed into our living rooms 24 hours a day. Does this invitation to make yourself over represent a new sense of empowerment or merely encourage overload as life becomes a never-ending dance between new possibilities and new insecurities?"

In this chapter, we look at how cultural expectations and the pressures they bring do so easily lead to overload and tap into insecurities about:

- Body image and self esteem
- Age and attractiveness

Few women start therapy because of appearance problems. If appearance has been troubling them, they tend to head for the gym or the nutritionist or the plastic surgeon, they buy diet books, free weights and yoga mats, they revamp their wardrobes. What we do see, however, is the woman who perhaps has tried one or all those avenues of improvement, had little success or not as much success as she thinks she should have, and is deeply unhappy. Appearance ties to damage in other areas of life, and yet it's the aspect of the self we most ardently believe can be fixed.

Lauren's Story

"I really can't stand my body."

Anyone would consider Lauren, twenty-eight, an attracive woman with a great shape. A self-confessed "gym nut, since I was a teen," she worked hard at building and maintaining her body—an hour or more a day with weight training and aerobic exercise. In her work as a physical therapist, Lauren impressed on her clients the importance of strength, flexibility, and health. In herself, however, she focused on looks. She was deeply discontent with her appearance. In fact, she *hated* her appearance. It was never good enough.

When she came for therapy, Lauren described herself as mildly depressed, anxious much of the time, and maybe becoming obsessive about her attractiveness. Lately she'd been overspending, buying clothes that she believed would make her feel better and that she often didn't wear. Although she'd been with her boyfriend since college graduation, she had become increasingly less interested in having sex with him.

We asked Lauren to identify the greatest areas of stress in her life, and rate each on a scale of one to ten in severity, with one representing barely any stress and ten standing for nearly unbearable stress. Lauren listed eleven items; eight of them she indicated were significant stressors in her life, right up around a ten, and all eight were related to her negative body image and consequent low self-esteem. She felt a little embarrassed by how powerfully her feelings and mood were affected by endless concerns about her appearance.

Body dysmorphic disorder is a term used to describe the experience of people who worry excessively about their physical image and find it impossible to believe that they look perfectly okay, even when other people assure them they do. A woman may develop addictive attractions to one behavior, then switch to another; she may be obsessed with what she eats, then throw herself into ferocious working out. Concern with appearance seeps into other areas of life, including romantic relationships.

Lauren was toward the far end of a continuum, the large population of women who are in basically excellent shape but think they should look more excellent. And then there's the even larger population, within which so many women find themselves: maybe they're not obsessing constantly about their looks, but they don't like them much either. Maybe they never have.

To reach a more personal standard of attractiveness, make realistic choices about what to do and what to forget about, and just enjoy a greater degree of comfort, a woman's self-talk might start back—as is so often the story—with the earliest messages she received, this time about appearance.

Voice Mapping

"Don't eat so much, you'll get too fat."

That's what Lauren remembered her mother telling her midway through practically every meal of her youth. Here are some other voices from the family, reports from several of our clients (and how they "heard" the messages):

- "Eat everything on your plate, that's being a good girl." (*I shouldn't get thinner than my mother, because she won't like that.*)
- "When you're a little older, we can get you a really pretty nose." (*Everybody thinks my nose is grotesque.*)

- "You've got brains, you don't have to worry about your looks." (*Everybody thinks I'm ugly.*)

Peers, of course, can be cruel. One woman remembers a painful adolescence, other kids nicknaming her "Tubs," and her efforts to work harder at being sweet, funny, and smart—"the jolly fat girl." Another suffered through "zit-face" taunts, and had to force herself out the door to school every morning.

As you think about what and when you began to learn about how you *should* look, and what was wrong with the way you did, it helps to consider that women are trained from childhood not to like their bodies. We're always *too* something. And the earliest messages can start us on a lifetime of negative perceptions.

"Attractive women are young, thin, and lithe."

When a woman thinks about whom she is comparing herself to, the most obvious answer for many will be all those media images that stir up in us feelings of depression, guilt, or shame. The referent standard of beauty in our culture at this point in time is underweight and young, no getting away from it.

But for Lauren, as for many younger women, the ideal body image is no longer just about being slim. It's super fitness as well—the lean, muscular, hard shape. A personal trainer who works with individual clients noted that many of her customers are women in their late twenties and thirties, some of them with a child or two. They elect to pursue intense regimens of yoga, weight lifting, aerobics, Pilates—and they are "tiny little things," she said. "These women wear size 2 and size 4. Working out is like a career for them." For most women, that's an impossible standard to meet, of course, and attempting to do so might sometimes be unhealthy as well.

"You can't be happy if you don't look great."

Lauren's self-image was affecting the rest of her life in negative ways. For one thing, she was aware of the creeping lack of interest in sex with her boyfriend. After careful focusing, she also recognized that she was picking fights with him on a fairly regular basis; the fights usually stemmed from her conviction that he was admiring some other woman when they were out together. She herself tended to start it up. "We'll be in a restaurant, and I'll say, 'Look at this woman walking in, isn't she great looking?' Vince says, 'I guess so,' or whatever, and five minutes later I'm arguing about something completely irrelevant. Vince has no idea where this is coming from."

For many women who are unhappy with appearance, social skills can become tied in to the sense of body. Relationships may be analyzed through the self-perception of attractiveness and unattractiveness: "I'm not getting any dates because my nose is too big."

Reframing

Is my perception of my appearance shared by my partner? Or by my physician? My family? My friends? Am I in an environment, a neighborhood, a work setting, a circle of friends against whom I'm constantly comparing myself, and finding my appearance lacking?

An objective reading, as far as one is possible, may be the first useful step in broadening your perceptions.

Stop focusing on body parts.

In talking about their body unhappiness, women describe particular perceived deficiencies:

"Look at these shaky thighs and that cellulite, disgusting!"
"My breasts are too small and flat."
"My breasts are too huge."
"My breasts aren't the same size."

One woman, conversely, who considered herself a total loss in almost all aspects of her body found comfort in her "perfect ears," the lobes of which she had never had pierced, because a boyfriend in her distant past "used to like to nibble on my ears, and called them so beautifully shaped."

If you find yourself tending to fixate with dislike on a part of the body—jiggly thighs, floppy underarms, saggy jaw—reframing might include resolving to look at the whole picture or focus on your good features. Or think about the body part you're unhappy with, and consider where on the continuum you fit, from "Yes, it would be nice if it were different, but no big deal," to "I'm really seriously upset and disturbed about this part of my looks."

What if I did look the way I think I should look? Or, why exactly do I want to change what I'm unhappy with?
If you land near the "seriously upset and disturbed" end of the scale, adopt a "what-if?" strategy. Suppose you did acquire the nose you've always wanted. Suppose you did have the thick, luxurious head of hair you wish you had. Suppose you did get down to the size 8. See yourself "in" that appearance. What then?

In therapy dealing with body image issues, including pervasive body hatred, this is one way we might push a woman to examine what meaning or fantasy she's attached to those desired changes.

The meaning or the rationale might be persuasive and make sense (my husband would really like it if I was slimmer. . . . in my business, it's important to present a youthful image. . . . I just want to get back some of my old jawline and I can afford the surgery to do it). On the other hand, do you detect avoidance behavior behind your wishes (if I obsess about this one thing, I don't have to deal with that other thing)?

Or are you pursuing an external ideal out of fear? Could your thoughts about possible cosmetic surgery be the beginning of more seriously compulsive behavior concerning your looks? One woman who said that she was "always searching for little lines in my face, pulling my hair back to see how I'd look if my skin was tighter," realized her deep anxiety about nearing her fiftieth birthday.

It's no sin to opt for elective cosmetic surgery or nonsurgical procedures, of course, but think about your motivations. You may feel confident that getting to the physical place you want to be will free you up to move ahead in the life you desire. One woman decided to undergo a face-lift when she was sixty-five. Today, at age seventy-five, she refers to that decision as "the best thing I ever did." She feels attractive and fit, and happier because of it. She also feels she has been able to age more comfortably. "When I tell people I'm seventy-five," she said, "they can't believe it." This gives her pleasure. And what's wrong with that?

Think health.

Am I telling myself that all my efforts are in the cause of strength and health, when in fact they amount to obsessive rumination about my physical appearance? Replace the goal of losing weight, let's say, with the goal of feeling healthy. That inevitably will involve at some point accepting what you are and being in control of what you do with it. The result may be an uneasy resolution—you're a size 14, you accept it, you'd still be happier as a size 8. But you can come to peace with it.

Lead with my brain.

If you can't change your *feelings* that your body is too gross, too fat, too whatever, despite realistic information to the contrary, try at least to remind yourself that your perception isn't entirely accurate, and build your life or adopt certain behaviors on that. Statistics vary concerning body size, but the average American woman is between 5 feet 3½ inches and 5 feet 4 inches and weighs between 140 and 152 pounds. The average fashion model is 5 feet 9 inches to 5 feet 11 inches and weighs around 117 pounds. It's often observed that Marilyn Monroe was about 5 feet 5 inches tall and weighed 135 pounds, which would make her appear overweight and on the short side today, compared to the models we look at in fashion magazines.

All this is good to think about now and then, when your brain knows one truth but your emotions continue to exert their pull towards an opposite message. The brain is the strongest organ in the body. Lead with it, and things can change for the better, even if your feelings don't follow—at least, not at first.

Movement Strategies

I can learn to accept positive feedback.

If you haven't taken that objective reading from family, friends, or coworkers, do so. If those individuals have agreeable and pleasant things to say about how you look, resolve to believe them.

A phenomenon called cognitive dissonance tells us that when an individual says something about you that *confirms* what you think about yourself, your reaction is "Um-hmm, she's right, she knows what she's talking about." When an individual says something about you that *contradicts* your self-image, your reaction is "Oh please, what does she know, she's got it all wrong." In order to maintain a negative self-perception, in other words, you diminish and undervalue the person who's telling you the good news.

I need to try to eliminate cognitive dissonance.

Allow yourself to take in and accept positive feedback. People pay other people casual compliments all the time. A coworker says, "What a great dress!" or "I like your haircut." A woman struggling with these issues typically discounts such small praises. She may smile and say thanks, all the while thinking, "Yeah, great dress but I can't fit into my jeans from last month anymore," or "I'm just having a good hair day, and also, she should have seen the way I looked before I spent half an hour blow drying this morning." Instead, assume the coworker is correct. By anyone's measure but your own, you're wearing a great dress and your hair looks pretty.

If you had the unfortunate experience of growing up with many negative messages at home, if the culture within which you were raised is not valued by mainstream society, or if you looked different from other girls because of your skin color or hair or size, you may need to work on getting yourself unstuck from child mode. Were you led to believe that while you were the amusing one your sister was the pretty one? Did you have a family label—"our little klutz"—that was damaging, even if meant affectionately? Were you made fun of because the clothes you were taught to wear did not conform to what other girls wore? Positive feedback now, maybe from a caring friend, can amount to a sort of grown-up mothering of a good sort.

I can write down the positive voices that oppose my negative voices.

This is a specific, mechanical exercise that can help you start to turn around negative thinking, gain a greater capacity to see yourself objectively, and install a new self-descriptive vocabulary. It's an exercise Lauren undertook, with good results. Here's how it works. Carry with you a stack of index cards, and try to write down on one card a negative message as it comes to mind. For example, after one workout Lauren looked in the mirror and thought, instantly, "God, I look positively yellow, I'm going to get sick!" Before going out for dinner one evening, the message popped into her head, "I can't wear these slacks, they make my butt look huge." She remembered to write these down on her cards a little later; by the end of two weeks, she had a stack of them.

On the third week, Lauren crossed out the negative messages one by one, and wrote the opposite positive message on the back: "I feel fine, I'm not sick." "The slacks fit, my rear is a normal size for my body." Then, feeling a little self-conscious but forging on, she read each positive statement out loud three times, as we'd suggested, to make the message more real. She continued identifying the negative voices and converting them into positive ones, until one day she caught herself actively disputing the negative voice and saying to herself that she didn't look so bad after all.

The index card exercise is useful because the woman who constantly finds nothing but fault about her body usually has absolutely no idea how persistently negative—and how persuasive—those voices can be.

I need to switch physical to mental imaging.

Instead of counting repetitions every time you're lifting weights, for example, figure out once how many minutes it takes to complete the number of lifts you're after, and in the future substitute a chant or a little mantra: "I can do it." The chant becomes a self-esteem booster for mental health, like an affirmation. If you're doing thirty repetitions in a typical workout, that's thirty psychological boosts to correlate with a muscular boost and the accompanied physiological changes. Think of it as a useful mind-body connection.

I will eliminate abstract goals.

Ask, for example: Is my weight goal realistic considering my body type? Is it realistic considering my age? If you keep trying to weigh 125, because the number sounds good or because that was your weight twenty years ago, you will probably never feel peace.

The woman who's struggling with weight problems can seek out a doctor or nutritionist for an analysis of her body type, bone structure, bone density, and so on. The goal is that instead of a vague "get thinner" in her head or an arbitrary number to shoot for, she will obtain information that allows her to adjust her own parameters and conceive a realistic image, one that reflects what's sensible for herself at this point in time. Then she can decide what she wants to do about it: I'll stay a little on the chubby side, or I'm willing to work hard at getting less chubby.

Eliminate the abstract goal, in other words, and focus on choices that are more contextual, relating to your real life and your real body, right here and now.

Sally's Story

"I'm fifty-three and just divorced and I feel like a neuter."

Sally had lately become "hideously self-conscious" about her body, which appeared to be a perfectly normal body for a fifty-three-year-old woman. Indeed, the thought of possibly being intimate with a new man caused her acute anxiety. "Most women my age just look so much better these days than I do," she believed, while at the same time she deplored the unfairness of it all. "A man can walk around with a potbelly and hair coming out of his ears, and still be considered attractive!"

This was the particular issue about which Sally initiated therapy. She had had a couple of enjoyable dates, and then had turned down the man's further invitations out of fear that a relationship would begin—and her clothes might come off. The divorce and the dating stirred up these anxieties, which in her more logical moments, she found humiliating and beneath her. Even before those epic events, Sally was experiencing feelings of rejection as a woman, aside from the wife part. "After a certain age," she said, "it seems you turn invisible. No man passing you on the street gives you a glance."

It was depressing, she said, and discouraging. But Sally was an intelligent, non-neurotic individual who wasn't going to spend a lot of energy ruing the passage of time. "I've got a wonderful daughter who's great company, a very decent job, a few tried and true friends. Life, in general, has been good to me." She liked men, she said, remembered the early years of her marriage fondly, and believed she'd enjoy being in a relationship with a new man. Finding one wasn't easy, but—urged on by her daughter and two close friends, and by her own common sense—Sally had been taking steps: getting out to socialize more, joining a volunteer organization, signing up for a public speaking class. "Just to broaden my horizons, get new people in my life."

The hangup, though, was her new obsession with her body, which was definitely getting in the way of her self-confidence: "You wake up one morning and overnight, it seems, the skin on your arms and legs has turned papery. How did that happen? I literally just can't stand looking at my arms and hands!"

Interestingly, many women seem to exhibit the same pattern of insecurities during and immediately after menopause as are typical during puberty and adolescence—self-consciousness, excessive focus on the body, and anxiety. They often seem unsure what to make of this changing body that is unfamiliar and perhaps unreliable, or what men will make of the changes. The good news is that for both transitional phases, most women find their equilibrium as the changes become complete and they adapt to the altered body. Sally needed to self-talk her way toward equilibrium.

Voice Mapping

"Older women should and can look great."

Again, popular expectations pressure us, telling us that even if young, underweight, and gorgeous is the ideal, you can be *older*, underweight, and gorgeous. Advertisers are boldly, bravely forging new ground, it's suggested, by showing some older women (great bones, silvery hair, and a few charming wrinkles) modeling Gap jackets or Eileen Fisher pants. The late Diana Vreeland was applauded for having taken her "ugly" face (as one of her contemporaries labeled it) and creating an iconoclastic beauty.

However, the natural, unreconstructed older women walking among us get our scorn. If you have the opportunity to take ten years off your appearance through cosmetic surgery, nonsurgical procedures, dieting, and exercise, and you haven't done so, what's wrong with you? Don't you care? Are you lazy? Are you not trying hard enough?

"If I looked great, I could attract a man."

That might sound positive, unless you're ambivalent about meeting a man and potential romantic partner. One woman—highly attractive, somewhat overweight, recently divorced—absolutely could not go out and attempt to meet a new man. She believed, powerfully and overwhelmingly, that she was not pretty enough, not good enough, and that there was only one man in the universe who would ever want her and now that man was gone. Holding that self-image, although she was unhappy and quite lonely, was a self-protective device. (*If I stay out of the arena, there's no chance I'll be rejected; if I enter the arena—by accepting a more realistic appraisal of myself—I'll be terribly vulnerable to being hurt.*)

Reframing

Many women who are no longer in the bloom of youth and were never raving beauties to start with get men.

What is it about them that's working?

This is not a frivolous exercise, or an invitation to brood over how much more successful a friend or coworker seems to be at attracting positive or romantic attention. Try to find a woman or two in your bracket in terms of age, size, marital status, and so on, who seems to be enjoying an active social life, and consider what "other" qualities she emanates. Perhaps those qualities fall in the areas of friendliness, cheerfulness, elan, curiosity, energy, confidence. Men often find a warm, accepting, happy woman highly attractive.

Five years from now, how do I want to think about my body?

Sally said she'd like not to think about it much at all, "Just accept it as a decent body that serves me well, thank God, and assume any man who wants to be with me is not going to run screaming away from my naked self."

That was a mindset that was both sensible and wise. As psychologists we have too often become aware that a woman's embarrassment about her aging body can have dangerous repercussions. She'll avoid medical checkups, for example, or be less than candid in talking to a doctor about bodily concerns.

What do men my age and older look like naked? What do other "real" women my age look like naked?

Even without the opportunity to see the older men and the older women she knew without their clothes on, Sally could appreciate that very few of them had "perfect" bodies.

Movement Strategies

I can learn by deconstructing my looks.

Older women tend either to peer obsessively at themselves in the mirror, hunting up any new wrinkle, or to consider the mirror merely utilitarian, something to glance in as infrequently as possible and only for purposes of applying lipstick. But at a time in which you're overwhelmed with "I look old and terrible," it might be a good strategy to revisit your image in a way that is both more objectively useful and more compassionately supportive. There's probably something about your appearance that you like.

Stand in front of a full-length mirror and take in the whole picture. Then peer into the bathroom medicine chest mirror or a hand-held one, and study your face. The point is to consider, as objectively and compassionately as possible, how you look, what's good about how you look, and what you might be able to and want to change somewhat. You may identify some "flaws," and say, so what? You may identify some that are able to be improved, and then ask yourself what you're willing to do and how hard you're willing to work at it. If changing your diet, working out, and dropping twenty pounds would help, do you want to put in the effort? Or will you say, the hell with it? Either way, you've made a conscious choice. Sally gave it a try: "Good teeth, nice smile, shapely legs. Also, I do have the remnants of a waist, which is nice."

I can try writing a personals ad about me. How much of "me" is what I look like?

Physical attractiveness *is* a component of healthy self-esteem. There's no denying the fact that knowing she looks good helps a woman feel good. Looks matter, from the time a child first starts making social comparisons between herself and her peers, and right on into adulthood. Anytime you perceive yourself as different in appearance from the norm—extremely short, extremely tall, disabled in some physical way, too dark-skinned, kinky hair, large nose—that perception is intimately tied in with self-esteem. Appearance, after all, is the first thing we pick up on, the first basis on which we decide something or other about another person—within seconds. One client struggling with obesity said, "A person who drinks too much or smokes can hide that fact for a few hours, say in a party or another group. But the minute I walk into a room people form a judgment about me, just by how I look."

So it's easy to treat appearance as 99 percent of what we are. But moving on from there, consider recasting the notion of "you," and think about your other assets as a possible dating person. Write a description of yourself, pretending you're writing a personals ad, even if you have no intention of posting it. Try hard.

You may find it surprisingly difficult to describe yourself. Ask some friends to evaluate your list, and maybe they'll add a few charming qualities that didn't occur to you.

I can seek out some professional reimaging advice.

If you really feel your looks no longer fit who you want to be, consider hunting up a personal consultant for an image remake. It might make you happier. It did for Sally; she hired a woman who spent one day with her, reorganizing her wardrobe and suggesting several new clothing purchases to revitalize her looks.

I should indulge myself a little more, the way I used to do when I was younger.

Sally hadn't devoted any real time to herself in years. Suddenly daunted by the emotions involving her sense of herself as a desirable female ("I feel like a neuter"), she was somewhat paralyzed into inaction. One possibility, she thought, might bring her more in touch with her physicality: Start a yoga class to gain greater flexibility and a better posture. But she began also to reintroduce into her routine some self-caring habits she'd abandoned long ago, "just little things, like giving myself regular pedicures. Just because it makes me feel good. It's a pleasant, small indulgence."

The bigger goal with all these action strategies is to consign the matter of your appearance to a lesser position of importance in your mind, as you strive to forge a new kind of life for yourself. Regarding your appearance, consider it objectively, take pleasure in what's appealing about it, change or don't change what's less appealing, and then forget about it. A cartoon in a national magazine shows a woman wearing a giant "lampshade" dog collar, the kind that prevents the animal from chewing on itself to relieve an itch. "It keeps me from obsessing about my body," she tells a friend. Adopt the mental equivalent of the dog collar.

Appearance, body image in particular, occupies a somewhat special position in our self-talk discussions. In the other issues with which women wrestle, and which we're addressing in this book—a love partner, a career, a child—a woman can to a large degree create her own image of rightness, the ideal, or the good-enough-for-me. She may decide about a potential mate, for example, Well, he's not what I'd like as far as A, B, and C, but on X, Y, and Z, he's terrific—and then she may adjust her sights, look at him through different eyes. When it comes to body image, as the experiences in this chapter have demonstrated, one ideal is put forth. Others have defined for us what's "right," and that picture is particular and narrow.

The reframing and movement strategies we have suggested say that appearance does count—both for a woman's sense of self-satisfaction and in the way she may be perceived by the world. But ignore as much as possible the popularly promoted image of the desirable body, and consider what choices you do or do not wish to make to reach your personal good-enough.

11

The Self-Esteem Expectation: "I Believe in Myself"

In her grand rallying cry, "I Am Woman," Helen Reddy sang, "If I have to, I can do anything. . . . I am strong, I am invincible." Accepting a Grammy music award, she thanked God, "because *she* makes everything possible."

That was over thirty years ago. In that time, we seven psychologists have listened to thousands of stories from thousands of women. Most women experience some of the confidence and self-esteem expressed in those words. Most also are quick to point out how and where they come up short. The following statements, from three of our clients, all of whom were leading active lives and leading them well, are not uncommon:

"My goals in life seem trivial compared to other people I know."
"I'd have to say there's nothing noteworthy about me, nothing too special."
"I always think that I should be doing a more terrific job at practically everything."

That last comment reveals a significant difference in the self-perceptions of many men and many women: a man tends to believe he's *better* at a thing he's doing than he actually is; a woman tends to believe she's *less good* than in fact she is. Seeing oneself and one's accomplishments clearly and calling them perfectly acceptable is at the heart of self-esteem, which has been defined as "The experience of being capable of meeting life's challenges and being worthy of happiness." What contributes to such a state has been the subject of research in recent years, much of it concerned with the development of self-esteem in children—how it forms, how it is fostered by parents and the other significant individuals in children's lives. Those findings tell us a lot about ourselves, because the encouragement and the expression of self-esteem in childhood isn't that different from the same in adulthood.

We know that it's not simply a matter of feeling good about oneself, and neither does feeling good about oneself translate into being a good person. Indeed, serial killers and other undesirables often hold themselves in high regard. Or, as the philosopher Bertrand Russell once wrote, "The whole problem with the world is that fools and fanatics are always so certain of themselves, and wiser people so full of doubts." A key concept to remember is that self-esteem doesn't exist apart from the social fabric and the relationships of a woman's life. It is largely through the ongoing interactional aspects of her journey—how others see her, the degree to which she is able to make herself known, the positive feedback she receives (and allows herself to take in)—that she grows in healthy self-esteem.

In the following stories, we look at how old voices and misguided self-talk can interfere with the experience of being capable of meeting life's challenges and being worthy of happiness. Each woman pushed the positives about herself to the far back corner of her mind, while the negatives remained up front, speaking to her loudly and clearly. That tendency often takes root in the earliest years and within the family of origin; it can lead to:

- A lack of appropriate assertiveness
- A sense of paltry accomplishment
- Fear of failing

But the good news is that low or inadequate self-esteem isn't a character flaw. It's a characteristic that is, essentially, learned—and that can be unlearned by seeking out new life experiences, perhaps beginning with the kinds of reframing and strategies we explore in this chapter.

Julia's Story

"Other people are running my life."

Julia, forty-five, admitted that she wasn't an expecially confident person. "I've always been sort of insecure. I guess I never thought I was bright enough or I don't have very good judgment about a lot of things." Nevertheless, she believed she was "a good mother, a good wife." She had married a solid, hard-working man, a man with strong opinions. "Joe is a take-charge guy," she said, "and I've always liked that about him."

Julia came to therapy not to talk about her marriage or about her feelings of insecurity. She had a particular problem for which she wanted help: "My problem is named Michelle. This woman is taking over my life." For the past three years, Michelle had been the office manager for Julia's husband, who owned a small contracting company in the town where they lived. Michelle handled the phones, helped schedule the work crews, did the company billing, and, said Julia, "according to Joe, she's the best manager he ever had." When Joe decided to make minor renovations to the kitchen in his and Julia's home, he sent Michelle around to do preliminary work and to be on the premises when two of his men were installing new cabinets and light fixtures. During that time, Michelle also made suggestions about other possible improvements, such as ripping out a wall in order to create one larger family space. "She went through the house like it was hers," Julia said, "and at first, that sort of startled me." But she didn't mind. "Michelle knows a lot. And she was terrific at talking to the workmen."

That was over a year ago. Since then, Michelle had essentially stayed on. Lately, Julia felt things were going too far. She gave some examples. When the construction work was under way, Joe had given Michelle a key to the house. Julia subsequently never asked for the key back, Joe either forgot about it or didn't think it was important, and Michelle sometimes let herself in when others weren't there. Julia came home one evening to find the blinds in a bedroom had been replaced with Roman shades, a decorating change Michelle had urged but Julia wasn't sure she wanted. On another occasion, Julia returned from her job in a bank to this scene:

"My son and his fiancée, Erin, had come by. Michelle was sitting talking to them and she looked over at me and said something like, 'Oh hi, Erin and I were just arranging to go to this furnishings outlet I know, she can pick up some great stuff for their apartment.' And I thought, now this woman has taken over my future daughter-in-law too."

Before she could come to grips with her Michelle dilemma, Julia needed to explore the roots of her insecurity, and think about why she allowed others—including her devoted husband—to dictate so many circumstances of her life for her.

Voice Mapping

"Everybody else knows better than me."

That was a voice she developed as a child, growing up in a home with two brothers, a dominant father, a sweetly quiescent mother, and the understanding that men were the ones who made the decisions.

Filling out the picture, Julia was never a strong student and not happy in school. She described herself as shy and "slow on the uptake. I could never keep up with the other kids. By the time I thought of what to say, everybody was on to the next thing." Later she learned she may have been hampered by a mild form of dyslexia.

It is not uncommon for children with perceptual or reading problems like dyslexia to think of themselves as slow, or as dumber than other people, even when they may have other significant strengths and talents. That sense of self often carries over long after school days are past. In interviews with celebrities—such as Cher, in discussing her dyslexia—this pattern of negative school experience is often reported.

Julia never doubted that she was loved by her parents; there was nothing abusive or obviously dysfunctional about her family. She simply had no model or support to help her feel comfortable about speaking her piece, no input to teach her. The mirror was not there. This is how life and relationships are structured, she believed; others know better than I, and that's all right. The "others" had been her father, her brothers, her husband; "others" had come to include the particularly self-assured Michelle.

Julia had to buoy up her shaky confidence, and supplant the old voice with an adjusted one that might sound something like this: "Other people may know a lot about a lot of things, but that doesn't mean I know nothing about anything—and it certainly doesn't mean I should have no say in matters that affect me directly."

Reframing

Do I have some investment in being "less than" other people?

The facts were stark: Julia had a woman in the middle of her life who was not a relative or good friend, who was establishing close relationships with her family members, and who had access to her home and apparently believed that she was free to rearrange it. And Julia allowed her to be there. She had no idea what to do about that, what to say to Michelle or, significantly, if she even was entitled to feel uncomfortable about the situation. "I know I should be appreciative, I guess. She does have so many good ideas about houses and furniture, and I certainly don't have any suspicions about anything going on between her and my husband."

The flip side of that argument might be: "Michelle is another person who's willing to run things for me. I'm used to that. And it feels safe. Besides, other people should be *more*, so I have to keep myself *less*." Julia didn't actively perceive herself that way. What moved her reframing along was the question: What am I gaining and what am I losing by leaving the decision making to others?

For her, the first part was easy to answer: somebody who knows more than I do has brought about improvements in my home and helped me out. The second part of the equation was more difficult to define. We suggested she ask herself whether allowing another person so much influence was feeding into her lifelong belief that she was not quite the equal of everybody else. By ceding control, was she losing a degree of trust in her own abilities to construct her life? Was she losing some self-respect, or the respect of people who were important to her? By electing not to be the decision maker, was she hoping to avoid responsibility for possibly being wrong? For Julia, a gentle soul, the bottom line was her uncomfortable impression of being "taken over." She wanted to change the picture.

Movement Strategies

I must learn to stop asking everybody what I should do.

Eleanor Roosevelt once said, "No one can make you feel inferior without your consent." Julia essentially gave her consent by, for one thing, gathering votes from everyone she knew.

It wasn't only her husband that Julia looked to for how to proceed on this or that; it wasn't only the intrusive Michelle. In the course of our talks, it became clear that Julia relied on her friends and her young-adult children when she needed to make up her mind about virtually anything. "Is this a good time to buy a new mattress?" "Should I tell my brother we don't want to go to his house for Thanksgiving dinner this year?" Julia was constantly trying to round up a consensus. This was a tough habit to break, but she resolved to take some small steps—simple strategies such as not calling a girlfriend before she went out to do some comparison shopping, or not seeking a stamp of approval from her sons when she was considering joining a woman's group at the community center.

At one point, at our urging, Julia brought her husband in for a session. This was a macho man; he didn't see the point of therapy. But as we talked, Joe revealed that he was "sort of glad she dragged me in." As a matter of fact, he said, he'd like it if his wife challenged him more. He wouldn't mind if, sometimes, she insisted on having her way or at least spoke up about what she wanted. Somewhat to Julia's surprise, he was extremely validating of her in this manner. She mentioned the business of Michelle's key to the house. "What?" Joe said. "Just tell her to give it back. Or I'll tell her." In a show of brave determination, Julia said she'd take care of it.

Even such simple strategies can feel risky to the woman who's used to gathering group support and a comforting go-ahead before making a move. But the sense of competence that promotes self-esteem builds up little by little with a few reasonable risks taken.

I will seek applause, or social recognition.

Here's one way to do that: develop an expertise that others can enjoy or admire. Or go public with an expertise you already possess.

Like many women with low self-esteem, Julia constructed her life so that she remained largely invisible. She was "a good wife, a good mother," that was it. In fact, however, Julia enjoyed a pastime at which she was quite skilled. An accomplished seamstress, for years she had sewn almost all her mother's and her own clothes. We asked her if there was a way she might bring that talent out into the light of day, and she immediately had an idea. "I saw a pattern for making large, stuffed toy bears, and I thought how cute they'd look if you sewed them in rose velvet, maybe with white lace collars. I could make some for the fund-raising fair at church." Julia made half a dozen velvet bears. They were hugely admired at the fair. All the bears sold. Julia was thrilled.

We know that *being* good at something helps children *feel* good about themselves; it works that way in adulthood too. Then there's everything to be said for seeking a little applause. It's a wonderful, self-esteem building strategy to go public with your gifts, as small as you may think they are. Applause—the kind of affirmation that can come from taking a personal talent and delivering it to the world—is something everybody wants.

I need to set boundaries that are more comfortable for me.
This matter of establishing psychological or emotional boundaries is one that threads through so many of the issues we address in this book, and it's one that presents a special challenge for the woman who feels perpetually "less than" everybody else. The simple act of saying, "No, I'm sorry, I will not be able to . . . [run the clothing drive this year, walk your dog while you're away, put up your sister for the weekend]" can create feelings of intense anxiety, primarily over the fear of making someone angry. But boundaries have to do, in part, with how a woman allows others to treat her. For Julia, key questions in the future would be:

- Am I doing something that I don't want to do?
- Is something happening that I don't want to happen?
- Is it in my power to change that?

Never an assertive individual, especially when compelled to deal with a forceful personality like Michelle, Julia nevertheless found the strength to ask that the spare house key—that highly symbolic demonstration of how her life had been "taken over"—be returned. That was a major step, and the beginning of further efforts to reclaim her territory.

Amy's Story

"I didn't get very far in life."

Amy, thirty-three, had done well for herself. It didn't seem so to her, however. Her family history had not been kind to her. With his first wife, Amy's father had three children, two sons and a daughter. When those children were in their late teens, he married for the second time, and he and his new wife produced Amy. The older children lived with the family. Amy's mother died when Amy was six, and from that time on she was essentially raised by her half-siblings. As a child, she said, "lots of times I felt like a fish out of water in that bunch. Like the alien kid."

She left as early as she could, finding a job immediately after high school. Although she considered herself a working woman, "not a big career person," she went on to take extensive computer training and at the time we met, was holding down an excellent job in a management placement firm. And Amy had been quite purposeful in her choice of employment; it was important for her to have a job where she left at six, closed the door, and had her own time. She had recently bought a small condo, which she loved.

In fact, Amy was tough, a self-contained little dynamo. But over the years, she had taken another path from that followed by her brothers and sister. All three married (their spouses were equally ambitious, with good jobs), had children, and lived in large houses in the suburbs. And compared to her siblings, Amy felt inferior. Actually, she still considered herself the fish out of water: she had no husband, no kids, no house in the suburbs, no profession. Looking at her life, she saw not much; she thought she was "ordinary."

That was the image she projected and how she expected the world to see her as well. Amy offered a list of things that she was *not*: "I'm not very verbal," she said. "I'm not a very giving person." She had few friends, which bothered her, although it became clear that her behaviors effectively ensured that Amy remained something of a loner and an outsider. The women at her job often went out after work together and didn't ask her; she never thought she might invite herself along. Her issues seemed to include this one: how do you acquire self-esteem if you're just an ordinary, regular Jane?

Voice Mapping

"My siblings, especially my brothers, are the success story in this family."

Amy's background sent her this message: girls don't amount to much, while boys are valued and favored. Often, that scenario occurs in a family with a stern, ruling-the-roost father and a self-effacing mother who lacks confidence. Amy's story was slightly different. Her brothers and sister were all articulate and quick-witted. There was a lot of repartee flying around the kitchen table in the evenings, joshing and one-upmanship, and Amy was routinely made fun of and belittled. One brother, the middle child of the older threesome, was openly quite mean to her, and not in an affectionate or teasing way. For reasons she could never understand, her father, when he was home, encouraged this behavior. Far from coming to her defense, he seemed to take away the impression that his older children were superior specimens, and he too was frequently harshly critical of Amy.

To a real extent, Amy had been compelled to parent herself, to grow up fast. Many women who have similarly been on their own for a long time and starting from a young age often are lacking in self-esteem. Forced to assume caretaking responsibilities for which she is not developmentally capable, the child reaches maturity under an aura of inadequacy. Her challenge, then, is to build up a store of positive self-feelings, to fill in some missing pieces from the past.

"Someone who never went to college isn't worth very much."

It's not uncommon for a woman to base her self-worth on the level of her education—as if being better educated makes one a better person. And as more and more women take the college path, the sense of inadequacy becomes stronger in some non-college-educated women, like Amy.

Reframing

Adopt a new mindset: No one is going to like me better than I like myself. And no one will treat me better than I treat myself.

There's a starting point, a reframing validation that empowers a woman to bring about change. It's in her hands, not everyone else's. Although Amy functioned well, she experienced bouts of depression; she wished to maintain a relationship with her siblings, her only family, but on a more equal footing, and she hoped to establish closer friendships. But she'd never learned to value herself or even to like herself much.

For a woman who grew up being belittled and criticized, it can be tremendously difficult to develop a dose of healthy narcissism. Liking herself, treating herself well, may feel like too much selfishness or egotism and not enough self-sacrificing. But if it's hard to like *herself*, she can surely find something to like about what she has done or can do.

What accomplishments can I point to with pride?

In our talks, we struggled to look for, first, what Amy was good at—and then, what she actually valued. And sadly, it took a long time for her to find anything at all. To a large degree, she continued to hang her self-esteem on the number of labels she could pin on herself, and they weren't many—not even "career woman," just a woman with a job.

Eventually, Amy said she was pretty pleased about one thing. "My boss is a difficult, demanding, impossible guy," she said. "I've been working for him for three years now, and nobody before ever lasted in this job longer than six months. And you know what? If I left for another job, whatever situation I land in I'm pretty sure I could handle it, because in some ways it couldn't be tougher than this one."

In fact, there was a great deal more Amy could look at with a sense of pride; the very accomplishments that she tended to minimize could be considered rather impressive. It took her a while to reframe in this way, but Amy came to appreciate these realities about her life. "I support myself. I bought an apartment, without the luxury of two salaries as my brothers and sister have. I made the decision myself, without consulting anyone else. I have the freedom and the curiosity to travel, and I can spend my money however I want. Not bad!"

The point is, self-esteem doesn't require the possession of many labels, unique talents, or high levels of mastery. Self-esteem can be built around ordinary, everyday accomplishments. Consider this: Can you point with satisfaction to something you've done? About what can you say, "That was pretty good"? What skills or accomplishments do you value in yourself, even if many women you know share them as well (such as raising a decent child, balancing a checkbook, putting a home-cooked meal on the table every evening)?

One client who went through our "point with pride" exercise said with a shy smile, "Well, I do feel quietly proud that I painted the living room and bedroom ceilings in my apartment without getting paint on the floor." Why wouldn't she feel quietly proud?

Movement Strategies

I can find ways to talk to my relatives with a new voice.
Are they still treating me as if I haven't amounted to much?

Returning to the scene of childhood—or more accurately, being in the company of the individuals who peopled that scene—can feel as if nothing is much different at all. One client who grew up in the kind of atmosphere we've described, with critical and fault-finding relatives, said that when she returns for a visit, "I feel like Alice just after she's swallowed the 'Drink Me!' bottle, ten inches high. After I leave, I resume my normal adult size."

Changing the old dance between you and those significant people in your life, the ones who are part of the picture of your low self-esteem, isn't easy. Amy thought her siblings were "nasty" to her, always had been, and always would be. During holiday visits, she expected to be treated like "the alien" of old, and in small ways, she was. She needed to learn how to present the new, evolved Amy to her brothers and sister. In fact, once she started admiring herself a bit more, she was able for one thing to view her siblings less accusingly. Consequently, she no longer projected the vibe of a little girl just waiting for the next verbal put-down to come her way. They, in turn, gradually become more responsive and even more respectful toward her.

I can seek out positive feedback.

The question is this: How can you get the esteem-building input now that you missed as a child? Or is the case closed? Young children grow in self-esteem when a parent or other significant adults in their lives identify and support their unique qualities, strengths, and talents. If you were short-changed back then, if you failed because of critical parents, dismissive teachers, or for whatever reason to receive such validation, seek it for yourself now. Build a new repertoire. Talk to two of your closest friends, and ask what it is they like about you, what they value or admire.

I need to present myself with more confidence to the people around me.

One element that contributes enormously to healthy self-esteem is a woman's (or a child's) sense that she's socially accepted. She doesn't have to be the most popular one in the crowd, but she does know that the people with whom she spends some or much of her time like her, respect her, maybe even enjoy her company.

Amy didn't allow herself to believe any of that. She quietly did her job, and did it extremely well—and stopped there. She wished she had more friends, and wished she could feel more at ease around her coworkers. She needed to hear how she probably sounded to others, and then find the courage to take small social risks.

Think about how you talk, or don't talk, when you're out in the world—in the office, at a community or school meeting, in a mixed group at a party, even when you run into an acquaintance at the store. Can you present yourself with a more assured tone, knowing that sending out a quiet aura of self-respect invites respect from others?

If you're constantly putting yourself down or remaining silent out of a belief that what you have to say isn't so important, you reinforce and send yourself a message that deflates your self-esteem. Because no one will treat you better than you treat yourself, you may be setting up a self-fulfilling prophecy. Amy took these ideas to heart, and gradually began to edge her way into the social life at her office. One day, a big day, she asked two women who were heading out after work if they felt like joining her for a glass of wine at the nearby restaurant. To her delight, they said, "Great idea, let's go."

That can do more to boost a woman's self-esteem than anything—to know it is within her power to obtain a desired response
from others, to realize that she is liked and worthy of being liked.

Valerie's Story

"I feel like a fraud."

Since she was a young child, Valerie, twenty-nine, had been en-
tranced by all aspects of the arts. She was a voracious reader, she
loved the theater, and by the time she entered college she had
resolved to become a writer. A small incident in a freshman class
proved to be a marker of Valerie's approach to her experiences over
the next ten years of her life. She described it. "We had an assignment
to write a critique of *David Copperfield*. I was making the point that
Dickens painted such vivid word portraits, his characters become the
ultimate personification of a certain idea or quality. So you can refer
to someone you know as 'a real Rosa Dartle type,' and anyone who
likes Dickens knows what you're talking about. When I got the paper
back, the professor had written in the margin, 'Have you ever actually called someone a real Rosa Dartle? Or known anyone who did?'"

Valerie was mortified. No, she never had used the term; she was
just "showing off, trying to sound profound, not thinking the thing
through. What I wrote was totally fake." In fact, that was about the
only bone the professor had to pick. Valerie received an A minus on
her overall essay. But the thing that burned in her mind was that
"fake" observation.

When we talked, Valerie had been in graduate school for several
years, working toward a doctorate in English literature. She hoped
to find a university teaching position and continue her fiction writing, the passion that drove her. Two circumstances were troubling
her. "I can't settle on a thesis topic. The first one I worked up I had
approved by my adviser, but then I began to think it was going to
be more than I could handle. I came up with another idea and my
adviser thought it was excellent, but that one too just doesn't feel
right to me now. So many other people have done work in the field,
I don't see how I could add anything really substantial."

Her adviser was losing patience and telling her it was time to fish or cut bait, which was the same message she'd been hearing from her writers group. "We've been meeting for the last three years," Valerie said, "we read each others' works-in-progress and give suggestions. We're critically supportive of each other, or maybe that's supportively critical. Now I have two stories that everybody in the group says are terrific, ready to go. Publishable. But I just haven't felt okay about sending them out. I know they can be better."

Actually, there was a third event that bothered her, and that was the one to persuade her to seek some counseling. Valerie and Katherine, her younger sister (by five years), had had a major blowup over a troublesome situation. Their widowed father, a man in his sixties, had been hospitalized for two weeks following surgery. He was now on the mend, but both sisters felt his post-surgery treatment in the hospital had been appalling, and actually delayed his recovery and contributed to a depression that he still fought. They decided to write a letter of complaint to the hospital administrator; Katherine drew up the letter and Valerie was to review it. Valerie wasn't entirely happy with the letter; then she wasn't happy with her redrafts; the letter never got sent. It had been five months since their father left the hospital.

Katherine was disgusted with her. "Kat basically said to me, 'What the hell is your problem? You're never satisfied with anything, you always think you can do better than everybody else, why don't you try to join the real world?'" But Valerie thought her sister had it backward. "I don't think I can do better than anybody. I just think I'm not as good as I should be. And if a thing isn't perfect, it's no good at all."

She was a procrastinator. She had the sense of "spinning my wheels, I should have finished up my degree long ago." Nearing thirty, Valerie wanted to uncover the reasons why she seemed to have so much trouble moving forward.

Voice Mapping

"Whatever I'm doing, it should be better."

Tell us a little about your family, we asked, what it was like for you growing up, and an interesting and not unusual picture emerged. The two sisters assumed separate roles over the course of childhood. Valerie was the serious one, the ace student. Katherine was the pretty one, the social butterfly. Probably without any such aim, their mother and father tended to reinforce those identities: "Dad used to refer to me as 'our little scholar,' 'the brains of the family,' things like that. They were always extremely proud of how well I did in school. Actually, by the time I was a preteen, I figured they were trying to make me feel better because Kat was the acknowledged beauty."

Valerie was by no means unattractive. However, when she showed us a recent photo of herself and her sister, it was possible to appreciate her sense of differentness. Katherine was strikingly lovely, with a vivacious air that came across even in a snapshot.

Like it or not, looks do matter in terms of self-worth. In an earlier chapter, we've talked about how a woman might strike a balance between making appropriate efforts to develop pride and confidence in her physical self and, on the other hand, being caught up in unhealthy obsessions from media images, fear of aging, or old voices from the past. Valerie wasn't unhappy about her appearance. But she did hold herself to extremely high standards as the grown-up "little scholar," the identity on which her childhood sense of self rested. Anything she felt was below the top rung just wasn't good enough.

"I have to be the perfect brain in order to be loved."

That was an internalized belief: Dad, and now everyone else, would only love her if she continued being the little scholar. The message was probably not true, but Valerie lived her life as if it were. She needed to challenge those powerful voices.

Reframing

Consider this: To whom am I comparing myself? Or to what standard?

For her, the standard of comparison was an idealized self-image. For another woman who's sharply critical of her achievements, the comparison may be with the one or two or three peers who are after the same goals and seem to be winning. For another, the standard may be a composite of all the best traits of every woman she knows.

Many women see only the strengths, not the weaknesses, of the women around them and individuals they read about in the media. Any such means of comparison do little for her self-esteem.

Studies have demonstrated that the child who engages in a competitive activity—for example, a sport involving highly developed individual skills, such as gymnastics—may be an excellent performer and yet feel anything but excellent. And that's because she looks around at the relatively tiny group of elite gymnasts with whom she practices or against whom she competes, ranks herself (perhaps accurately) as more toward the bottom than the top within that population, and so deems herself inferior. The fact that among all the kids in the world who take part in gymnastics she'd clearly stand out as a star is not on her radar screen.

It's also true that a woman who perpetually pooh-poohs her accomplishments often looks way above her—to the finished product, so to speak—for her standard of comparison. For example, one client who was in the early stages of pursuing a career in industrial psychology considered two older, seasoned women her informal mentors and role models. But paradoxically, they didn't make her feel more confident about her own chances, because both were "brilliant," "totally self-assured," "overachievers"—everything she believed she wasn't and would never be. What she failed to consider was that each probably reached her current success only after struggle, practice, and many years of work. And that perhaps if she was in the skin of either of those overachieving women, she'd experience some of the anxieties and worries she imagined each was immune to.

Put a stopper on the internal voice that says, "If they only knew the truth about me. . . ." Or "Well, they don't have the whole story. If they did have the whole story, they'd find out that the real me is not so hot."

This was a voice that contributed to Valerie's experience of being stuck, not moving forward. She acknowledged that she took every less-than-perfect performance as a revelation of her inadequacy. Why had she written that "fake" comment in her school essay? Her professor surely realized that she was just "trying to sound profound." If she pursued the new thesis topic and finally wrote the thing, it would eventually become clear to anybody who read it that she wasn't up to the job.

Years ago psychologist Pauline Clance described "the imposter syndrome" so common among high-achieving women, who have a nagging fear that they really don't deserve the accolades and they'll be found out and embarrassed. Instead of accepting the probability that an effort turned out *well* because of her own abilities and hard work, the woman who feels she's an imposter comes up with a raft of alternate explanations: that was just dumb luck, or good timing, or knowing the right people, or the thing wasn't so difficult in the first place—and she'd certainly never be able to pull off that success a second time. When her efforts *don't* turn out so well, she's got an answer for that too: "I did badly because I'm no good."

These feelings are not unusual, based on our socialization. But we need to overcome them. If a woman attributes her successful outcome to what are called "unstable external causes" (it was luck, knowing the right people, good timing), she can build her self-esteem voice by reframing those beliefs—for example, "Well, it's not luck actually, I worked hard to get here." "Stable internal causes" include her own hard work and intelligence, but also such negative messages as "I did well because it wasn't so difficult in the first place." She needs to reframe by telling herself that the task wasn't so easy, or "Maybe it wasn't difficult, but I still can do the hard stuff well too." Or "I didn't do my best that time but it was a pretty good job anyway."

Movement Strategies

I need to stick with it.

When you begin a project, do you too quickly decide, "This is never going to be great, so why bother?" Would it be wise to make yourself carry on anyway, and at least hope for the best? This is a huge stumbling block for the woman who puts high demands on herself. It was a major difficulty Valerie had to conquer, and she was able to see that while she sometimes got off to a good start, following through to a logical conclusion hung her up. Following through would mean telling herself she'd done well, or good enough, and that was a voice she still hadn't developed for herself. Valerie had a habit of quitting shortly before she got to the payoff.

Interestingly, she kept mulling over that unfinished letter to the hospital administrator, wondering if some aspect of her relationship with her sister had been involved in how it all played out. She decided it wasn't anything to do with sibling rivalry; it was just that she, Valerie, was the writer, the letter had to be written perfectly, and she felt she could never reach perfection. So she took one small but important movement strategy, one step toward breaking an old, self-defeating habit: even though months had passed, she rewrote the letter and mailed it off.

I can focus a little less on mastery and a little more on enjoyment.

Yes, mastery—being good at a thing—can contribute hugely to increased self-esteem. But the woman who feels like a fraud, who considers even her fine achievements the result of some quirk of fate or circumstance and not of her own commitment and talents, might need to try simply to take more pleasure and satisfaction from the process of doing what she's doing.

I will seek out realistic feedback.

Think about what you're hearing from people you know and trust. How do they value or judge your efforts? Can you believe what they're telling you?

Feedback is an important ingredient in building self-esteem. But if what you're getting is all sunny news, all the time, it doesn't feel reliable. Clinical work with children is telling in this regard. The child who receives endless praise from her parents for every slight effort comes, over time, not to trust any of it. She fails to gain what she herself senses is a true barometer against which to make an adequate assessment of her self-worth.

So feedback must be realistic. But women so often don't *internalize* the sense of having done something well or of being on the right track, even when ample, reliable proof from the outside world says that such is the case. Valerie, for example, had a couple of great resources in her corner. Presumably, her graduate adviser was offering a realistic appraisal of her proposed thesis topics; he told her the ideas were valid and she was capable of the work. Certainly, that highly supportive writers group had no interest in steering her down a wrong path; they told her her stories were good enough to send out into the world and see what happened. The hard part for

Valerie was overcoming her inability to *take in* those positive messages. People she trusted were validating her work; she needed to believe it.

Here is where the kind of self-talk group sessions we suggest at the end of this book can be invaluable. Assume you are with a small coterie of friends or friendly acquaintances. You have expressed the stated wish to talk—openly, honestly, and caringly—about issues on each others' minds. You know you are in a safe place, with individuals who will neither tell you simply what they think you want to hear, nor bring in a negative agenda that will put you on the attack. Within that group, seek and expect to receive honest feedback.

I should realize that sometimes I may take a blow to my self-esteem, and I won't be destroyed by it.

At the beginning of this chapter, we noted that low self-esteem isn't a character flaw; rather, it's a characteristic that's learned through life experiences, and that can be unlearned by building a base of new, better, validating experiences. It would be delightful if the base remained firm as a rock, forever in place. Sometimes, however, it will take a hit; for a while you may feel on shaky ground again. But you are simply in a time of transition, not a permanent state. Think of what you need to do to get over the hump and regain a good sense of yourself.

The woman with an adequate supply of self-esteem perceives herself as a basically capable human being who can handle what comes at her with some degree of courage, grace, good judgment, and strength. She trusts that her efforts are, overall, good enough. Whether it's on the job, or at mothering, or in being a valued friend, or in pursuing a hobby with passion and talent, she's able to say, "I've persevered and I've done well. I'm capable of meeting life's challenges and I'm worthy of happiness."

12

Self-Talk among Friends:
Beginning the Conversation

From the dialogue that's taken place over the preceding chapters, some hopeful and encouraging themes have emerged. Women have enormous psychological and emotional strengths. Indeed, being "stuck" in the ways that our clients have described emerges most often from values and characteristics that are admirable and humane: the instinct to care for others, the capacity for intimacy and connection, the wish to engage in honest communication, the ability to have a lot on our plates and see to it all.

Striving for the best—even the high bar, popularly promoted expectation of the twenty-first-century woman—is perfectly fine, as long as the effort does not lead a woman to a deeply, perpetually dissatisfied sense of her self, her goals, and her accomplishments.

There are many paths to a fruitful life; multiple truths; countless ways to grow, actualize, cope, adapt, and contribute. Among those paths, for many women, will be the need sooner or later to confront a personal crisis—illness, the death of a loved one, financial loss, betrayal. Indeed, none of us gets to live long without facing painful events at some stage of the journey. How a woman meets the challenge has much to do with her individual experience, with the presence or absence of support in her life, and with any number of other factors.

What we have learned from our work with thousands of women, however, is that times of upheaval or emergency can lead to wondrous new strengths, deeper insight, greater compassion. Progress isn't always so obvious; there may be one step back for every two steps forward. But like pruning the limb of a tree makes the plant stronger and enables new shoots to emerge, coming through a crisis—and dealing with the trauma it may produce—is another way to grow. And to grow according to your own voice.

As psychologists, we wouldn't say: Now believe this. Rather, we hope, our message throughout this book has been: Stop believing that all the voices you have allowed to guide you know *your* truth. Explore your needs and wishes through self-talk, separate the external roadblocks or dead ends that you cannot change from the internal barriers that you can, and come closer to understanding and finding your own voice.

And then, begin the conversation.

From Self-Talk to Group Talk

After reading about the women we have introduced in the previous chapters, you surely have some feelings about the challenges they faced, and about their efforts to reframe their perceptions and put new strategies into effect. Perhaps now you think it would be productive to share those feelings with other women you know. That might be two close and trusted friends, or a dozen or more acquaintances you'd like to gather together and get to know better. Maybe you already belong to a book club, a sewing sorority ("Hand Job," "Stitch and Bitch"), a woman's service organization, a "Wine and Whine" group, or your company's women's softball team, and you have a ready-made assemblage that might be expanded in this added direction. Or, consider rounding up several women from among the mothers in your children's school or playgroup. Start a brown bag lunch bunch at work. Create a self-talk chatroom on the Internet, if you're too pressed for time to meet in person.

If this sounds like something you're ready for, if you are interested in exploring the possibility of a self-talk group, here are some suggestions:

- Decide at the outset how many weeks your group will meet. At the end of that period you may or may not agree to continue.
- Find a comfortable setting for your meetings, one that will ensure privacy and few interruptions. The right setting enhances the process you're embarking on.

- Use *Finding Your Voice* as the launching pad for your discussion. If you're starting a new group, suggest that the members read the book before you begin.
- You may decide to focus on it chapter by chapter, or pick the issue of most interest or relevance to you and your companions. Groups work best with some structure, at least initially. So in the begining, start with one topic and see where it goes.
- Decide if you would like at first to take up less intimate issues, such as parenting or money, and save the discussion of sex for later. Or you may decide you don't want to talk about some of the topics at all. It's important that all members feel safe.
- You may want to use one of the women's lives discussed in the chapter you select, or introduce your own experiences. The discussions may take various directions. See what works for you and your group.
- Accept different styles and solutions; embrace diversity.
- Seek cooperation, discourage competition.
- Avoid groupthink. Remember, the goal is not consensual voices, but helping one another overcome the "shoulds" of a woman's life so each finds her own individual voice.
- Reduce distractions. Try to adhere to a beginning and ending time; agree that cell phones will be turned off or answering machines will handle calls, as we have done throughout our own process of writing this book.
- Not everyone may elect to continue in the group; don't let that dissuade the others from continuing.
- Inevitably, some conflict will arise. Meet conflict with an attitude of acceptance that says, "we agree to differ." Trust, intimacy, and comfort grow over time.
- Pledge confidentiality to each other. Each woman is free beyond the group to talk about her own life experiences, but she is not free to discuss the details she has heard from others within the group.
- Groups frequently have questions. Visit our Web site if you feel a need to consult with us.

In this next section we offer some chapter-by-chapter questions to facilitate your dialogue. See where they lead you.

The Friendship Expectation:
"I've Always Got My Girlfriends"

A woman's friends can be at times her greatest joy, and at times the source of pain, disappointment, and anger. There are many reasons. We expect a lot from a woman friend, such as that she will always know what we think and what we need. When friends drift out of our lives, it's not easy to find new ones; establishing solid, intimate friendships gets harder as time goes on. And then, in the midst of busy family and career lives, keeping up with girlfriends gets dropped to the bottom of the list.

Questions for discussion:

- What do you look for in a friend? How would you identify a good friend?
- There are a couple of aspects of my life that I wouldn't think of telling anybody I know, even my best friend; I'd only feel comfortable talking to a stranger. Is that unusual?
- When your life changes dramatically—because of divorce, or marriage—do your friendships shift? Are the same women going to be there for you in the same way?
- The woman I trusted more than anybody just disappeared when I was going through a bad time. Can I ever feel really close to her again?
- Can your mother be your best friend? Or your sister?
- Do my gay guy friends count as "girlfriends"?

The Dating Expectation: "I Can Find
the Perfect Partner (but If I Don't,
I'll Be Just Fine without One)"

Relationships are harder than ever to bring about, it seems. Women have their long shopping lists of expectations (tall, dark, handsome, graduate degrees, good job, good money-earning potential, and on and on). Men have their notorious fear of commitment. Who has time to find a partner and develop a relationship, anyway, working the hours we do? And yet as much as ever, women want to find love and a life's partner. Some, still, feel they're nothing much without a man.

Questions for discussion:

- Are women too picky these days? Or is it that our potential romantic partners are really not a good match for us?
- Where and when does a woman compromise, and say, "He's not great but he's good enough?" Should she ever?
- Does every heterosexual woman really need a man? Can she really have a full, happy, satisfying life without one?
- How come some women (not necessarily gorgeous, rich, brilliant, or anything else) always find guys? What do they have, or know?
- In a love relationship, do women look for the kind of emotional intimacy that they're going to get only from their good girl-friends? Are they thus dooming themselves to disappointment?

The Sex Expectation:
"I'm Healthily, Happily, Wildly Sexual"

Sex isn't so easy, as it turns out. Sometimes a woman wants more sex than her partner does; sometimes it's the other way around. One half of American women consider themselves sexually dysfunctional. Middle-aged, middle-income women are the fastest growing group contracting HIV and AIDS infections, usually from sex with a male partner who refuses to use a condom. Young women are at risk for chlamydia, a sexually transmitted disease that can cause sterility.

Questions for discussion:

- Is pornography a harmless, useful aid in increasing sexual interest or libido? Is liking pornography more acceptable in men and not so acceptable for women?
- Self-arousal to orgasm—is it worth the time and effort?
- If you had a sexual relationship with another woman in college, is it common to still feel confused about that?

- Is it normal to fantasize about taking another sexual partner? When can that become dangerous?
- Should I worry if my partner doesn't want me to see what he or she is up to on the Internet?
- Can I become assertive enough to demand my partner use a condom and talk about HIV, AIDS, and sexually transmitted diseases?

The Marriage Expectation: "I Can Achieve the Marriage I Want (but If I Don't, I'll End the Marriage)"

We no longer have to marry for many of the reasons of a past age— for financial support, or because of social convention, or in order to have children. But despite our independence and freedom of choice, marriage is difficult and not all that satisfying for many women. Often, she's grown and moved on in one way or another, and he has not. And if divorce is more acceptable than it once was, it's still a scary prospect.

Questions for discussion:

- Why do I feel it's up to me to make the marriage "work"? What about him?
- Is it truly possible to feel contented, even happy, within a marriage that's gone stale? A marriage that's not downright awful, but that's no fun at all?
- How can you know if you'd be better off living a single life once again?
- Does couples therapy help? What if that's the last thing he'd ever consider?
- In the absence of physical abuse, alcoholism, or other devastating problems, is staying together always better for the children?
- Do you feel different about staying in a marriage if you have children? Or if you don't?

The Child-Rearing Expectation: "I'm Raising a Perfect Child, and Loving Every Minute of It"

In some ways, it's harder than ever to do a good job at parenting: kids grow up fast; they're almost scarily savvy about things like sex. We want to be in charge without being dictatorial or authoritarian, but it's hard to figure out the right boundaries to draw. Plus, with all the incredible advantages children enjoy these days, they should turn out just right. When it looks like maybe they're not, a woman wonders what she's done wrong.

Questions for discussion:

- Do kids learn what they need to know about sex in school and from their peers? How can a mother have the sex talk without her child getting embarrassed?
- Are we all raising a generation of indulged children who feel entitled to the world?
- Do you ever wonder if you would have enjoyed some things more if you hadn't had children? Do you think about what you gave up?
- What do we really want for our kids?
- What are the really important things children need from their mothers in today's world? How can we provide them?
- How is it that my child is less respectful to me than I ever dared to be with my own mother?
- What do you do when you hear your mother's voice coming out of your mouth?

The Work Expectation: "I'm Happy with My Career (or Happy without One)"

Choose to be a working mother or a stay-at-home mother, you can't win either way. The woman leaving her child with the nanny or in daycare feels guilty; the woman at home with her child feels defensive. Aside from child-raising pressures, careers often aren't as fulfilling as we anticipated they would be. Sometimes that's because a woman expects coworkers to be like family. Often, it's because the workplace is still designed for men.

Questions for discussion:

- Why do mothers feel terrible about leaving their kids to go to work, while fathers don't?
- Based on your experiences, what would you tell your daughter now about the work world and choosing a career? If you had to start over again, how would you do it differently?
- In a business meeting, do men really want to listen to women give their opinions?
- Somebody handed you a million dollars. Would you still want to work? At what?
- How much of my self-image, and my self-respect, is tied into my job?

The Money Expectation: "I Have My Financial Life Well in Hand"

Money matters—thinking about money, investing it, making plans with it—still make women break out in a cold sweat. Maybe that's because it seems, even now, not very feminine to deal with this important life resource. Maybe it helps us feel more secure when somebody else handles it. Besides, is it okay to spend money on everybody else but not ourselves? Or okay to spend on ourselves when we're feeling lonely, worried, or unloved? The trouble is, we have a hard time talking about all this, because money (and all it represents) is perhaps the last great taboo.

Questions for discussion:
- Can money ever be a substitute for love?
- Are women at a disadvantage because, typically, unlike boys we were never encouraged to get smart about economics, mathematics, finances?
- When I buy some new clothes for myself, I bury the shopping bag in the closet for a few days and don't tell my partner about it. Why do I do that?

- If a wife earns more than her husband, what is the impact on their relationship? Are there special strains because we live in a society that still assumes husbands will earn more than wives?
- In a committed relationship, should each partner know all the details about the other's money matters?

The Balancing Act Expectation: "I'm Running My Life, It's Not Running Me"

Yeah, your life is running you. The overloaded woman is working a job, taking care of the kids and maybe the older generation too, seeing to the housekeeping—and way at the bottom of her list is time for herself. Stress is a factor in the modern woman's life that must be addressed. The unequal division of family responsibilities between husband and wife is another one that should be addressed. But that's difficult to do, because we're all operating under the assumption that she manages the home and kids, and he helps her out.

Questions for discussion:

- How do you divide up household chores 50–50, and make it stick?
- Why is it so hard for me to say no to taking on one more task, when I know I should in order to protect my well-being?
- Suppose you took off for a weekend all by yourself. What would happen on the home front?
- What's the one thing you'd like your partner to understand about you and the balancing act you're trying to achieve?
- What is your surefire way to feel less tense and stressed?

The Appearance Expectation: "I Love My Body, Just as It Is"

We don't love our bodies at all, even the gorgeous among us. We wish to be taller, thinner, smoother-skinned, and anything but looking the way we do actually look. The aging body is a source of depression for many women, who feel wrinkles and crepey skin make them undesirable love partners.

Questions for discussion:

- Botox, collagen injections, plastic surgery—if you could afford them, would you go for it? Are these possibilities just putting more pressure on women to reach for the impossible?
- What messages did we receive about our bodies when we were children?
- What ideal image do you think you should achieve? And if you managed to get there, how do you think your life will change?
- How about those super-toned gym nuts all over the place? Do we hate them? Envy them? Feel superior? Am I one of them?
- Why is it so hard to accept a compliment about one's appearance?

The Self-Esteem Expectation: "I Believe in Myself"

Accomplished, productive, nurturing women so often say they don't have a great deal of self-esteem at all. Always, there's the thing they could have done better, the second-guessing, the sneaking suspicion that they're something of a fraud. And when an effort does come out well, they chalk up their success to other factors besides their own abilities. We women hold ourselves to very high standards, and see ourselves as falling short of the mark.

Questions for discussion:

- I procrastinate, because I always think I need more time or help or information before I can do the job right. What's going on there?
- Is it a good idea to want a little praise or recognition when I have done a job right?
- If there's nothing rarified or unusual about you, can you be both ordinary and unique?

- How does low self-esteem start? Does it have to do mostly with old, damaging family messages?
- I didn't grow up with a lot of self-esteem. Is it too late to get some now?
- How can I shut off my own mother's critical messages in my head?

Finding Your Voice has been a group-talk project from the start.

We are seven psychologists, each of whom had been elected president of a national professional organization. We didn't know each other all that well at first. But the conversations began, and continued, and we came to realize that in our experiences—as professional women, as wives, mothers, daughters, friends—there was much we wanted to share. And so this book took shape.

You'd assume that seven leaders working together would be entirely too competitive to collaborate. But we tolerated each other's idiosyncracies—like the one who doesn't read her e-mail and the one who urged us all to swim in the algae-filled pond near her home. We accepted that not all would be able to make every meeting we scheduled. We trusted each other, nurtured each other, and supported each other through all the crises that can occur over five years in the lives of seven women with families.

We learned a lot—for one thing, what a good clinician each of us is, a professional validation we hadn't expected. We resolved conflict. Thinking about it in retrospect, however, we realized there had been almost none, because we allowed each to lead with her strength and relied on each other's resources. Talking it over now, we can name each other's strengths, just as each is able to own her own strengths and acknowledge her weaknesses.

Here's the best payoff. We really like each other, and find in our developing relationships great comfort, stimulation, and excitement. We hope that's a payoff you will discover from your own group talk.

Support works to keep women healthy. As you're exploring your reframing and movement strategies, the encouragement of others can help you to know yourself better and perhaps acquire a little cheering section behind your efforts at reinventing aspects of your life. And as you find points of connection with other women, celebrate your differences, and practice communication skills in real relationships, you develop strength and resilience. Listening to other women's stories can expand your awareness of the cultural climate we live in. It will enable you to feel a little less isolated, a little more whole.

Index

About the Authors

Dorothy W. Cantor, Psy.D., is a psychologist who has been practicing for over twenty-five years in Westfield, New Jersey, since earning her doctorate at the Graduate School of Applied and Professional Psychology, Rutgers University. She served as president of the American Psychological Association in 1996, and is currently president of the American Psychological Foundation. She is the author of five books, including *Women in Power: The Secrets of Leadership*, and *What Do You Want to Do When You Grow Up? Starting the Next Chapter of Your Life*. She has appeared on national television on such programs as the *Today Show* and *Good Morning, America*. She is long married, and has two children and seven grandchildren. Visit her Web site at www.drdorothycantor.com.

Carol D. Goodheart, Ed.D., is a psychologist in Princeton, New Jersey, who has been practicing for twenty-five years since earning her doctorate in Counseling Psychology at Rutgers University. She serves currently as a member of the American Psychological Association Board of Directors, is a past president of Psychologists in Independent Practice, and is a Distinguished Practitioner in the National Academy of Psychology. She is an author and editor of numerous articles and four books, including *Living with Childhood Cancer: A Practical Guide to Help Families Cope*, and the forthcoming *Handbook of Girls' and Women's Psychological Health: Gender and Well-Being across the Life Span*. She is married, has three children and five grandchildren, and a passion for creating gardens.

Sandra Haber, Ph.D., was awarded her doctorate from the Graduate Center, City University of New York, and has practiced psychology in New York City for the past twenty-five years. In 1998, she was the president of the Psychologists in Independent Practice, a division of the American Psychological Association. In addition to coauthoring three books, including *Breast Cancer: A Psychological Treatment Manual*, she has appeared on national television and radio and is frequently interviewed in newspapers and magazines. Video clips and excerpts of her articles may be viewed through her Web site at www.DrHaber.com. Along with her husband, children, grandchildren, and friends, she frequently retreats to her tree farm in northeast Pennsylvania.

Ellen McGrath, Ph.D., is a clinical psychologist and head of the Behavioral Section of the La Palestra Weight Management Program in New York City. For the past five years, she was the director of the Outpatient Eating Disorders Clinic at University of California–Irvine Medical School. For twelve years, Dr. McGrath has been a full-time faculty member at the University of California–Irvine Medical School, the University of Rochester School of Medicine, and a part-time faculty member at New York University. She is a past president of both the Media Psychology Division and the Division of Psychotherapy of the American Psychological Association, and an APA Council Representative. Dr. McGrath is the author of three books on stress and depression management. Listed by three national women's magazines as one of the top therapists in the country, Dr. McGrath was honored again in 2001 as the Outstanding Psychologist of the year by the Psychotherapy Division of the American Psychological Association.

Alice Rubenstein, Ed.D., completed her doctorate at the University of Rochester and has been a practicing psychologist in Rochester, New York, for more than twenty-five years. She is founding partner of Monroe Psychotherapy and Consultation Center. Dr. Rubenstein served as president of the American Psychological Association Division of Psychotherapy, and was the 1996 recipient of its Distinguished Psychologist Award. She has been elected a Distinguished Practitioner to the National Academies of Practice. Dr. Rubenstein's book *The Inside Story on Teen Girls*, coauthored with Dr. Karen Zager, is based on more than two years of research and offers expert answers to the questions that are most important to today's adolescent girls and their parents. She has served on the American Psychological Association Presidential Task Forces on Women and Depression and on Adolescent Girls: Strengths and Stresses. Dr. Rubenstein is married to an academic psychologist and has two daughters and two stepdaughters. Her mother is one of her very best friends and her most important role model.

 **Lenore Walker, Ed.D.,** has been in the independent practice of psychology since she received her doctorate in psychology from Rutgers University, New Jersey, in 1972. Currently she is professor of psychology at Nova Southeastern University in Fort Lauderdale, Florida. She has been president of several divisions of the American Psychological Association, including the Society for the Psychology of Women, Psychologists in Independent Practice of Psychology, and Media Psychology. Dr. Walker has written twelve books in the area of violence against women including the now classic *The Battered Woman*, published in 1979. It was her research that named the Battered Woman syndrome. She has testified numerous times before the U.S. Congress and in over four hundred cases where battered women have killed their husbands in self-defense. A veteran of many television news shows, Dr. Walker has traveled all over the world at the invitation of many countries trying to improve safety and life choices for women and children. She has two grown children, five stepchildren, and four grandchildren and lives with her psychologist partner at the beach.

 **Karen Zager, Ph.D.,** is a psychologist who has been in full-time private practice in New York since she received her doctorate in clinical psychology from Fordham University in 1981. She served as president of Psychologists in Independent Practice, a division of the American Psychological Association, and received a Presidential Citation from the American Psychological Association for her contribution to the field of psychology. She is coauthor of a recent book, *The Inside Story on Teen Girls*, and consulted on the film *5 Girls*, which aired on PBS. She has made frequent radio and TV appearances, including *Good Morning America, The Donohue Show, Sally Jesse Raphael,* and the *O'Reilly Report*, and she is interviewed regularly for magazines such as *Parenting, YM, Newsweek,* and *Time*. She has been married for more than thirty years, and has two sons attending college.

Andrea Thompson, a former editor at *McCall's* magazine, has published numerous articles in the areas of women's issues, psychology, parenting, and health. She has cowritten twelve books, including *Couple Fits, The Friendship Factor,* and *Joining Hands and Hearts*. She lives in New York City with her family.

Printed in the USA
CPSIA information can be obtained
at www.ICGtesting.com
JSHW082158140824
68134JS00014B/305